BLACK WOMEN NOVELISTS

The Development of a Tradition, 1892–1976

Barbara Christian

Contributions in Afro-American and African Studies, Number 52

GREENWOOD PRESS
WESTPORT, CONNECTICUT • LONDON, ENGLAND

Library of Congress Cataloging in Publication Data

Christian, Barbara.
    Black women novelists.

    (Contributions in Afro-American and African
studies;   no. 52   ISSN 0069-9624)
    Bibliography: p.
    Includes index.
    1.   American fiction—Afro-American authors—
History and criticism.   2.   American fiction—
Women authors—History and criticism.   3.   American
fiction—20th century—History and criticism.
4.   Afro-American women in literature.   I.   Title.
II.   Series.
PS374.N4C5   813'.09'9287   79-8953
ISBN 0-313-20750-X lib. bdg.

Library of Congress Catalog Card Number: 79-8953
ISBN: 0-313-20750-X
ISSN: 0069-9624

First published in 1980

Greenwood Press
A division of Congressional Information Service, Inc.
88 Post Road West, Westport, Connecticut 06881

Printed in the United States of America

10 9 8 7 6 5 4 3 2

This book is dedicated to my daughter Najuma, whose birth inspired it, and to my parents, without whom it could never have happened.

Contents

Preface

This book was being written long before I thought of writing it. For some years I had been working with Women Studies and Ethnic Studies divisions in the Berkeley Unified School District, trying to devise a curriculum that would engage black girls, the forgotten group in the classroom. At the same time, as a black woman involved in the appreciation and teaching of contemporary black literature, I was searching for words that expressed the configuration of my own life, my own history. Although I was a student of Afro-American literature and had read much of it, I knew little about black women, their history, or their literature.

In 1974 I had an opportunity to develop a course on black women writers at the University of California, Berkeley. Black women students there were also seeking some evidence of their own history and experience in the books they were reading. So they asked that such a course be developed. In the process of researching that course, I began to see the recurrence of certain images (images I had seen before but did not fully understand) that needed some thought, some analysis. These images and reactions to them permeated the works by black women. I found, not surprisingly, that very little work had been done on the black woman in literature and that she seldom appeared in a focal position in the black novel.

Since my subject is contemporary black literature, I began with that period and found that during the last twenty years, more and more black women were appearing in print. Many of their works were brilliant and indicated a tradition unheard of, unseen, that preceded them. I was especially interested in the novel, because through it a writer could construct a world of her own, affected by her developing personal vision, yet tempered by reality and informed by social change. I felt that the development of a writer's vision would seldom happen in the course of writing one novel and that a novelist would need the opportunity to write at least two novels to understand her craft as well as her ideas.

I discovered only a few black women, either in the past or the recent past, who had had the chance to publish one novel, far less two. But these few novelists were successful in expressing their own ideas and feelings and were also pivotal in the development of the black novel. Through their craft they were indicators of the relationship between racism and sexism in this country. Although few black women writers got their works into print, they managed to create a tradition that would reach fruition in the works of black women novelists of the present.

This book is an attempt to describe that tradition, to articulate its existence, to examine its origins, and to trace the development of stereotypical images imposed on black women and assess how these images have affected the works of black women artists.

The first three chapters are historical, in which I trace the development of these images and the impact they had on the beginnings of the black novel. Although they cover a lot of time, from 1860 to 1960, it must be remembered that few, although important, novels by black women were published during that period.

Each of the next three chapters is devoted to the novels of a contemporary black woman novelist who is very much a part of the tradition that preceded her, but who is also developing it in some critical way. The three writers are Paule Marshall, Toni Morrison, and Alice Walker. Each has written two novels and is in the process of developing her own critical vision.* Each has affected and enlarged the form of the novel itself, and each is from a different region of the United States. Although I did not originally intend regional contrast, the patterns of similarities and differences among these three writers from different backgrounds do reveal the variety and richness of the black woman's experience and guard against any easy generalizations. The emphasis in each of these chapters is on the craft as well as the major ideas of the artist, since little attention is ever paid to the creativity and artistry of the black woman writer. In addition, each of these chapters has been written so the reader, student, or teacher who is interested in one of the writers can use that particular chapter without having to digest the entire book. I am hopeful, too, that readers of one particular writer will be inspired by my presentation of other writers so they will read their books as well.

In the final chapter, I look at the whole tradition, as I have articulated it, and try to draw some conclusions about its major characteristics and about what direction it may be moving in. Not surprisingly, an important theme in this chapter is the relationship between sexism and racism as expressed

---

*Toni Morrison also published a third novel, *Song of Solomon* (New York: Knopf, 1977).

in the literature and the pattern of overt and covert restrictions on the black woman writer.

Obviously this book is not intended to be a definitive work. I am not commenting on every black woman who has ever written a novel. Rather it is a beginning study that I hope will help readers appreciate the works of these brilliant writers and will alert an interested audience to the fact that there is a rich and powerful tradition of black women writers who have woven works of lasting beauty despite the odds against them.

Since the works I discuss have received little critical attention either individually or collectively, I have attempted to illuminate the novels of these writers rather than to set them up against inappropriate criteria. That is, I have attempted to let the essential qualities of their works shine forth so readers can judge for themselves what is effective and what is not. I believe contemporary black women novelists, with the help of their audience, are wresting free from a set of standards that have inhibited or distorted their visions and are attempting to develop measures of their own potential. Finally, I have chosen contemporary writers whose beauty and substance have engaged my spirit and whose work represents lasting expressions of the black woman's creativity.

Acknowledgments

While working on this book I received invaluable assistance from so many people that I cannot possibly name all of them. I am especially grateful to the poet Thalia Kitrilakis and to Gloria Bowles, coordinator of the Women Studies Program at the University of California, Berkeley, who saw me through the many versions of the manuscripts, and to my colleagues, Professor Erskine Peters and Catherine Macklin, whose marvelous intelligence and precision in language always sharpened my insights. Susan Groves of the Women Studies Department at the Berkeley Unified School District and Professor Margaret Wilkerson at the Women's Center, University of California, Berkeley, provided opportunities for me to discuss my research with others. I am also grateful to Daphne Muse and Kathy Sloane, who read various sections of the manuscript, and to Waldo Martin, whose library I pilfered. Special thanks to Grace Rutledge, who typed most of this manuscript with intelligence and care, and to the students of the Images of Black Women in Literature classes, with whom I had fruitful and delightful dialogue.

I also want to thank my women friends, Cathy and Daphne, Peggy and Jean, and Jean, Mildred, and Yvonne, who provided me with child care and emotional support.

Thanks are due to the following for permission to include copyrighted selections:

Howard B. Odum and Guy B. Johnson, *Negro Workaday Songs*. Copyright 1926, The University of North Carolina Press. Reprinted by permission of the publisher.

Saint Peter Relates An Incident, by James Weldon Johnson. Copyright 1935 by James Weldon Johnson. Copyright © renewed 1963 by Grace Nail Johnson. All rights reserved. Reprinted by permission of Viking Penguin, Inc.

"Harlem Dancer," from *Selected Poems of Claude McKay*. Copyright 1953 by Twayne Publishers, Inc. Reprinted with the permission of Twayne Publishers, A Division of G. K. Hall and Company, in Boston.

Alain Locke, "The New Negro," from *The New Negro*, ed. Alain Locke (1925). New York: Atheneum, 1968.

Specified material from *Their Eyes Were Watching God*, by Zora Neale Hurston (J. B. Lippincott Company). Copyright 1937 by J. P. Lippincott Company, renewed 1965 by John C. Hurston and Joel Hurston. Reprinted by permission of Harper and Row, Publishers, Inc.

Specified material from *The Street*, by Ann Petry, copyright 1946 and © renewed 1974 by Ann Petry. Reprinted by permission of Houghton Mifflin Company.

Specified material from "Maud Martha," in *The World of Gwendolyn Brooks*, by Gwendolyn Brooks. Copyright 1953 by Gwendolyn Brooks Blakely. Reprinted by permission of Harper and Row, Publishers, Inc.

Material from *Browngirl, Brownstones* and *The Chosen Place, The Timeless People*, used with permission from Paule Marshall.

Material from *The Bluest Eye*, by Toni Morrison, used with permission from Holt, Rinehart and Winston. CBS Educational Publishing, A Division of CBS, Inc. Copyright © 1970 by Toni Morrison.

Grateful acknowledgement is made to Alfred A. Knopf, Inc., for permission to quote from *Sula*, by Toni Morrison. Copyright © 1973 by Toni Morrison.

Excerpt from *Revolutionary Petunias* © 1970 by Alice Walker. Reprinted from her volume *Revolutionary Petunias And Other Poems*, by permission of Harcourt Brace Jovanovich, Inc.

Excerpts from Alice Walker's "In Our Mothers' Garden," printed with permission from the author.

Excerpts from *The Third Life of Grange Copeland* and *Meridian* by Alice Walker are reprinted by permission of Harcourt Brace Jovanovich, Inc.; © 1970, 1976 by Alice Walker.

Book I
From Stereotype
to Character

1

_____ Shadows Uplifted _____

O whitened head entwined in turban gay
O kind black face, O crude but tender hand,
O foster mother in whose arms there lay
The race whose sons are masters of the land!
It was thine arms that sheltered in their fold,
It was thine eyes that followed through the length
Of infant days these sons. In times of old
It was thy breast that nourished them to strength.

So often hast thou to thy bosom pressed
The golden head, the face and brow of snow;
So often has it 'gainst thy broad, dark breast
Lain, set off like a quickened cameo.
Thou simple soul, as cuddling down that babe
With thy sweet croon, so plaintive and so wild
Came ne'er the thought to thee, swift like a stab
That it some day might crush thy own black child?[1]
—*The Black Mammy*, by James Weldon Johnson

PART I

Shadows . . .

Iola LeRoy, Shadows Uplifted, by Frances Ellen Watkins Harper, considered by many to be the first novel by an Afro-American woman to be published, appeared in 1892.[2] By that time, the country had experienced historic traumas during the Civil War and Reconstruction periods that

3

affected the nature of life for black people and for women. As an abolitionist and a black feminist, Frances Harper had been one of the leading figures
in the national struggle to free blacks from slavery, as well as a longtime
spokesperson for the many black women who were not yet free to speak.
She had spent her life lecturing against slavery, had written ten volumes of
poetry, had taken an active part in the 1856 Women's Rights Convention,
and had helped to found the National Association of Colored Women. Many
of her newspaper articles, such as "Black Women in the Reconstruction
South" (1878), reflect her involvement with the problems of black women
in this country. William Still, her contemporary and the black editor of the
Underground Railroad, said of her that:

> I know of no other woman white or colored, who has come so inti-
> mately in contact with the colored people in the South as Mrs. Harper.
> Since emancipation she has labored in every Southern state in the
> Union, save two, Arkansas and Texas; in the colleges, schools, churches
> and the cabins. . . . With her, it was no uncommon occurrence in visit-
> ing cities and towns, to speak at two, three or four meetings a day. . . .
> But the kind of meetings she took greatest interest in were meetings
> called exclusively for women. . . . She felt their needs were far more
> pressing than any other class.[3]

Yet Harper's novel, *Iola LeRoy*, does not dwell on those pressing needs
but is the heavily moralistic tale of a refined and educated octoroon, who
but for the devilry of her white father's friend would have lived as a white
woman in the South, not even knowing herself that she possessed a few drops
of black blood. Certainly the novel does not contain much of the realistic
experiences Harper herself describes in her articles about the lives of black
women of the time. For example, in "Black Women in the Reconstruction
South," she tells us about Mrs. Hill, a widow who

> has rented, cultivated and solely managed a farm of five acres for five
> years. She makes her garden, raises poultry, and cultivates enough corn
> and cotton to live comfortably and keep a surplus in the bank. She
> saves something every year, and this is much, considering the low price
> of cotton and infavorable seasons. . . .[4]

and about Mrs. Madison who,

> although living in a humble and unpretentious home, has succeeded
> in getting up a home for aged coloured women. By organized effort
> women have been enabled to help each other in sickness and provide
> respectable funerals for the dead.[5]

Yet in *Iola LeRoy* the salient element of the story is the heroine's willingness to be known as a black woman, although she has all the physical and cultural attributes of the white woman. This notwithstanding, Iola is a feminist of the time in that she believes women should work for a living, when in fact most black women had no choice but to work to survive.

Certainly there is a great discrepancy between the substance of her novel and Harper's detailed observations of the life most black women were leading in the period of Reconstruction, a discrepancy that has something to do with the form of the novel at that time and the images of black women in American society. *Iola LeRoy* is an important novel, not because it is a "first" or because it is a good novel, but because it so clearly delineates the relationship between the images of black women held at large in society and the novelist's struggle to refute these images—all of this even as the novelist attempts to create a world of characters and situations that can be viewed as suitable to the form of the novel, yet realistic enough somehow to resemble life.

What images of black women was Harper struggling against, and why was it important for her to use the novel as a form in refuting them?

Black women were brought as slaves to this country to fulfill specifically female roles and to work in the fields. At first the planters thought slavery would be a short-range measure. But by the early 1700s, because of the demands of labor and the myths they entertained about the nature of black people, they maintained and defended black slavery as a permanent institution essential to the American economy.[6] Particularly after it became obvious to them that "black gold" would not forever be available in Africa, either because of growing European political resistance to the slave trade or because of the cunning of local African dealers, the planters must have realized the importance of American-born black slaves.

But even as the colonists solidified the institution of slavery by enacting slave codes, many like Benjamin Franklin feared that the presence of large numbers of blacks might endanger the character of American settlements as white colonies.[7] As English planters, they were at first concerned also that other European settlers might usurp the British characteristics of the colonies. But even more threatening was the presence of blacks who, the planters believed, were obviously and distinctly different.

From the beginnings of the thirteen colonies, black people, although not at first identified with slavery, were certainly designated as inferior.[8] As a means of protecting whites from the taint of black blood, some states as early as 1680 banned interracial marriages.[9] By the early 1700s blacks had become associated in the American mind with the ape, especially the orangutan.[10]

In the first two centuries of the colonies' existence, much of their literature is obsessed with the establishment of blacks as a species, different from and lower than whites, the link so to speak in the Great Chain of Being between animal and man.[11] Whether animal or man, blacks were seen as "lewd, lascivious and wanton."[12] Based on reports they had heard from slave traders and travelers, the planters believed the black female was sexually aggressive and sometimes mated with orangutan males, while the black male, because of his nature, hankered uncontrollably after the next link in the chain, the white woman.[13] These arguments about the nature of the black race were part of the European's initial groping into new areas of the natural sciences, as well as his increasing awareness that there were seemingly different groups of men all over the world. Coincidentally, in America these pseudo-scientific discussions were used as rationalizations for slavery, a condition the English themselves abhorred.

From the first century of this nation's history, then, race and sex were interrelated and the problem of interracial sex was foremost in the minds of the colonists. However, although there might have been popular discussion about racial concepts, a clear intellectual definition of race was not formulated until the mid-nineteenth century. In the seventeenth and eighteenth centuries the inferiority of blacks was couched in terms of the concept of "civilization." George Stocking, in his book *Race, Culture and Evolution*, pointed out that initially civilization was seen by naturalists as the "natural capacity" of all races. Savages would eventually become civilized. With the expansion of industrial civilization, however, the gap between the savage and the civilized European widened.

> When the ideas of primitivism and progress in civilization separated, "civilization" lent itself quite easily—indeed to some even seemed to call for—a racial interpretation.[14]

In keeping with their beliefs about the inferiority of blacks to whites, the newly independent Americans also saw miscegenation as an unnatural thing. One of the most prominent antislavery proponents, Thomas Jefferson, believed Negroes were inferior to whites. He, as well as many of his countrymen, thought that blacks lacked beauty, intellect, and imagination. Their essence, it seemed to him, was that of crude sensation.[15] Jefferson agreed with Judge Sewell of Boston who succinctly exclaimed that "Negroes cannot mix with us and become members of society . . . never embody with us and grow up into orderly families, to the peopling of the land."[16] Given the powerful language that the planters used to attack miscegenation, one could conclude that they saw it as a crime against the body politic. Yet given their belief in the sexual aggressiveness of the black female, they also allowed that white men would fall prey to her wiles.[17]

Since blacks were obviously needed for labor, and since the planters accepted miscegenation between white men and black females as inevitable, they charged the white woman with the responsibility of being "the repository of white civilization."[18] By giving birth to the white man's legitimate heirs, she became actually and symbolically his greatest treasure. Thus the fear of rape of the white woman by the black man reached mammoth proportions in the mind of the southern planter. For any sexual activity between these two actors would constitute, from the white man's perspective, the rape of his birthright and legacy.

The planters attempted to resolve the tension between their need for slave labor and their insistence that the American colonies and later the American Republic retain its whiteness by designating the black woman as the bearer of black slaves and the white woman as the bearer of free whites. Just as white women were seen as pivotal to the preservation of white civilization, black women were central to the continuation of the slave system as an essential part of the American economy.

Although it has not been confirmed by contemporary historians that black slave women in America were forced to breed in the strict sense that they were in the Caribbean, there is no doubt that "an essential value of the adult slave women rested in their capacity to produce the labor force."[19] Perhaps the fact that planters in America saw that land as their home while those in the Caribbean saw themselves as transient Europeans accounts for the difference in their respective approaches. According to Winthrop Jordan, American "slave owners acquired valuable young Negroes not by forcing their slaves to mate (clear instances of this being very rare), but by doing little to interfere with a system which gave every encouragement to early and frequent sexual intercourse among their slaves."[20] That the black woman was valued for her reproductive capacity, however, was established as early as the 1660s, "when Negro women brought a high price because their issue was valuable and because they could be used for field work while white women generally were not."[21]

As the previous statement indicates, the black woman was also seen as different from the white woman in her capacity to do man's work. From the beginnings of the colonies, white women did not ordinarily work in the fields. As early as 1643, before slavery became established in the colonies, Virginia's tax law provided that

> all adult men were tithable and in addition Negro women. This official discrimination between Negro and other women was made by men who were accustomed to thinking of field work as being ordinarily the work of men rather than women.[22]

The black slave women were not identified, as white women were, with the roles of wife and mother, but primarily and specifically with the roles of mother and worker. Not surprisingly, then, the black woman as mammy

was one of the most dominant images to emerge in southern life and literature, an image that has proved to be a most enduring one even to the present.

The mammy image is extremely complex, because the concept of motherhood was already rife with contradictions among the planters of the South.
Motherhood, within the confines of marriage, was of course revered, for
through it the white man was ensured his heirs. The late eighteenth- and early
nineteenth-century southern white woman was taught from early childhood
an image to which she was expected to conform. As Anne Firor Scott put
it in her book, *The Southern Lady*:

> This marvelous creation was described as a submissive wife whose
> reason for being was to love, honor, obey and occasionally amuse her
> husband, to bring up his children and manage his household. Physi-
> cally weak, and "formed for the less laborious occupations," she de-
> pended upon male protection. To secure this protection she was
> endowed with the capacity to "create a magic spell" over any man in
> her vicinity. She was timid and modest, beautiful and graceful . . . the
> most fascinating being in creation . . . the delight and charm of every
> circle she moved in.[23]

This image could, of course, only be that—an image; alabaster ladies could
not possibly have endured life in a frontier land. As the diaries and letters
of antebellum southern women so clearly illustrate, most of them, even those
of the upper class, worked hard.[24] Even the mistresses of large plantations
were managers of huge households designed to be self-sufficient, isolated
from each other and from the world except when gala events were held.
Nonetheless, the image persisted, even in the minds of southern women
themselves, who knew the reality of their lives but felt somehow they did
not live up to the ideal.

Beyond the question of its relationship to truth, the image itself contained
contradictions. A lady was expected to be a wife, a mother, and a manager;
yet she was supposed to be delicate, ornamental, virginal, and timid. How
then could she endure the sexual appetites of her husband and survive the
nine months of pregnancy, not to mention the ordeal of childbirth necessary
to produce his heirs? These tasks were unavoidable. But given a system of
mistress and slave, she need not nurse, be chained to her babies' continuous
demands, or do heavy housework, elaborate cooking, tedious weaving, and
sewing to maintain, nourish, and clothe her family. If the image of the delicate alabaster lady were to retain some semblance of truth, it would be
necessary to create the image of another female who was tougher, less sensitive, and who could perform with efficiency and grace the duties of motherhood for her mistress and of course for herself. The image of the southern

lady, based as it was on a patriarchal plantation myth, demanded another female image, that of the mammy.

Why was the image of the lady, and therefore the corresponding image of the mammy, so important to the South? Early nineteenth-century planters rationalized the institution of slavery in two ways, by using scientific proofs to cast doubts upon the humanness of blacks and by perceiving themselves as patriarchs, such as existed in the Bible.[25] The characteristics of blacks' racial inferiority, which Jefferson had so impressionistically discussed in the 1790s, were, by the 1830s, buttressed by scientific arguments. Ethnological writers such as Richard Colfax, Samuel Cartwright, and Josiah Nott detailed the physical deficiencies of the Negro, his cranial characteristics, his facial angles, and concluded that intellectually the Negro was incapable of being the equal of whites. Their utterances quickly became a racist ideology in the United States. This school of thought also had polygenist tendencies, however. That is, many ethnological writers believed that different races of men had different origins and that God created many pairs of the human race.[26] Therein lay the weakness of its appeal to many southern aristocrat writers, for they were devoted to the Bible and such a thrust seemed to go against the Adam and Eve biblical story.

On the other hand, advocates of patriarchy, like George Fitzhugh, maintained that the patriarchal concept was the best societal model for the South and that slavery was necessary to that order; William Byrd, an eighteenth-century Virginian planter, expressed the quintessence of the patriarch image in his letter to Charles, earl of Orkney:

> Like one of the Patriarchs, I have my Flocks and my Herds, my Bonds-men and Bondswomen and every Soart of Trade amongst my Servants, so that I live in a kind of Independence on everyone but Providence. However tho' this Sort of Life is without expense, it is attended a great deal of trouble. I must take care to keep all my people to their Duty, to set all the Springs to motion and to make everyone draw his equal Share to carry the Machine forward.[27]

Our main concern here is with the patriarchal concept, since the plantation myth was the subject matter of southern antebellum literature. But clearly the scientific arguments of mid-nineteenth-century ethnologists strengthened the proslavery argument of the patriarchal concept and eventually dominated it, since patriarchy also demanded subordination of poor and middle-class whites.[28] Although these two schools differed in their emphasis, both reiterated the importance of the white woman in maintaining a superior society. Ethnologists such as Josiah Nott insisted that ethnic purity had to be maintained or the world would retrograde instead of advance in civilization, and Brinton, his disciple, in the 1890s, came straight to the point:

> The "ethnic purity" of the whites must be maintained. White women had no holier duty, no more sacred mission, than that of transmitting in its integrity the heritage of ethnic endowment gained by the race through thousands of generations of struggle.[29]

In like manner, the lady was essential to the concept of patriarchy, for pivotal to that concept was the domestic metaphor, which contained within it the idea of a domestic hierarchy. To emphasize the maleness of the perfect patriarch, the perfect wife was expected to be submissive, weak, and dependent. Men as patriarchs were to be obeyed by wives, children, and slaves.

The contradictions within the patriarchal system of belief are related to the way in which work was viewed by the society. The truly civilized lady did not work, for work, although necessary, is demeaning. Work (here meaning man's work, since until recently women's work was hardly seen as comparable) involves participation in the world, an activity best left to the masculine members of the species, who know how to deal with the sulliness of competitiveness and striving. How well the man succeeds in making his work profitable is measured by the extent to which his wife does or does not work. So the lady is symbolic of the patriarch's success, her state a visual representation of his power. But the acquisition of power or wealth demanded such specialization that work in the home was necessarily left to women. The southern mind, though, did not dismiss motherhood, or housekeeping, as nonwork. It could not, for such work was necessary to the plantation's self-sufficiency. These activities in fact were obviously continuous, unrelenting, and necessary. Thus an even further indication of a man's power was his ability to relieve his wife even of this involvement. Only then could she emerge as a completely helpless, totally dependent being whose identity and worth flowed from the male patriarch.

Of course, for most people in the South, this version of reality was sheer fantasy. Most people, slave or free, did not even live on large plantations but on small farms.[30] Yet the rhetoric of patriarchy and the myth of the plantation transformed the realities of the slave system into a benevolent institution. The domestic metaphor that insisted that "we are all one great big happy family, both black and white" implied that there was an irrevocable bond between the nature of the family, the nature of man and woman, and the concept of slavery.[31]

Women of the servant class had of course performed unavoidable and tedious women's work for the lords and ladies of England; here in America the fact that the slave woman in question was black and, according to the prevailing philosophy, possibly the female of a lower species should have caused the patriarch and the lady some concern. But black women had a high regard for motherhood, since in much of Africa the relationship between mother and child is seen as sacred, symbolic of the relationship between the earth and creativity.[32] Whites seemed to misinterpret this cornerstone of African thought in much the same way that Melville's naive Captain Delano, in *Benito Cereno*, does when he characterizes the affection of the "uncivilized Negresses" for their babies as "naked nature."

When the black woman first began to experience and understand the contradictions about motherhood among the southern planters, she must have been truly appalled. Nonetheless, her tendency to see maternal duties as natural and sacred must have reinforced the southern planters' stereotype that black women were perfectly suited to be mammies. But this assertion, too, must be qualified. Even as the planters praised the black woman as the "contented mammy," they also insisted that black slave women neglected their own children.[33] Above and beyond these factors stands a major contradiction: that the planters could relegate the duties of motherhood, a revered and honored state, to a being supposedly lower than human, reveals their own confusion about the value of motherhood. That they could separate spiritual aspects of motherhood, which they acknowledged in their religion, from the physical aspects and give the duties of childrearing to a "subhuman" gives us some indication about the value they placed on women's work. As a white woman character says in a book by William Thompson, the antebellum proslavery humorist:

> "I could never bear to see a white gal toatin' my child about, waiting on me like a nigger. It would hurt my conscience to keep anybody 'bout me in that condition, who was as white and as good as me."[34]

Despite the contradictions inherent in the image of the lady and its correlate, the image of the mammy, these concepts were essential parts of the South's public dream and therefore of its literature. The lady was, of course, at the center of that dream. But although the black woman is seldom focused on in antebellum literature, she almost always appears in the background as the contented and loyal mammy.

The mammy is a consistent, if minor, mainstay among the stock characters of white antebellum and Reconstruction novels. From J. P. Kennedy's *Swallow Barn* (1832) through the nostalgic darky novels of Thomas Nelson Page to the vindictive Reconstruction trilogy of Thomas Dixon, the black woman as a mammy appears as a normal part of the southern fabric.[35] Enduring, strong, and calm, her physical characteristics remain the same. She is black in color as well as race and fat, with enormous breasts that are full enough to nourish all the children of the world; her head is perpetually covered with her trademark kerchief to hide the kinky hair that marks her as ugly. Tied to her physical characteristics are her personality traits: she is strong, for she certainly has enough girth, but this strength is used in the service of her white master and as a way of keeping her male counterparts in check; she is kind and loyal, for she is a mother; she is sexless, for she is ugly; and she is religious and superstitious, because she is black. She prefers the master's children to her own, for as a member of a lower species, she acknowledges almost instinctively the superiority of the higher race. Caroline Hentz describes a typical mammy in her sentimental and popular romance *Linda* (1857):

> Aunt Judy's African blood had not been corrupted by the base mingling of a paler strain. Black as ebony was her smooth and shining skin, in which the dazzling ivory of her teeth gleams bright as the moon at midnight. Judy had loved—admired, reverenced her, as being of a superior, holier race than her own.[36]

This image of the mammy persisted beyond the Civil War into the literature of the 1890s. And even so fine a writer as Kate Chopin focused on this version of the black mammy in her short stories, "Beyond the Bayou" and "A No Account Creole" (1894).

I have specifically mentioned fiction written by white southern women writers of the antebellum and postbellum periods. It is true, as Anne Firor Scott pointed out, that ladies and mammies were often on intimate terms and that many southern women were private abolitionists in their diaries (Mary Chestnut's comment, "there is no slave like a wife," comes to mind). No doubt many southern women were weary of the institution of slavery, for they were expected to be supervisor, teacher, doctor, and minister to a large family of slaves.[37] Nonetheless, when southern women wrote, that is, when they participated in the South's public dream, they emphasized as did the male writers the qualities of contentment, self-sacrifice, and loyalty in the mammy. Their books reveal that they accepted society's image of themselves as southern ladies (whether they lived it or not) and therefore projected the corresponding image of the black mammy. Their books heighten Eugene Genovese's assertion that "to understand her [the mammy] is to move toward understanding the tragedy of plantation paternalism."[38] The image of the mammy, then, cannot be seen in a vacuum; she is a necessary correlate to the lady. If one was to be, the other had to be.

The same holds true for the other stereotypical images of the black woman that developed during slavery and continue today. If the southern lady was to be chaste except for producing heirs, it would be necessary to have another woman who could become the object of men's sexual needs and desires. There is some reason to believe that the image of the sexless southern lady is really a reflection of difficulties white women faced because of the lack of effective contraceptives. Southern women feared "the misery of endless pregnancies with attendant illnesses and the dreadful fear of childbirth was a fear based in fact. The number of women who died in childbirth was high."[39] Even if a woman survived many pregnancies, she could expect that some of her children would not survive their first year. If they did, each additional child increased her labor and responsibility.

The image of the black woman as "lewd" and "impure" develops partially in response to the lady's "enforced" chastity and partially as a result of the planters' myths about the sexuality of blacks. Certainly this image fits neatly into the dualism of white (good, pure) and black (bad, evil). At the crux of the "loose woman" image is the belief that black women, unlike white women, craved sex inordinately. Given that the black woman was perceived as the female of an inferior species, such an assumption would be logical. The rape of black women by white men or the use of their bodies for pleasure could be rationalized as the natural craving of the black woman for sex, rather than the licentiousness of the white man. "For by calling the Negro woman passionate, they [white men] were offering the best possible justification for their own passions."[40] Despite their public statements about the horror of miscegenation, many planters felt it their right to possess whatever slave girls they desired.[41]

Of course the southern antebellum novels did not stress the image of the loose black woman. Since the literature projected the domestic metaphor of a harmonious patriarchal system, it could not introduce the theme of miscegenation. But the popular and light literature of the day did include many references to the image of the black woman as overtly sexual, usually because she came from a hot climate:

> Next comes a warmer race, from sable sprung,
> To love each thought, to lust each nerve is strung:
> The Samboe dark, and the Mullatoe brown,
> The Mestize fair, the well-lim'd Quaderoon,
> And jetty Afric, from no spurious sire,
> Warm as her soil, and as her sun—on fire.
> These sooty dames, well vers'd in Venus' school
> Make love an art, and boast they kiss by rule.[42]

Although expressions like these appeared only in worldly places such as the Charleston newspapers, their existence does indicate that this sentiment was held by many who might not have been so forthright.

In any case, the image of the loose black woman who was naturally lascivious occurs frequently in the diaries of southern white women who resented their husbands' sexual freedom and their own lack of it. Mary

Chestnut, like so many of her sisters, undercut the harmonious image of the plantation when she wrote in her diary:

> Under slavery, we live surrounded by prostitutes. Like patriarchs of old, our men live in one house with their wives and concubines. . . . Any lady is ready to tell you who is the father of all the mulatto children in everybody's household but her own.[43]

Again, contradictions abound within the content of the image itself. If the black woman was indeed subhuman, and that after all was what her incredible sexuality was based on, then white men were mating with creatures of a lower species, an act of perversion at the very least. But given the southern planters' definition of sex as an animal function, which was unfortunately necessary for the male to maintain his health and power, the black woman's animality fit well into the scheme of the division between mind and body, spirit and matter. Rooted in this particular image is the sense of sex as base, even violent, and an act of domination rather than sharing. "The English word *sex* itself derived from terms indicating cutting, separation, division."[44]

Although the image of the loose black woman is a correlate of the image of the chaste lady, this particular stereotype, in real life, further separated the slave woman from the white woman. Many mistresses resented slave girls because of the apparent sexual freedom black women could exhibit. Since the loose woman image emphasized that black women solicited these attentions, many white women would view them with jealousy and anger. The myth of the licentious, exotic black woman became so much a part of the consciousness of the South that even the black abolitionist William Wells Brown began *Clotel* (1861), the first black novel to be published in this country, with this observation:

> When we take into consideration the fact that no safeguard was ever thrown around virtue, and no inducement held out to slave women to be pure and chaste, we will not be surprised when told that immorality pervades the domestic circle in the cities and towns of the South to an extent unknown in Northern states. Many a planter's wife has dragged out a miserable existence, with an aching heart, at seeing her place in the husband's affection usurped by the unadorned beauty and captivating smiles of her waiting maid. Indeed, the greater portion of the colored women, in the days of slavery, had no greater aspiration than that of becoming the finely-dressed mistress of some white man.[45]

Yet historical documents consistently demonstrate that the comely slave girl who was taken by her master not only had to deal with his attentions under the threat of the lash but also with his wife's wrath. Caught between two evils, black parents prayed that their daughters would not be too attractive.[46]

Like the mammy, the loose black woman has certain physical characteristics. She is brown-skinned, rather than black, and voluptuous, rather than fat, and she possesses a sensuous mouth and a high behind. She is known to have an "evil" disposition, a characteristic that constitutes rather than distracts from her sexiness, which is contrasted with the sweet demeanor of the lady. She is good looking and passionate, but never beautiful, for her animal nature rather than her human qualities are foremost in her makeup. She ensnares men with her body rather than uplifting them with her beauty. Her corresponding image, the chaste lady, would function as a vessel of beauty, that spiritual flower who could aid men in their ascent toward God and culture. In contrast, the loose black woman would be seen as yet another version of one of the pitfalls of men, this particular one being the Flesh, rather than the World or the Devil. As such, the loose black woman is the quintessence of an aspect of woman that men feared, the power of sexual allure that might waylay even the best men's minds and spirits. This image surely reveals the philosophical discomfort that the southern mind, derived as it was from medieval Christian philosophy, experienced in regard to the nature and place of sex in their world. Although not as dominant as the mammy in white southern novels, the image of the loose black woman is almost always present in the planters' discussions on the nature of blacks, often as a means of explaining the waywardness of otherwise moral white men and therefore the existence of so many slaves of mixed blood.

Like the mammy, the loose black woman image demonstrates how complicated stereotypes can be. The assignment of the black woman to the sexual aspects of women's work is further heightened by the fact that many African cultures did not view sex as a separate entity distinct from or lower than the mind and spirit. Given the many traditional rituals that African societies developed around the union of woman and man, the African woman who was transported to America must have been at a loss to determine what sexual behavior meant to her master and mistress. Dance, religion, song, and music in the African world view are also characteristically sensual, for the body and soul are seen as one.[47] Again, the culturally determined judgments about the value of sensuality could easily be used by the already predisposed southern gentry to reinforce their beliefs that black women were sex crazed. When this configuration is complicated by the obvious fact that sometimes the use of sexual allure was the only means by which she could survive, the natural role that sex would play in the life of the slave woman had to be crucially distorted.

Since miscegenation obviously occurred, it is not surprising that some antebellum novelists of the plantation tradition used the image of the mulatta in their works. In fact, the image has been with us since the beginnings of the American novel. Cora Munro, one of the minor characters in Cooper's *The Last of the Mohicans* (1826), is an octoroon, and she is a foreshadowing of the many octoroons who appear in the literature of the nineteenth century, for she meets with a tragic end.

Unlike the abolitionists' literature of the antebellum period, the southern writers' literature focused on the black woman as the contented mammy rather than the mulatta, since they tried to sweep the existence of miscegenation under the rug. Still, when they did present this image, the mulatta is tragic.[48] Often she is shown as caught between two worlds, and since she is obviously the result of an illicit relationship, she suffers from a melancholy of the blood that inevitably leads to tragedy. In contrast to the southern lady, whose beauty, refinement, and charm bring her admiration, love, and happiness, the fruit of miscegenation is Tragedy, regardless of what other positive characteristics the mulatta might possess. The word *mulatto* itself etymologically is derived from the word *mule* and echoes the debate Americans engaged in about whether blacks were of the same species as whites.[49] If they were not, the result would be similar to a mule, a cross between the donkey and the horse and a being that itself was incapable of producing life. The etymology of the word also brings to mind the conclusions of the ethnologist Josiah Nott, who claimed that "the mulatta was a genuine hybrid, weaker and less fertile than either parent."[50] It is interesting in this context to note how many black jokes there are about mules, animals who are also identified with unrelenting labor.

Like the tragic mulatta image, the image of the conjure woman is not nearly so dominant in the literature of the southern writers as the mammy image. Yet it persists throughout antebellum literature and thought. This image is extremely elusive. On one hand, the conjure woman image incorporates the signs of traditional African religions that the southern gentry pointed to as dark and evil, heathen forces. The value judgment they made about the religion of the slave was both practically and philosophically to their advantage, for they used it as a rationalization for the entire system of slavery. Much of early southern literature argues that slavery was really a blessing for the Africans, since it separated them from the dark effects of heathenism and introduced them to the saving light of Christianity. In this context, it was necessary continually to keep alive the image of African heathenism, so the slavemaster could use slavery as part of an overall Christian crusade to elevate otherwise damned souls to possible levels of salvation. Even this point of view was rather liberal, though, for many writers insisted that slaves, because they were inferior to whites, could not really become Christians, or that if they were allowed the Gospel, they might become discontented under slavery.[51] In any case, the antebellum literature does emphasize the heathenism of blacks by pointing up the "ridiculous" superstitions of black folk, a characteristic the southern mind believed in so intensely that when the Ku Klux Klan (KKK) began its infamous career, it chose sheets for disguise since blacks were so afraid of "haints."

On the other hand, the image of the conjurer was, in southern literature, treated with some measure of respect and awe, as if the dark, incomprehensible forces did exist and had some power to affect the fortunes of men. The slave narratives also testify to this quality of respect among whites. Ex-slave Susan Snow told an interviewer, "My ma was a black African and she sure was wild and mean. Dey couldn't whip her. Dey used to say she was a 'conjer' and dey was all scared of her."[52]

Perhaps mammies communicated their respect for conjurers to the white children they reared.[53] No doubt human beings have always been fascinated by the unknown, particularly in the realm of the unseen and the intangible. But even more, the hidden guilt that the Southerners must have felt, whatever their rationalizations about slavery, could give rise to fears about what the slaves might allay themselves with in an attempt to free themselves. For example, conspirators tried to use the slave folk religion but capitulated to Gabriel Prosser's more political approach, when they put together their plans for Gabriel's Rebellion in 1800.[54] The Haitian Revolution, with its overtones of dark, unknown forces turning against the masters and the victory of the hypnotic drum, could only reinforce the planters' fears all the more. The African drum, of course, was outlawed in the United States, but the reality of its threat was kept alive in the image of the conjurer, who, although potentially dangerous, was certainly kept under some degree of control, if only because he or she maintained a definite role in plantation society.

Of course the southern gentry's own heritage contained large doses of lore about the intrusion of evil spirits into the lives of human beings.[55] Certainly the war between God and the Devil provided ample seeds for many unorthodox beliefs about the battle between the forces of good and evil. But the southern gentleman was not a Manichean, a sect outlawed by Christianity for its belief in the existence of good and evil forces, at least not openly; much of his feeling about evil forces was relegated to underground caverns of the mind. Superstition was as much a part of his world view as the tenets of Christianity. Particularly in the sections dominated by Catholicism, the conjure woman image flourished for the Catholic hierarchy of saints further heightened the contrast between God and the Devil. Whatever their actual power, black women like Marie LaVeau in New Orleans and Mary Ellen Pleasant in San Francisco would use their knowledge of the white man's fear of the supernatural to become real-life conjure women, wielding power over matters of state and politics.

Not surprisingly, the conjure woman image has a direct relationship to the southern lady. Above all her other attributes, the lady was expected to be a Christian; in fact, her qualities of submissiveness and purity were based on her deep Christian faith. Her devotion to her husband and her children was, in effect, a reflection of her devotion to God.[56] But although southern ladies were expected to be intensely religious, they certainly were not supposed to have the intellectual fibre necessary to be ministers in the church. The fact that the black conjurer could be a woman might have reinforced the planters' belief that such a religion was intellectually deficient, conditioned as they were to Christianity where men were undoubtedly the leaders and women were primarily associated with emotive roles. Coincidentally, many male conjurers were ministers in the Christian church as well.

The conjure woman image, although a stereotype, includes within it true elements—in this case that black people not only kept alive certain aspects of various African religions such as herbal medicine, folk wisdom, and ritual, but also that women were also able to be leaders in the rituals of many African religions.[57]

Of course, black male images were also evident in antebellum literature, and they were often the counterparts of the female images. The mammy, for example, is often paired with the plantation uncle. Just as the black female images emphasize lewdness and strength, negative qualities in the ideal southern lady, and omit the essential feminine attributes of beauty and delicacy, so the comic, submissive, irrational qualities of the black male images are an inversion of the dignified, strong, rational image of the male patriarch. Both female and male black images run decidedly counter to the masculine and feminine norms of antebellum southern society, thus strengthening the myth that the Negro had to be contained by a superior being and was naturally suited to the condition of slavery.

The images in southern antebellum literature that developed as stereotypes of black women reveal much, not only about the southern attitude toward black people but also about their definition of woman. Each black woman image was created to keep a particular image about white women intact. Another way of putting it is that the aspects of woman that had negative connotations in the society were ascribed to black women so white women could be viewed, as Alice Walker would later phrase it, to be "perfect in the eyes of the world." Significantly, the qualities that distinguished woman from man—her ability to be a mother, her distinct sexual relationship to man, and her supposed tendency toward emotionality and spirituality—are seen as problematic. The definition of a proper woman within the southern context of patriarchy erases those areas in which women naturally could exhibit power—power that was based on their physical nature as well as their place in society. Like the race theories of the nineteenth century, which associated physical characteristics with certain personality traits, all of the images of women, both black and white, are pointedly physical, emphasizing body type and appearance as the essence of woman's being.

The breaking of any of these images was seen as a threat to the entire society. George Fitzhugh, one of the South's most articulate spokesmen for slavery, made clear that "any change in the role of women (and here, he means white women) or in the institution of slavery would cause the downfall of the family and the consequent demise of society."[58] The image of the southern lady, which visually contained the South's philosophical tenets for the status of women, could not be effective without the corresponding images of the black woman.

PART II

... Uplifted

Black abolitionists, such as William Wells Brown and Frances Harper, were certainly aware of the images of black people that had developed during slavery. In fact, from the 1830s to the beginning of the Civil War, a battle of images raged between the writers of the proslavery South and the Abolitionist Movement. Just as antebellum southern writers projected their images of blacks as a servile, inferior race, so the abolitionists countered with their own images through their lectures and writings. The black abolitionists were particularly important in this context, for their oratorical and literary skills were direct refutations of the South's image of blacks as ineducable. Orators like Frederick Douglass, William Brown, and Frances Harper were concerned with countering southern images not only of black men but of black women as well, since many of their supporters were white women involved in the struggle for women's rights; also, black abolitionists had proclaimed themselves on the side of female equality when the Abolitionist Movement split over the woman issue.[59]

In the struggle against slavery, the novel as a means of exposing its evils was an effective medium, since, as a genre, it could be used as a source of both moral instruction and entertainment. Harriet Beecher Stowe's *Uncle Tom's Cabin* had proved the effectiveness of the romance novel, for amidst controversy it had created much support for the Abolitionist Movement. Black abolitionists were also eager to create literary works, since one of the most hurtful accusations made against them by proslavery advocates was that black people were culturally inferior and had not produced, and never would be capable of producing, works of art.

Such reasons, to a large extent, conditioned the form of the black abolitionist novel. *Uncle Tom's Cabin*, *Clotel*, and *Iola LeRoy* were activated, as James Baldwin in his essay "Everybody's Protest Novel" so beautifully put it, by a "theological terror," where the concepts of good and evil, salvation and damnation, are pitted against each other.[60] This version of the novel, Baldwin argued, could not reveal the complexity, the truth, of a human being living within a particular society. It would necessarily rely on the motif of sentimentality, that is, an excessive display of emotion as well as a prettifying of ugliness, to move the reader, to set him on the right side of the question. Nor was it possible for early black novelists, like Brown or Harper, to do otherwise, since the existence of black people in America had been couched in such extreme moral terms.

No doubt, the black abolitionist writers were influenced by Mrs. Stowe's extremely popular novel, for it caused more discussion about slavery than all of the abolitionists' previous pamphlets and lectures. *Uncle Tom's Cabin* was especially effective because it attacked one of the two major arguments Southerners used to buttress slavery—the concept of the patriarchy and the domestic metaphor. "In her letter to Gamiel Becky in 1851, offering the series of sketches to the National Era, Mrs. Stowe explained that she would give 'the lights and shadows of the patriarchal institution . . . the best side of the thing and something faintly approaching the worst.' "[61] Throughout the novel, she translates her intention into gripping melodrama, as she shows how the big, happy family of the southern plantation is beset by the shadows of separation of slave parent from child, slave husband from wife, slave brother from sister, and that the patriarch, whether his nature is kind or cruel, cannot merely abide by familial ties when he is dealing with slaves but must primarily be concerned with economic considerations.

Mrs. Stowe's attack on the domestic metaphor of the South did not go unnoticed by Southerners. Her book unleashed volumes of critical reviews from the South, the like of which had never been seen before. Her opponents chafed at her precise attack on their most cherished argument in any number of ways—by insisting that she did not understand the concept of patriarchy, and by deriding the "little woman" for entering into such masculine affairs.[62] They understood, too, that her particular antislavery thrust was also an attack on the domestic order and therefore on the condition of southern women. Instinctively, the South called upon southern ladies, who dutifully obliged, "to put the Yankee woman in her place."[63] Many southern men like the novelist George Simms knew that some southern women privately opposed slavery because of the effects of miscegenation on their domestic order. In a valiant attempt to put the novelist and her novel beyond the realm of intellectual concern, he remarked that Mrs. Stowe had reasoned "sensuously" from the "woman nature" and had "misused the mode of romance for the purpose of sociological criticism."[64]

Simms's comment illuminates some of the other dominant characteristics of *Uncle Tom's Cabin*, which were reflections of various abolitionist positions. Mrs. Stowe graphically presented the nature of the Negro in direct comparison to the "woman nature." Both groups, she insisted, were "natural Christians" whose qualities of gentleness and willingness to serve made them superior to the materialistic, intellectual white male. Her vision was not hers alone. In 1863 Theodore Tilton, the editor of the New York *Independent*, said in a speech he gave at Cooper Institute in New York:

> In all the intellectual activities which take their strange quickening from the moral faculties—which we call instincts, intuitions—the negro is superior to the white man—equal to the white woman. It is sometimes said . . . that the negro race is the feminine race of the world. This is not only because of his social and affectionate nature, but because he possesses that strange moral instinctive insight that belongs more to women than to men.[65]

Many abolitionists expressed the view that these feminine qualities were sadly lacking in white American civilization and that the rise of the Negro and the woman would "take the hard edges off of the Anglo Saxon."[66] The idealized Negro, then, pointed up the deficiencies of the white race, and again the Negro was perceived by these thinkers as a means of serving the white race, this time for its own moral betterment.

Ironically, the "feminine" image of the Negro that Mrs. Stowe so dramatically expressed resembled very closely the servile mammies and uncles of antebellum southern literature. What she and other abolitionists who agreed with her emphasized were these qualities, not as reasons for the Negro's inferiority but for his superiority, not as reasons for his enslavement but for his freedom. The effect in literature was the creation of the Negro as a dramatic focal character rather than a comic minor image.

Despite Mrs. Stowe's claim that Negroes were superior because of their Christian virtues, she could not romanticize reality to the extent that she thought these gentle beings could survive as freedmen and as natural Christians in the competitive Anglo-Saxon world of America. So she ended her novel with another idea, which many abolitionists advocated, that the Negroes should go back to Africa where their "special potentialities could be fully realized."[67] Obviously the implication of statements such as these was that slavery, as a national crime, should be abolished, but also that the Negro could never become a part of the American nationality.

If the Negro was naturally gentle, how then could Mrs. Stowe and other abolitionists dramatize his resistance? In keeping with their view that Negroes were "natural Christians" and Anglo-Saxons were inherently competitive and restive, they presented mulattoes as the rebellious segment of the black population. Unconsciously, perhaps, they reversed the "taint of black blood" motif of antebellum novels into the "taint of white blood" syndrome, for their mulattoes, both male and female, exhibit some of the restiveness and unwillingness to serve associated with the Anglo-Saxon personality. But in doing so, these writers revealed their own ambivalences about the superiority of the Negro as a natural Christian. Sterling Brown quoted, in his discussion of the rebellious mulatto stereotype in abolitionist literature, one critic who said:

> This was an indirect admission that a white man in chains was more pitiful, than the African similarly. Their most impassioned plea was in behalf of a person little resembling their swarthy proteges.[68]

In writing their own novels, black writers used some of the elements they found in Mrs. Stowe's novel: the inherent duplicity of the patriarchal system and the Negro as a natural Christian. Often they combined the qualities of the natural Christian as Negro and as woman by focusing on the black woman in their novels. If their heroines were to be effective, however, they would have to combat the negative images of black women in southern ante-bellum literature. They did this by creating a "positive" black woman image. Since positive female qualities were all attributed to the white lady, these writers based their counterimage on her ideal qualities more than on the qualities of any real black woman. The closest black women could come to such an ideal, at least physically, would of course have to be the mulatta, quadroon, or octoroon. Since there was such a close correlation between physical type and spiritual qualities, at least in the area of woman images, it was absolutely necessary to begin with a positive physical type.

The literary conventions of the novel at that time, also legislated that the heroine of a story be beautiful, since physical beauty, at least for a woman, was an indication of her spiritual excellence—but not just any kind of physical beauty. The nineteenth-century novel promoted a rather fragile beauty as the norm; qualities of helplessness, chastity, and refinement rather than, say, strength, endurance, and intelligence were touted as the essential characteristics of femininity. The nineteenth-century heroine not only had to be beautiful physically; she had to be fragile and well bred as well.

The black woman could not possibly fulfill these requirements since by definition to be black in color meant the opposite of beauty, and *well bred* was a term applied only to the upper class. The mulatta, then, according to the literary convention of the nineteenth century as well as half of the twentieth century, could be the only type of black woman beautiful enough to be a popular heroine and close enough to wealth vis-à-vis her father to be well bred. Again, it is interesting to see how social conventions determine literary ones. The social philosophy that denied the beauty of black women and the economic policy of slavery that relegated black people to the bottom of the economic ladder made it very difficult for anyone to write a novel in which a credible black woman could be the major focus of attention. Consequently, from 1861, when *Clotel* was published, until the publication of Ann Petry's *The Street* in 1945, a disproportionate number of black novels adhered to the literary convention of the mulatta heroine.

Although antebellum southern writers had occasionally featured mulattas, it was the abolitionist novelists, both black and white, who would etch her image into the national consciousness. *Clotel*, the first novel to be published by a black man in America, uses the mulatta as the center of the novel. William Wells Brown's descriptions of the mulatta became the model for other black novels:

> Her tall and well developed figure; her long silky black hair, falling in curls down her swan-like neck; her bright, black eyes lighting up her olive-tinted face, and a set of teeth that a Tuscarora might envy, she was a picture of tropical-ripened beauty. At times, there was a heavenly smile upon her countenance which would have warmed the heart of an anchorite.[69]

He went on to tell us about mulattas in general:

> Bottles of ink, and reams of paper, have been used to portray the finely-cut and well-moulded features, the "silken curls," the dark and brilliant eyes, "the splendid forms," the "fascinating smiles and accomplished manners" of these impassioned and voluptuous daughters of the races—the unlawful product of the crime of human bondage.[70]

Doubtless true, Brown contributed his bottle of ink to the number, for one of Clotel's major attributes is her beauty as a mulatta, the fine mixture of two races in which the physical features are predominantly white, although touched enough with black blood to be considered "exotic" or "voluptuous."

Brown played upon Clotel's beauty so heavily that we cannot help but remember the assertions of so many whites, from the time of Jefferson through the mid-nineteenth century, that blacks were inferior because they lacked beauty. Perhaps Brown's characterization of Clotel was influenced by the effect runaway mulattas such as Ellen Craft had on white northern audiences. He had been in charge of her tour throughout the North, had introduced Craft to white sympathizers who were struck by her beauty and refinement, and had remarked on their difficulty in distinguishing her from a white woman.[71]

Clotel's beauty, however, is not her only attribute. In fact, her beauty, like the southern lady's, is primarily a reflection of her spiritual qualities, for she is a natural Christian. Brown emphasizes this quality of hers in all three published versions of his novel, transforming the stereotypical tragic mulatta, Clotel, of the first version into the beautiful Angel of Mercy in the second and third versions. Clotel is beautiful, pure, and Christian, in contrast to the black woman of the antebellum southern writers.

Brown's *Clotel*, however, differs from Mrs. Stowe's *Uncle Tom's Cabin* in two significant ways. These differences reflect the concerns of black abolitionists as well as the view of William Lloyd Garrison, the most important white leader of the Abolitionist Movement. Brown flatly rejects the idea of colonization in Africa, for although the Clotel of the second and third versions lives in Europe for a while, she returns to America, her home, where she nurses soldiers during the Civil War. Africa is seldom mentioned in the novel and certainly not as a place where Clotel's potentialities as a natural Christian would be fulfilled. Many black abolitionists, as well as the Garrisonites, had harshly criticized the colonization movement, calling it an indication that even white abolitionists doubted blacks were the equals of whites and were a part of the American nation.[72]

The second significant way in which Brown differs somewhat from Stowe is in his treatment of rebellious Negroes. Although many of his minor characters are the stock comic mammies and uncles of antebellum southern literature, his rebellious hero, Jerome, is a dark-skinned, although curly-haired, Negro. Jerome is not only rebellious, he is interested in learning and the finer things of life, in contrast to the view of many Northerners who believed that Negroes, once freed, became indolent and degraded.[73] Brown's Jerome is a vivid example of the self-help philosophy of the black abolitionists.[74] But beyond that, he is a natural gentleman of learning well befitting Clotel, the beautiful Angel of Mercy.

Brown's three versions of *Clotel*, written before, during, and immediately following the Civil War, reflect some of the events of that traumatic period. By the time Harper's *Iola LeRoy* was published in 1892, the country had gone through years of Reconstruction, as tumultous a time as the Civil War period. After they saw their dream of abolition realized, black abolitionists were to experience a steady stream of defeats, for as W. E. B. DuBois put it, "the planters, having lost the war for slavery, sought to begin again where they left off in 1860, merely substituting for the individual ownership of slaves, a new state of serfdom of black folk."[75] Once slavery was abolished, the racist prejudices of many Northerners, as well as Southerners, surfaced, for neither region was committed to the idea that blacks were equal to whites. Many white Americans of that period would have responded to Captain Delano's query, "you are Saved, who has cast a shadow upon you?" as Melville's Benito Cereno did when he muttered, "the Negro."

Frances Harper had participated not only in the fight against slavery, but also in the struggle for Negro suffrage and the passage of the Fifteenth Amendment. She must have known that political expediency, the need for a strong Republican party in the South, rather than a belief in Negro rights, was the major reason for its passage.[76] Before its passage, she had watched Northerners project the image of docile black soldiers, despite their fine record in the Civil War; she had seen the enactment of the Black Codes in the South, the discussions that raged about whether the Negro was inherently inferior, and the renewal of colonization schemes.[77] After the achievement of Negro suffrage, she must have cringed at the rise of white supremacy and the popularity of ethnological, "scientific" proofs that the Negro was a sub-human species.[78] She must have noted that many pre-Civil War abolitionists now asserted that the Negro was a vanishing species destined to extinction before the march of the superior white race.[79] She must have reacted with alarm to the intensification of the myth of the degenerate Negro, which emanated from the old eighteenth-century notion that black men had un-controlled passions for white women and that black women were, by nature, sexually loose.[80] As an abolitionist elder, she participated in the founding of the Anti-Lynching Societies with younger black women, such as Ida B. Wells and Mary Church Terrell, whose investigations proved that it usually was not black men who raped white women, but white men who raped black women.[81] In 1891, at the meeting of the National Council of Women of the United States, Harper made this incisive statement about a government that allowed lynchings:

> A government which has power to tax a man in peace, draft him in war, should have power to defend his life in the hour of peril. A gov-ernment which can protect and defend its citizens from wrong and outrage and does not is vicious. A government which would do it and cannot is weak; and where human life is insecure through either weak-ness or viciousness in the administration of law, there must be a lack of justice and where this is wanting, nothing can make up for the deficiency.[82]

On the literary front, the battle of images between pro-Negro and anti-Negro forces continued. Although new southern writers like Albion Tourgée and George Washington Cable eloquently called for Negro rights, Harper was certainly aware that popular American writers, such as Joel Chandler Harris and Thomas Nelson Page, were recreating in their fiction the happy plantation myth of the antebellum period. More to the point, they and less celebrated writers were erasing the horrors of slavery in the American public mind and intensifying their thrust by dramatizing the idea that the contented slave reverted to a savage when freed from the necessary control of whites.[83]

It is no wonder then that the sixty-seven-year-old Harper began her novel not during Reconstruction but during slavery, and that she used many of the elements of the abolitionist novel that had been successful in the initial drive for the freedom of blacks. She made clear her purpose when she stated about her novel that "her story's mission would not be in vain if it awaken in the heart of our countrymen a stronger sense of justice and a more Christ-tian-like humanity. . . ."[84]

One of the main themes of *Iola LeRoy, Shadows Uplifted* is the horror of slavery as visited upon the most effective heroine of the antebellum abolitionist novel, the beautiful, refined, Christian octoroon. Our first glimpse of Iola LeRoy is through the eyes of one of the black slaves:

> "My! but she's putty. Beautiful long hair comes way down her back; putty blue eyes, an' jis' ez white ez anybody's in dis place. I'd jis' wish you could see her yoresef. I heard Marse Tom talkin' 'bout her last night to his brudder; telling him she war mighty airish, but he meant to break her in."[85]

The attempt at black dialect notwithstanding, Harper's Iola LeRoy physically resembles Brown's Clotel. But Harper goes one step further than Brown, for Iola has gone to the finest New England schools and thus fits into the culture's description of what the quintessence of refinement should be. Nor is Iola merely the offspring of some illicit relationship between a white aristocrat and a black slave. Although *Clotel* had originally been subtitled *The President's Daughter*, for it was popularly thought that Thomas Jefferson had a black slave concubine. Iola LeRoy is the fruit of a lawful marriage between a wealthy New Orleans plantation owner and a quadroon whom he educates and frees before he marries her. The children, of course, are not told that their refined, well-educated mother is black. So not only is Iola a mulatta, she is initially an upper-class white woman with privileges most white women of her day could only dream of. Ironically, before Iola painfully discovers that she is black, as a southern lady and a slaveholder's daughter, she had always defended slavery—this despite her high spiritual qualities. It is only when she is cast into the dark condition of slavery that she changes her opinion. Undoubtedly many white women could identify with the beautiful woman who looked as white as they did, who was certainly more wealthy and privileged than they were, and who, despite all this, is instantly pummeled into the pit of servitude only because she has a few drops of black blood in her veins.

Harper's presentation of what slavery meant for Iola is also indicative of the images the writer must refute as well as the atmosphere of the Reconstruction period during which the novel was published. For Iola's virtue, her chastity, is what is at stake, and our heroine spends much of her short time in the shadow of slavery successfully resisting attempts of sex-crazed white men to drag her virtue down. Iola is no loose black woman, nor is she coarse or loud, and therefore being a woman of high Christian morals, the novel insists, she does not deserve the brutal, immoral treatment that is part of the tradition of slavery.

Even more than Brown, Harper emphasized the immoral, un-Christian effects of slavery in the area of brutal and wanton sex. Perhaps she was particularly forceful about the area of rape, because by 1892 there was substantial evidence from congressional investigations about the KKK, proving that many black women were being raped by white men, rather than the popular conception that white women were constantly being raped by black men. The investigations had also proved that the rape of black women was a political tool used to intimidate black men so they could not exercise their political rights.[86] The excessive power of the slavemaster results in immorality not only for the slave, Harper insisted, but for the master class as well. Brown presented a case for the many white women who pined their lives away because their husbands chased after slave girls, therefore making a strong bid for the sympathy of women who knew what it was to be betrayed by a man. Harper did an interesting variation on this theme. She had Iola LeRoy's father tell us about the effects of slavery on the personalities of slavemistresses and therefore the reason he prefers his quadroon sweetheart to them:

> "No! but I think that slavery and the lack of outside interests are beginning to tell on the lives of our women. They lean too much on their slaves, have too much irresponsible power in their hands, are narrowly compressed by the routine of plantation life and the lack of intellectual stimulus."[87]

Although Brown and Harper had similar views, this excerpt points to some of their differences—differences that could certainly be attributed to the thirty years that passed between the publication of *Clotel* and *Iola LeRoy*. Brown was content to have Clotel be a refined, beautiful, Christian mulatta. But Harper had fought for women's rights during this period and had experienced the South's unwillingness to be reconstructed. Thus attention in her novel is placed on the need women feel to work, to be given an education, and to be able to participate in intellectual matters.

In the first part of the novel, Harper also touched on other distorted myths that had developed about blacks since the Civil War. She recounted how black soldiers fought bravely for the Union. She emphasized one of the most terrible effects of slavery, the breakup of families and the attempt of the newly freed slaves to find their kin. In some of the most authentic, although small, moments of the novel, she used her experience as a Reconstruction journalist to narrate briefly the story of a few southern ex-slaves who worked hard, against great odds, to improve their lot.

In fact, her theme in the second half of the novel, as indicated by her subtitle, *Shadows Uplifted*, is a presentation of how professional blacks are lifting themselves up to the standards of middle-class American virtue and thrift. One of the most incredible sections of *Iola LeRoy* is the chapter "Friends in Council." In this chapter, Iola and her circle of high-bred, race-conscious, hardworking Negroes, as well as a few intellectual whites, meet to discuss issues that will benefit the race. Harper sets the mood of this meeting by calling it a *conversizione*, thereby giving it an aura of high culture. The object of the *conversizione* is:

> to gather some of the thinkers and leaders of the race to consult on subjects of vital interest to our welfare. He has invited Dr. Latimer, Professor Cradnor of North Carolina, Mr. Forest of New York, Hons. Dugdale, R vs. Carmicle, Cantmor, Tumster, Professor Langhorne of Georgia and a few ladies, Mrs. Watson, Miss Brown and others.[88]

When Iola LeRoy says she is glad that this meeting is not a dance and her uncle prods her by asking if she does not believe young people should have a good time, she responds in solemn tones:

> "Oh yes, I believe in young people having amusements and recreations, but the times are too serious for us to attempt to make our lives a long holiday."[89]

At this gathering Iola LeRoy appropriately delivers a paper called "The Education of Mothers." Her paper is based on her mother's comment that:

> "we were thrown upon the nation a homeless race to be gathered into the homes and a legally unmarried race to be taught the sacredness of the marriage relation. We must instill into our young people that the true strength of a race means purity in women and uprightness in men; who can say, with Sir Galahad:
> 'My strength is the strength of ten
> Because my heart is pure'
> "And where this is wanting neither wealth nor culture can make up the deficiency."[90]

Although sentimental and puritanical in tone, the *conversizione* does communicate Harper's sense that women, particularly black women, must be involved in working for the race. But note that the tone is one of uplifting the race, of rescuing it from its own culture, of molding black women and men superior to white people according to their own Christian mores. In this section Harper bent over backward to refute the popular stereotype of the day that blacks were degenerates who could not advance either economically or culturally and that they needed white tutelage to be part of the American social order.

In emphasizing this ability among professional blacks to be socially responsible, Harper embellished one of the most important qualities of Clotel and other literary mulattas. Like them, Iola LeRoy is a cultural conductor between the white race and the black because of her education, refinement, and beauty. She gives to the black race what she has learned from the white culture. And what culture means is Western Christian civilization at its best. She becomes, then, a cultural missionary to the ignorant, the loudmouthed, the coarse but essentially good-natured blacks, who need only to be shown the way. Like Clotel, the Angel of Mercy, Iola LeRoy, when freed, nurses wounded soldiers. But Harper emphasized even more than Brown her heroine's commitment to the race, for Iola LeRoy has the opportunity to marry a white doctor and pass into the white race. This she rejects. Instead, she marries a mulatto doctor who himself has rejected the opportunity to pass. Together they work, Iola in a Sunday School where she plans meetings for the special benefit of mothers and children, while her husband, the Good Doctor, inspired by his lovely wife, is a true patriot and good citizen. He

> has great faith in the possibilities of the negro, and believes that, enlightened and Christianized, he will sink the old animosities of slavery into the new community of interests arising from freedom, and that his influence upon the South will be as the influence of the sun upon the earth.[91]

Iola LeRoy, Shadows Uplifted describes the rise of a black middle class headed by mulattoes who feel the grave responsibility of defining for the black race what is best for it, who work within the context of moral Christian ethics, and whose faith in the country and its culture enables them to be conservative in all matters except race. Harper, then, responded to charges that the Negro is and always will be a degenerate by idealizing this segment of the black community. At the center of this upward striving class is the mulatta, no longer tragic or melancholy but a source of light for those below and around her.

The qualities with which Frances Harper endowed her heroine are the result of her reaction to images of black women she felt she had to refute. Iola LeRoy is decidedly not the contented mammy, whom novelists like Thomas Nelson Page continued to idealize. She, like Clotel, does not fit the physical type. She is emphatically not a loose woman; in fact, both she and Clotel rise to the heights of angelic purity, a state that seems sentimental at best, boring at worst. Like Clotel, she is decidedly Christian, and no African spirits lurk in the background as in the Uncle Remus stories of Joel Chandler Harris. Nor is she a tragic mulatta in which the mingling of blood renders her perpetually unhappy. Significantly, however, unlike Clotel, who is a singular beacon of light in Brown's novel, Iola LeRoy now belongs to a society of intelligent and superior black people. Because of her physical beauty and her spiritual virtue, she inspires her society toward the higher values of life. She is, in fact, except for her race, invisible; although her blackness may be to the undiscriminating eye the epitome of the image of the lady, the light by which the shadows will be uplifted.

Images were also fashioned by another tradition, the oral tradition, the witnessing of black people as seen through narrative and song. The slave narrative, as a genre, tended to be represented by those extraordinary slaves, usually men such as Frederick Douglass, who escaped from bondage. Yet there are many narratives of men and women slaves who considered themselves the common folk and who remained in slavery most or all of their lives.[92]

As would be expected, within the genre, the image of the mammy still persists. She is there as cook, housekeeper, nursemaid, and seamstress, always nurturing and caring for her folk. But unlike the white southern image of the mammy, she is cunning, prone to poisoning her master, and not at all content with her lot. It is interesting and ironic that Sojourner Truth, the flamboyant orator who advocated the abolition of slavery and fought for women's rights, would fit the stereotype, at least the physical stereotype, of the mammy southern gentlemen wanted to perceive as harmless. Sojourner Truth is not the only mammy who fought to protect her own children or who rose up against slavery. Mammies kicked, fought, connived, and plotted, most often covertly, to throw off the chains of bondage. The mammy saw herself as a mother, but to her that role embodied a certain dignity and responsibility, rather than a physical debasement, doubtless a carryover from the African view that every mother is a symbol of the marvelous creativity of the earth. The mammy is an important figure in the mythology of Africa. The way in which this theme of African culture is distorted by the white southern perspective testifies to its inability to relate femaleness and femininity—as countless southern belles in antebellum American movies illustrate.

The tragic mulatta, too, appears in slave narratives. And indeed, she is tragic, as are almost all of the accounts. The contrast of comic darky and tragic mulatto developed in the literature of that period certainly does not stand the test of reality. There is little romanticism in the accounts mulattas give of their lives. There are tales of mulattas who as mistresses are abused and sold, their children scattered to the ends of the land, mad mulattas who hate their fathers if they are acknowledged at all by them. There are sullen, cynical mulattas, reared to be sold as high-class courtesans. The narratives abound with tales of woman, be she field nigger or house nigger, mulatta or darky, as breeder, nursemaid, concubine, whipping block, put on the rack of everlasting work and debasing servitude. And in the tales of these women, be they "yaller" or "chocolate," the trivial underscored the abuses they faced: having to sleep outside the mistress' door so that little sexual relationship with one's husband was possible, having to take care of mistress' children so that one's babies were born dead, time after time. The narratives are especially poignant in the equalization of abuse they suggest, for the advantages that the mulatta might have because of her link to the master were easily offset by the disadvantages of alienation and frustration.[93]

The narratives tend to focus on the relationship between slave and master, but the work songs give us another view of how the black woman, during slavery and Reconstruction, viewed herself and was viewed. As music is usually so intensely personal, and need not be sanctioned by a publisher to be heard and spread, the folk songs about and by women tend to peer into the relationship between the black man and the black woman in their identity as man and woman. Courting, lovemaking, success, and disappointment in love—all of these aspects appear in the songs. Some men revel in their women. "Pretty Girl" is representative of this group:

> Rubber is a pretty thing.
> You rub it to make it shine.
> If you want to see a pretty girl,
> Take a peep at mine, take a peep at mine.
>
> Talking about a pretty girl,
> You jus' oughta see mine.
> She is not so pretty
> But she is jus' so fine.
>
> She gives me sugar,
> She gives me lard,
> She works all the while
> In the white folks' yard.[94]

At the same time there is often the recurring theme that:

> De woman am de cause of it all,
> De woman am de cause of it all,
> She's de cause of po' Adam's fall,
> De woman's de cause of it all.[95]

The songs, too, mirror the tingling clash between the dark woman and the "yaller" woman, often in a humorous tone:

> De mulatto gal got yaller skin, yaller skin,
> De mulatto gal got yaller skin, yaller skin,
> De mulatto gal got yaller skin, yaller skin,
> De mulatto gal got yaller skin,
> Den she got a devilish grin, daddy.

De chocolate gal got greasy hair, greasy hair,
De chocolate gal got greasy hair, greasy hair,
De chocolate gal got greasy hair, greasy hair,
De chocolate gal got greasy hair,
She is de gal can cuss and rare, daddy.[96]

Somehow, though, within the confines of their own space, threatened as it was by a more powerful society with different standards, there does not emerge a hard and fast line about the value of a woman simply because she has some white blood. Unlike the literary products of the day, the heroines of these songs might or might not be cinnamon, coffee, chocolate, or yaller:

If 'twant for de ter'pin pie
And sto-bought ham,
Dese country women
Couldn't git nowhere.

Some say, give me a high yaller,
I say, give me a teasin' brown,
For it takes a teasin' brown
To satisfy my soul.

For some folkses say
A yaller is low down,
But teasin' brown
Is what I's crazy about.[97]

Almost always, the substance of the work songs about or by women is sifted through the cry of hard times and how that affects relationships. The men who caught trains and left for whatever reasons, the lack of money, the pervasive sense of danger, the need for a woman to be independent of men, an independence imposed rather than desired, shapes the songs and gives even the gayest song an undertone of plaintiveness. Slave narrative and work song alike project black women as caught in the vise of "hard times," their spirits rising sometimes to the heights of heroism but more often tempered by the nibbling need always to be practical.

Why is there such a difference between the images of black women presented in the early black abolitionist novels and the images in the oral tradition? We must not forget that, by necessity, the first novelists were writing to white audiences. Few black people were literate at that time because of stringent laws against teaching slaves to read and write. The thrust of the black novel necessarily had to be a cry of protest directed at whites for their treatment of blacks. The problem was not whether black women were heroic, but whether they were women at all. I do not make this statement lightly.

According to the norms of society, a woman was physically weak but important to the male because of her ability through her beauty and refinement to rouse his higher instincts to the level of God and culture. The fact that Sojourner Truth could say, as she did at the Convention of the Equal Rights Association in 1867, that she had worked like any man and was yet a woman, that Harriet Tubman had been the only American woman to lead troops into battle, that Marie LaVeau and Mary Ellen Pleasant had wielded political power in New Orleans and San Francisco, or that Phyllis Wheatley had written poems of a quality as fine as that of most eighteenth-century white American poets—these facts complicated the issue rather than resolved it. The deeds of these women and many others less known seemed to indicate that the black woman lacked femininity, a necessary ingredient of womanhood, according to the norm. Further, the social need for a beautiful heroine in the novel tended to designate femininity as the necessary ingredient of female heroism. It is interesting to note that American novels up to that time seldom emphasized the heroism of white American women who had done much hard work toward the creation of the country.

By presenting an image of the black woman that would elicit sympathy and appreciation for her and therefore for black people as a whole, Brown and Harper sought to soften as many differences as possible between the images of the black woman and the white woman. Thus they appealed to the norm with a vengeance; consequently, their works were based on society's definition of their race as "shadows" who needed uplifting.

From the beginning, the black novel had to struggle with the cloak of "theological terror" that Baldwin elucidates in his discussion of protest literature. That is, black writers would constantly have to distinguish between black people as white Americans saw them (as a moral problem and a dumping ground for their fears) and as complex human beings. At the same time, black writers would have to wrestle with the ramifications of white American stereotypes that so strongly affected the lives of black people as a group. Black thinkers would have to articulate the concepts of their own culture, even as there was resistance to that articulation from within as well as from without. Only then could they dismiss Anglo-American cultural norms as their conceptual framework. Only then could they begin to draw inspiration and materials from the forms of their own culture that lay embedded in the rich oral and musical tradition of the folk. One of the important concepts they would have to articulate would be the images of female and male within the community of the black folk even as these images were being assaulted by the dominant society.

Certainly the works of Charles Chesnutt were a great step in that direction. Although Paul Laurence Dunbar is the acknowledged Negro poet of the turn of the century, his first three novels focused on whites and the promise of his last novel, *Sport of the Gods* (1904), a precursor of the

Harlem Renaissance city novel, was never realized because of his early death. Chesnutt was a writer of fiction and the first black novelist to rise to national prominence. Although he uses full-blown versions of the mammy, the loose woman, the tragic mulatta, and the conjure woman in his short stories and three novels, this pioneer in black fiction cautiously introduced elements of black folklore as frames for his fiction. Although his novels are primarily about the small, black middle class, he tries to present black characters and situations that are more in keeping with the reality that black people had to face at the turn of the century.

His racial identity unknown to the literary world, Chesnutt received considerable praise for his first collection of short stories, *The Conjure Woman and Other Stories* (1899). But when it became known that he was black, he received increasing pressure from his publishers to maintain the tone of sentimentality of the happy plantation darky story, popular at that time. His letters reveal his chafing sense of frustration at having to disguise his perceptions with overlays of sentimentality and caricature, because his white audience was not open to a view of blacks as complex human beings.[98] Nonetheless, he overstepped his boundaries when he wrote *The Marrow of Tradition* (1901), a novel based on the Wilmington Race Riot of 1898, and *The Colonel's Dream* (1905), a novel about the conflict between the South's racist prejudices and attempts at reform. These two novels were published at a time when Thomas Dixon's novels, *The Leopard's Spots* (1902) and *The Clansman* (1905), were extremely popular. Given the enactment of the Jim Crow laws and the disenfranchisement of most Negroes in the South, it is not surprising that white Americans reacted more favorably to Dixon's vindictive portrayal of the Negro as a brute rather than to Chesnutt's dramatization of racist concepts that permeated American society. Soon after, disappointed by the harsh reviews of his novels, which were not about his craftsmanship but about his racial views, Chesnutt retired from writing fiction and went back to his law practice.

His literary career clearly illustrates the plight of nineteenth-century black novelists as they struggled with the cloak of theological terror that was thrust upon them. They had the choice of being silent completely or of compromising their sense of reality if they were to publish. Without the freedom to write about life as they saw it, restricted by the concepts of good and evil that black people represented to the majority culture, it is no wonder that their expression lacked the imagination and richness of the folk expressions of the day. Without the atmosphere of experimentation, social conventions that were obviously stereotypical views hardened into literary conventions. The shadow of white racism hung over early black novelists. Many years would pass before it would be lifted, allowing glimpses of reality to revise the distorted black images of the eighteenth and nineteenth centuries.

2
The Rise and Fall
——— of the Proper Mulatta ———

Applauding youths laughed with young prostitutes
And watched her perfect, half-clothed body sway;
Her voice was like the sound of blended flutes
Blown by black players upon a picnic day.
She sang and danced on gracefully and calm,
The light gauze hanging loose about her form;
To me she seemed a proudly-swaying palm
Grown lovelier for passing through a storm.
Upon her swarthy neck black shiny curls
Luxuriant fell; and tossing coins in praise
The wine-flushed, bold-eyed boys, and even the girls
Devoured her shape with eager, passionate gaze;
But looking at her falsely-smiling face,
I knew her self was not in that strange place.[1]
　　　—*The Harlem Dancer*, by Claude McKay

Between 1906, when Charles Chesnutt stopped publishing, and 1917, when Claude McKay published the poem *Harlem Dancer*, monumental events occurred that greatly affected the life-styles of most Afro-Americans. One was the great migration of blacks from the South to the North, a journey that has become a structural framework for Afro-American cultural forms.

Blacks certainly had good reason to leave the South. At the turn of the century, partially because of the economic and social progress they had made, they were being energetically contained by overtly southern racist policies. In practically every southern state, blacks had been disenfranchised, while their lives in every social arena—housing, education, employment—were controlled by Jim Crow laws. They were increasingly threatened by the debt slavery system, by drastic penal measures, and ultimately by the possibility of being lynched.[2] Southern white writers such as Thomas Dixon were portraying blacks as brutes, and by 1915 the history-making film *Birth of a Nation: A White Southerner's View of the Civil War*, was playing to packed houses all over the nation.[3]

For these reasons, as well as more individualistic ones such as the desire to travel, a multitude of blacks left the largely agricultural South to try their luck in the industrial northern centers. For the first time, New York, Philadelphia, Washington, D.C., Boston, and Chicago found themselves absorbing sizeable numbers of the people they had so gallantly accused the South of abusing.

The First World War provided a peak for this already large exodus, since jobs in industry necessary to the conduct of the war were left vacant by departing soldiers, and since drought and then heavy rains and the boll weevil ruined the cotton crops of 1915 and 1916. By 1918 more than one million blacks were estimated to have left the South. A Negro song of this period succinctly expressed the reasons for this unprecedented mass exodus:

> Boll weevil in de cotton
> Cut worm in de cotton
> Debil in de white man
> Wah's goin' on?[4]

The years 1914-18 were a period of upward mobility for urban blacks as well as for black and white women, since jobs in the North were plentiful and lucrative. Along with an increase in the black population, racial discrimination intensified in the North, particularly when the war ended and the soldiers returned home. Of course, city life changed, to some extent, a previously rural black culture. The immediate result of the migration, and the First World War, was the development of black ghettoes in the larger cities and concurrently the grafting of new cultural patterns onto the old ones from the South.

Harlem became the most prominent of these black cities. Located in New York, the cultural capital of the United States, it evoked dreams not only of a better life but of glamour, excitement, and fame. Characterized by jazz, a new black music conceived in New Orleans and nurtured in Harlem's swanky clubs, the Negro metropolis became a legendary city within a city. Its bright lights, along with its elegant Dutch brownstones, proclaimed it the black capital of the world.

It was this image of Harlem that lured many black women and men to Harlem. To some extent the image carried some substance. For professionals or businessmen, the large black population meant economic opportunity and profit. One need only point to Madame Walker, who had become a millionaire by selling hair-straightening products to black women who wanted to be in style. For those with talent in the arts, this electric black city held the promise of fellowship and the possibility of making some impact on America, even the world. After all, intellectuals like James Weldon Johnson and W. E. B. Du Bois called Harlem their home. For men like Garvey, interested in the betterment of the race through politics, the large concentration of blacks was there, dormant perhaps, but waiting to be organized. The first political mass movement of blacks, Marcus Garvey's Universal Negro Improvement Association (UNIA), had its base in Harlem. Alain Locke, the black philosopher of the age, expressed the dominant feeling of the times when he said of his city:

> Here in Manhattan is not merely the largest Negro community in the world but the first concentration in history of so many diverse elements of Negro life. It has attracted the African, the West Indian, the Negro American, has brought together the Negro of the North and the Negro of the South; the man from the city and the man from the town and village; the peasant and the student, the businessman, the professional artist, poet, musician, adventurer, and worker, preacher and criminal, exploiter and social outcast. Each group has come with its own separate motives and for its own special ends, but their greatest experience has been the finding of one another. Prescription and prejudices have thrown these dissimilar elements into a common area of contact and interaction. Within this area, race sympathy and unity have determined a further fusing of sentiment and experience. So what began in terms of segregation becomes more and more as its elements mix and react, the laboratory of a great race welding. Hitherto, it must be admitted that American Negroes have been a race more in name than in fact, or to be exact, more in sentiment than in experience. The chief bond between them has been that of a common condition rather than a common consciousness; a problem in common rather than a life in common. In Harlem, Negro life is seizing upon its first chances for group expression and self-determination. It is—or promises at least to be— a race capitol. That is why our comparison is taken with those nascent centers of folk-expression and self-determination which are playing a creative part in the world today. Without pretense to their political significance, Harlem has the same role to play for the New Negro as Dublin has had for the New Ireland or Prague for the new Czechoslovakia.[5]

The intellectual and artistic movement that exploded in Harlem between 1917 and 1929 was called then, as it is now, the Harlem Renaissance, a name that indicates the self-consciousness of the age.[6] Intellectuals such as

Locke and Johnson, the oldest and most prestigious black writers of the day, proclaimed a new philosophy, the New Negro Philosophy. The New Negro, they insisted, was an assertive being who was both proud of his race and insistent on his rights as an American.

As George Kent pointed out, "the single unifying concept which places the achievement of the Harlem Renaissance in focus is that it moved to gain authority in its portrayal of black life by the attempt to assert, with varying degrees of radicality, a disassociation of sensibility from that enforced by American culture and its institutions."[7] Although seemingly straightforward, however, the New Negro Philosophy that informed the literature of the Renaissance embodied the contradictions of the age. The young poet Langston Hughes proclaimed:

> We young artists who create now intend to express our individual dark-skinned selves without fear or shame. If white people are pleased, we are glad. If they aren't, it doesn't matter. We know we are beautiful and ugly too. If colored are pleased we are glad. If they are not, their displeasure doesn't matter either. We build our temples for tomorrow, strong as we know how, and we stand on the top of the mountain, free within ourselves.[8]

Yet he agreed with Locke when he stated in his essay, "The New Negro," that:

> The Negro Mind reaches out as yet to *nothing but American wants, American ideals*. But this forced attempt to build his Americanism on race values is a unique social experiment and its ultimate success is impossible except through the fullest sharing of American culture and institutions.[9]

In hindsight the terms used to define the New Negro Philosophy themselves lacked definition. What in fact did American ideals mean, or more specifically, what was the essence of America? That question had yet to be answered since America itself, until the 1920s, had looked to Europe for its culture, its own definition. America had yet to manifest in its art the forms of its developing culture.[10] What then did the New Negro mean when he said he reached out to nothing but American wants? American ideals? What did these American ideals mean particularly, since only fifty years before, blacks had been seen not as Americans but as the property of Americans?

The problem of self-definition was further complicated during the Renaissance by the tendency of its leaders to view art as the means to social equality. White liberals such as Carl Van Vechten and Mrs. Mason Osgood concurred with Robert Park, the foremost white student of race relations of the period, when he wrote that "the Anglo Saxon was basically a pioneer while the Negro is primarily an artist living life for its own sake. . . . The Negro is the lady among the races."[11] In retrospect, the views of these negrophiles seem to be but another variation on the romantic theme of the superior Negro that nineteenth-century abolitionists had fostered. But Harlem Renaissance leaders also exploited this view, perhaps because blacks had not been able, through political means, to secure even a semblance of social equality. Certainly the atmosphere resulting from this aesthetic view of the Negro had a favorable effect on the artistic realm. In the theater, for example, white writers such as Eugene O'Neill (*Emperor Jones*, 1920), Ridgely Torrance (*Granny Maumee*, 1917), and Paul Green (*In Absalom's Bosom*, 1924) were helping to increase the acceptance of the Negro as a serious subject in literature.[12] Black intellectuals noted that doors were opening in artistic fields. James Weldon Johnson summed up a pervasive argument of that period when he insisted that "the demonstration of intellectual parity by the Negro through the production of literature and art" would be the most effective tool against racism.[13]

Such a stratagem would entangle the black writers of the twenties in a web of contradictions. On the one hand, they insisted on their own independence both as individuals and as black people, while on the other hand, they were seen as the true representatives of the race, as its image makers. The web became even more of a tangle since artistic models that were uniquely Afro-American had yet to develop. The logical step would be to look to Africa for those essential qualities that distinguished black art from white art. But Africa as an intellectual concept was little known to Afro-Americans who had learned to think of it as the dark continent and who had yet to distinguish between its value system and the value system of America. Nor had anyone articulated the impact of African culture on the Afro-American experience. Inevitably, then, this approach tended to lead the writer down the path of romanticism and sometimes dishonesty.

One could, of course, look to America for models. Although a seemingly simple approach, this path, too, posed many problems. If the Afro-American was merely an American, what distinguished his art and culture from the art and culture of Anglo-Americans? Americans themselves had yet to create functional cultural models that did not lean heavily on upper-class European images. For the Afro-American writer, such a route could only end in self-contempt. If American culture was essentially European, and if upper-class images were the ideals, then what role could Afro-Americans possibly play in that grand drama of European tradition? Such a position could only lead to the pathetic limbo James Baldwin felt himself to be in when, thirty years later, he gazed with wonder and envy at the cathedral in Chartres.

The questions hidden under the guise of the optimistic New Negro Philosophy were devastating, for they indicated that self-definition would be
no easy task for the Afro-American writers. Without a clear sense of self,
how much risk would they be able to take in creating new and engaging
forms? No matter how much black writers might assert their independence,
they had yet to reckon with the vacuum of an unarticulated tradition.

Such a dilemma is difficult enough to unravel, given the best of circumstances—a dialogue between the writer and the culture from which he or
she comes. But black writers of the twenties knew, as Frances Harper did,
that their reading audience was primarily white and one that also was
searching for its own definition through the process of contrast. Whether
the white reader would characterize black images as a shot in the arm for
an overcivilized West that had lost its passion, or whether he found solace
in the belief that he was morally and intellectually superior to blacks, he
was primarily interested in his concept of himself.

"The New Negro, as perceived by many whites, was simply the old
romantic conception of the Negro covered with a patina of the cultured
primitivism and exoticism fashionable in the 1920's."[14] As a result, Afro-
American literature in the twenties continued to struggle under the heavy
cloak of "theological terror" as it reacted to white society's view of blacks.
But during the Harlem Renaissance, the forms of struggle were outwardly
different from those of the nineteenth century. Some writers accepted the
fashionable belief that blacks were primitives who, because they lacked
inhibitions and succumbed to their passions, were noble and vital. Others,
seeing the venom in the "primitive" image, insisted that blacks were as
conventional, perhaps even more conventional, than their white counterparts. That is, blacks, like whites, accepted the American ideals of material-
ism, security, and conformity.

Not surprisingly, male writers explored the primitive view more intensely
than did the women novelists of the day. The garb of uninhibited passion
wears better on a male, who after all, does not have to carry the burden of
the race's morality or lack of it. In any case, the uninhibited, primitive female
image was too reminiscent of the loose woman image for most women
novelists to see any glamour in it. The harsh life of prostitution, which so
many black women were forced to accept, was all too evident in the Harlem
of the 1920s. Even Claude McKay, the most prominent proponent of the
primitive motif, acknowledged the pathos of the black prostitute and en-
titled his first American book of poems, *Harlem Shadows*, after the "little
dark girls who in slippered feet / go prowling through the night from street
to street."[15]

Instead, the female novelists of the 1920s chose to make their heroines
light-complexioned, upper-middle-class black women with taste and refinement. Two black women, Jessie Redmon Fauset and Nella Larsen, were

acknowledged during the Harlem Renaissance as significant novelists, and both exclusively focused attention on this image of the black woman.

Jessie Fauset was one of the more prolific writers of the period. She wrote four novels—*Three Is Confusion* (1924), *Plum Bun* (1929), *The China-berry Tree* (1931), and *Comedy, American Style* (1933)—and many short stories, articles, and light poems. As well as a writer, she was one of the intellectuals who "midwifed" the Harlem Renaissance,[16] to which end she wrote articles covering a wide range of interests, from Pan-Africanism to blacks in the American theater. Her article "The Gift of Laughter" is an incisive analysis of the black actor as the "funny man" of America. She quickly grasped in this article the paradox of this gift of laughter that the American Negro is contributing to the American theater:

> In passing one pauses to wonder if this picture of the black American as a living comic supplement has not been tainted in order to cam-ouflage the real feeling and knowledge of his white compatriot. Cer-tainly the plight of the slaves under even the mildest of masters could never have been one to awaken laughter. And no genuinely thinking person, no really astute observer, looking at the Negro in modern American life, could find his condition even now a first aid to laughter. That condition may be variously deemed hopeless, remarkable, ad-mirably inspiring, depressing; it can never be dubbed merely amusing.[17]

Yet, although she knows the image of the laughing Negro to be partly a ploy, she does not discount the quality of zest and the love of life that the black actor brings to the stage:

> The remarkable thought about this gift of ours is that it has its rise, I am convinced, in the very woes which beset us. Just as a person driven by great sorrow may finally go into an orgy of laughter, just so an op-pressed and too hard driven people breaks over into compensating laughter and merriment. It is our emotional salvation.[18]

Fauset, however, seldom mentions the depressing conditions under which most turn-of-the-century blacks lived in her novels. Her fiction is peopled by characters who are "trying for a life of reason and culture,"[19] culture in this case being Western refinement. Her novels insist that the upper-middle-class Negro has the same values as the upper-class white. This indeed may be true, and a presentation of upper-class Negro life is certainly interesting material for fiction. The problem with Fauset's novels is that she gives us this particular Negro exclusively and as the representative of what the race is capable of doing. "She records a class in order to praise a race."[20] Her Negroes become apologists for the race, indicators of the heights of refinement blacks might attain, given the opportunity. In her introduction to *The Chinaberry Tree*, Fauset tells us her reasons for writing this novel:

> Nothing—and the Muses themselves would bear witness to this—has ever been farther from my thoughts than writing to establish a thesis. Colored people have been the subjects which I have chosen for my novels partly because they are the ones I know best, partly because of all the other separate groups which constitute the American cosmogony, none of them, to me, seems so naturally endowed with the stuff of which chronicles may be made. To be a Negro in America posits a dramatic situation. The elements of the play fall together involuntarily; they are just waiting for Fate the Producer to quicken them into movement, for Chance the Prompter to interpret them with fidelity.
>
> The mere juxtaposition of the races brings into existence this fateful quality. But of course there are breathing spells, in-between spaces where colored men and women work and love and go their ways with no thought of the "problem." What are they like then? . . . So few of the other Americans know.[21]

She succinctly sums up the characteristics of the Negro she has chosen to write about by pointing out that:

> Finally he started out as a slave but he rarely thinks of that. To himself he is a citizen of the United States whose ancestors came over not along with the emigrants in the Mayflower, it is true, but merely a little earlier in the good year, 1619. His forebearers are to him quite simply the early settlers who played a prettily large part in making the land grow. He boasts no Association of the Sons and Daughters of the Revolution, but he knows that as a matter of fact and quite inevitably his sons and daughters date their ancestry as far back as any. So quite naturally as his white compatriots he speaks of his "old Boston families," "old Philadelphians," "old Charlestonians." And he has a wholesome respect for family and education and labor and the fruits of labor. He is still sufficiently conservative to lay a slightly greater stress on the first two of these four.
>
> Briefly he is a dark American who wears his joy and rue very much as does the white American. He may wear it with some differences but it is the same joy and the same rue.
>
> So in spite of other intentions I seem to have pointed a moral.[22]

Jessie Fauset could certainly write with authority about the upper-middle-class Negro of the day. She herself came from an old Philadelphian family and, in contrast to most black women of the day, received an extensive formal education. She received the B.A. at Cornell and the M.A. from the University of Pennsylvania and studied at the Sorbonne. She traveled extensively in Europe and was as aware of the European culture as she was of upper-class American Negro life. Nor was she a "puff" of refinement. She worked hard for black people, first as a teacher of Latin and French at the famous M Street High School of Washington, D.C., and then as literary editor of *The Crisis*, the magazine of the NAACP.[23] She wrote consistently about the problems and aims of the Negro, translated poems of French West Indians into English, and was committed to the betterment of the race. She was in many ways a fine example of W. E. B. Du Bois's "talented tenth."

Fauset did not write about upper-middle-class blacks only because she was a member of that class. In an interview, she related why she started writing fiction. She, as well as Nella Larsen, was greatly affected by the publication of T. S. Stribling's *Birthright* in 1922, a novel about a mulatto Harvard graduate who tries to improve his own people, a book that was considered at that time to be "the most significant novel on the negro written by a white American."[24] Fauset was impressed by Peter Siner, the protagonist, who was neither a primitive nor a poor peasant, but a well-educated, race-conscious black like herself. That this side of black life, as recreated by a black writer, was sadly lacking during the first years of the Renaissance is indicated by Fauset's difficulty in finding a publisher for her first novel. "Publishers rejected her manuscript because 'it contains no description of Harlem dives, no race riot, no picturesque abject poverty.' "[25]

Fauset, then, had at her disposal, because of her intimate knowledge of her class and because she was not fooled by the fad of primitivism, unique and significant subject matter. But because she was so conscious of being an image maker and because she accepted wholesale American values, except on the issue of race, her novels hardly communicate the intellectual depth that some of her articles do. Her fiction does not capture the essence of the upper-middle-class Negro society, a subject that certainly would show the relationship of class to race in America, because her characters lack critical insight and complexity, and because her plots seldom rise beyond the level of melodrama. In other words, her stories become bad fairytales in which she sacrifices the natural flow of life to the thesis that she feels she must prove—that blacks are as conventional as whites. Upper-middle-class blacks may have been as conventional, but Fauset's novels are so conditioned by her narrow mind set—the glorification of this position—that she does not allow her characters to become themselves.

Given her orientation, it is not surprising that Fauset's novels accepted the literary conventions of the nineteenth-century black novel. Her heroines are proper light-skinned women who unquestionably claim propriety as the highest ideal. They pursue the values of material success through marriage and inevitably believe that refinement is a reflection of spirituality. As a result, her heroines, like Laurentine Strange in *The Chinaberry Tree* and Angela Murray in *Plum Bun*, suffer crises because of a social mishap, either of birth or deportment. Nor does Fauset exercise any critical distance toward the unimportance of her heroines' major crises. She, too, believes that not being able to take up with the "right people" is a tragedy.

Her heroines, of course, are always beauties, according to the norms of the day. Light-skinned, long-haired, fine and graceful, they resemble princesses from a children's story who but for the complications of haphazard Negro birth would live happily ever after. *The Chinaberry Tree*, for example, is the story of Laurentine Strange, who is unfortunate enough to be the daughter of an ex-slave, Aunt Sal, and her former master, Captain Halloway. Far from having a primarily physical relationship, her parents were passionately in love with each other. "Halloway was a lad of serious bent but of tearing tyrannical passion. He loved her . . . he could not marry her."[26] Aunt Sal, a straight, brown-skinned woman, lives in the glow of her memorable passion, the only traces of which are her daughter Laurentine and her house protected by the chinaberry tree. The tree is ever present throughout the novel as comforter and solidifier until one wonders if Captain Halloway's spirit has entered it.

Although Aunt Sal might have been a woman of passion, her mulatta daughter Laurentine is a lady, except for her manner of birth and the strained strangeness that seems to come from her mixed blood. Appropriately, she is the finest beauty in the town, who except for the sordidness of her birth would have few social difficulties in life. But Laurentine Strange's background alienates her from upper-middle-class society to which, by virtue of shade and taste, she rightfully belongs. The novel is, to a large extent, the measure of her ability to step softly and straight, so she might be admitted into its shelter.

Fauset's novels also employ the theme of "passing," a phenomenon that exemplifies the shakiness of the upper middle class. If upper-middle-class blacks could successfully compete with whites, why then would they have to resort to passing? Ironically, passing is a major theme of the 1920s when race pride was supposedly at a peak. One might at first think that this theme fed into the American belief system that it is better to be white than black. In actuality, the theme, as it was presented in the twenties, heightened the white audience's awareness of the restrictions imposed upon talented blacks who then found it necessary to become white to fulfill themselves. Talented blacks, however, in the novels of Walter White, as well as Jessie Fauset, are the mulattoes, who are distinguished from other blacks by their restiveness and frustration, a motif reminiscent of the rebellious mulattoes of the abolitionist novels. Inevitably, though, in Fauset's novels as well as in most novels of the Renaissance, the passer returns to her race convinced that her loss of identity, as well as the values she must adopt to be in the white race, are too high a price to pay. Assailed by passion, the taint or glory of her black blood, depending on your point of view, these mulattas also resemble the tragic mulattas of antebellum novels.

It is significant, too, that the passer is often a woman who believes that through her marriage to a wealthy white man, she might gain economic security and more freedom of mobility. The process of passing could have peculiarly feminine overtones, for a woman can often cement her future according to the man she marries. This theme is so inordinately prevalent during this period, engaging the attention of black writers and white writers alike, that one is tempted to wonder if it offered vicarious wish fulfillment, as well as amusement for those blacks who would pass if they could, and titillating drama for a largely white reading audience. Sterling Brown summarized the characteristics of the passer in the Harlem Renaissance novel, underlining the difference in interpretation, according to the novelist's race:

> We have thus seen that the mulatto who "passes" has been a victim of opposing interpretations. Negro novelists urge his unhappiness, until he is summoned back to his people by the spirituals, or their full-throated laughter, or their simple, sweet ways. . . . White novelists insist upon the mulatto's unhappiness for other reasons. To them he is the anguished victim of a divided inheritance. Mathematically they work it out that his intellectual strivings and self-control come from his white blood, and his emotional urgings, indolence and potential savagery come from his Negro blood. Their favorite character, the octoroon, wretched because of the "single drop of midnight in her veins," desires a white lover above all else, and must therefore go down to a tragic end. The white version is nearly a century old; the negro version sprang up recently.[27]

In spite of their many social traumas, Fauset's heroines have great faith in America and in the American dream—that through hard work you can achieve equality. They even go one step further. They accept the precept that blacks must be superior to whites in their accomplishments to qualify. For what do they qualify? They qualify for freedom, yes, but not the freedom to experiment or experience. They want the highest of all American values: security.

Like Iola LeRoy, Laurentine's resolution is her marriage to a successful Negro doctor:

> But Laurentine and Melissa, so widely different, were thinking on none of these things. Caught up in an immense tide of feeling, they were unable to focus their minds on home, children, their men. . . . Rather like spent swimmers, who had given up the hope of rescue and then

had suddenly met with it, they were sensing with all their being, the feel of the solid ground beneath their feet, the grateful monotony of the skies above their heads . . . and everywhere about them the immanence of God. . . . The Chinaberry Tree became a Temple.[28]

Jessie Fauset's novels continue the tradition that *Iola LeRoy* started. In these novels the beautiful mulatta princess reigns, although in Fauset the heroine need not be technically a mulatta but merely light-complexioned. In both novels, much attention is placed on the efficacy of the upper-middle-class refinement. In Fauset, the details of refined living are voluptuously reported and the upper-middle-class family is so firmly entrenched that it can reject those from its ranks who do not measure up by virtue of parentage, shade, or life-style. Also, Fauset's heroines tend to be less independent than Iola LeRoy, closer to the image of the contemporary pampered young woman, the darling of her daddy, and the jewel of her lover's eye. Style replaced angelic pretensions:

> She drew on the stockings, put on a pair of shoes with the sides cut almost entirely away; arranged her hair with its not too permanent wave back from her extremely good forehead and into a small flat knot at the nape of her neck, got herself into a crushed strawberry tinted thin wool frock with squares of mulberry embroidery arranged distractingly about the skirt, the sleeves and the neck. A mulberry colored handkerchief and a few drops of some devastating perfume completed her ensemble.[29]

Appropriately, Laurentine is a seamstress and a very good dress designer—feminine skills that along with her light complexion recommend her to the upper class. No teacher of Sunday School or composer of papers on the education of black mothers, the heroine of *The Chinaberry Tree* is touted as the first Negro to introduce fashionable pajamas to her small New Jersey town. In Fauset, as in Harper, the upper middle class is interested in the betterment of the race, but for this Harlem Renaissance novelist, that concern is so connected with the individual's need to be successful or to maintain status that one gets the feeling that success is so rare among blacks that it in itself is enough of a contribution.

One extremely important difference exists between Iola LeRoy and Fauset's heroine. Iola LeRoy rejects any attempt to pass into the white race, for that would be totally against her sense of righteousness and would eliminate the intense need she feels to be part of the wonderful struggle to better the race. Fauset's heroines pass for social and economic advancement, thereby showing the crack in the assumption that the middle class of blacks are having as fine a time as middle-class whites. Fauset obviously knew that refinement and the American values of thrift and economy were not enough to achieve equality, for "The Problem," in her novels, is never too far away. Yet she does not take advantage of the discrepancy between the image and the reality of the upper middle class, for she does not question the values she insists they pursue.

We must remember that Fauset exemplified the dominant position of the Harlem intellectuals of her day. Her works were praised by critics and her images exalted.[30] However, her values also posed a serious threat to the New Negro Philosophy. If blacks were culturally no different from whites except when downtrodden, how could anyone posit a unique Negro genius, a specifically different culture? If Fauset's novels were to be believed, the Negro's peculiar contributions to America were a result of oppression rather than the consequence of a different cosmology or tradition. Also, what should one do with the issue of class? Why should lower-class Negroes rise up and change their situation if they only replaced one master with another, black like them, but master nonetheless. Fauset's novels indirectly pose the question of whether one could really be conservative about all things except race unless one were sitting in a position of relative comfort.

In contrast to Jessie Fauset, Nella Larsen consciously intensified the pathos and hollowness of the middle-class mulatta heroine image. Undoubtedly, her novels *Quicksand* (1928) and *Passing* (1929) are partially based on her life, the salient element of which was her position as a child of mixed parentage, comfortable in neither her father's nor her mother's world.

She was born in Chicago in 1893, the child of a Virgin Islander (Danish West Indian) and a Danish woman. Her father died when she was two and her mother later married a Dane like herself. Nella spent an unhappy childhood, for her race was a constant reminder to her stepfather of his wife's former life.

Her early experiences must have confused and embittered the sensitive girl. A singular image of difference, she was educated in Chicago schools, where all of the children were of northern European ancestry. When she was sixteen she went to Denmark where she spent three years with her mother's relatives only to return to the United States for her college education. She went to Fisk University for a year, certainly an attempt on her part somehow to belong to the Negro world. But the restrictive atmosphere there disturbed her and she left Fisk for the University of Copenhagen. By this time she was a moody, sensitive woman who seemed never to be at home wherever she was.

Her life was characterized by constant dissatisfaction and change. She returned from Copenhagen to New York where she entered nursing school. After graduating from Lincoln Hospital Training Program in 1915, she went to Tuskegee Hospital where she became the superintendent of nurses.

But again she became dissatisfied. She spent one year there and then returned to Lincoln Hospital. But the change in environment did not give her
a feeling of belonging. In 1918 she began studying to become a librarian
and finally became the children's librarian at the 135th Street branch (Harlem) of the New York Public Library. She remained there from 1921 to
1929 during which time she married Dr. Elmer S. Imes.

Imes was a physicist and a graduate of Fisk with a Ph.D. from the University of Michigan. The couple lived in Harlem and were certainly a part
of the educated and polished middle class. In 1929 Nella Larsen won the
bronze medal of the Harmon Foundation for distinguished achievement
among Negroes. Nonetheless, she felt restricted by America. In 1930 she
became the first black woman to win the Guggenheim Award. Its purpose
was to allow her to travel abroad so she could write a novel "on the different
effects of Europe and the U.S. on the intellectual and physical freedom of
the Negro."[31]

But Nella Larsen was still as uncomfortable in Europe as she had been
in upper-class Negro America. She soon returned from the continent, never
to complete her third novel. Instead, she and her husband were divorced,
whereupon she disappeared completely from public life. She became a super-
vising nurse at Bethel Hospital in Brooklyn and died virtually unknown in
1963.

Many critics have commented on Nella Larsen's mysterious disappear-
ance from the world of literature. Both of her novels, *Quicksand* and *Passing*, received considerable acclaim and showed great promise. Some believe
that as sensitive and insecure as she was, Larsen was discouraged by the
economically depressed America of the thirties, a world certainly not par-
tial to a black writer. Others remind us that Larsen was deeply wounded by
a widely publicized although false charge of plagiarism brought against her
when she published her "Sanctuary" (1930). In any case, Larsen, like
Jean Toomer, another important writer of the period, disappeared into the
wide world, to be neither black nor white, but merely apart.[32]

Larsen's novels, as well as her life, are the quintessence of the tragic
mulatta image and combine some of the qualities Sterling Brown distinguished in black and white novels about passing. *Quicksand* portrays Helga
Crane, a sensuous mulatta of questionable parentage who is repulsed by
the drab puritanism of middle-class Negro society, yet who cannot give herself up to the sensuality she feels dammed up inside her. Larsen's opening
description of Helga's room at Naxos, a distinguished Negro school, beautifully sets up this tension:

> Helga Crane sat alone in her room, which at that hour, eight in the
> evening, was in soft gloom. Only a single reading lamp, dimmed by a
> great black and red shade, made a pool of light on the blue Chinese

carpet, on the bright covers of the books which she had taken down
from their long shelves, on the white pages of the opened one selected,
on the shining brass bowl crowded with many-colored nasturtiums
beside her on the low table, and on the oriental silk which covered
the stool at her slim feet. It was a comfortable room, furnished with
rare and intensely personal taste, flooded with Southern sun in the
day, but shadowy just then with the drawn curtains and single shaded
light. Large, too. So large that the spot where Helga sat was a small
oasis in a desert of darkness. And eerily quiet. But that was what she
liked after her taxing day's work, after the hard classes, in which she
gave willingly, unsparingly of herself with no apparent return. She
loved this tranquility, this quiet, following the fret and strain of long
hours spent among fellow members of a carelessly unkind and gossip-
ing faculty, following the strenuous rigidity of conduct required in this
huge educational community of which she was an insignificant part.
This was her rest, this intentional isolation for a short while in the
evening, this little time in her own attractive room with her own books.
To the rapping of other teachers, bearing fresh scandals, or seeking
information or other more concrete favors, or merely talk, at that
hour Helga Crane never opened her door.[33]

Irritated by the school's insistence that Negroes have good sense and be
satisfied with being hewers of wood and drawers of water (obviously a reference to Tuskegee), she chafes at its conformity and lack of spirit:

This great community, she thought, was no longer a school. It had
grown into a machine. It was now a showplace in the Black Belt, ex-
emplification of the white man's magnanimity, refutation of the black
man's inefficacy. Life had died out of it. It was, Helga decided, now
only a big knife with cruelly sharp edges ruthlessly cutting all to a
pattern, the white man's pattern. Teachers as well as students were
subject to the paring process, for it tolerated no innovations, no indi-
vidualism. Ideas it rejected, and looked with open hostility on one
and all who had the temerity to offer a suggestion or ever so mildly
express a disapproval. Enthusiasm, spontaneity, if not actually sup-
pressed, were at least openly regretted as unladylike or ungentlemanly
qualities. The place was smug and fat with self-satisfaction.[34]

Unlike Ralph W. Ellison's unnamed narrator, Helga Crane sees the lie behind this distinguished Negro school. What is remarkable about Larsen's
treatment of her heroine is that she is able to communicate how Helga's
taste for fine objects and her love of natural things allow her to perceive
the truth about the black middle class' imitation of white values. Yet because

of her neurotic instability and her condescending tone, Helga uses this argument as a cover for a deeper problem, her inability to see herself as ordinary, precisely because of her problematic birth. At one point in the novel
Helga tells a colleague, Margaret, that she just cannot stand another minute
of teaching at Naxos and must leave immediately. Margaret is concerned
about what that might mean for Helga's career:

> "Heaven forbid," answered Helga fervently, "that I should ever again
> want work anywhere in the South. I hate it." And fell silent, wonder-
> ing for the hundredth time just what form of vanity it was that had
> induced an intelligent girl like Margaret Creighton to turn what was
> probably nice live crinkly hair, perfectly suited to her smooth dark
> skin and agreeable features into a dead straight, greasy ugly mess.[35]

This response comes from a girl with "skin like yellow satin and curly blue-
black hair, plentiful and always straying a little wayward, delightful way,"
whose physical attributes had certainly earned her whatever respectability
she enjoyed at Naxos.

Her interview with Dr. Anderson, the principal of the school, pushes her
over the edge. Although she is swayed by his talk of service and by her physical attraction to him, he inadvertently says the wrong thing, exposing the
hidden thorn that is always pricking her: "You're a lady. You have dignity
and breeding." To which Helga angrily retorts:

> "The joke is on you, Dr. Anderson. My father was a gambler who
> deserted my mother, a white immigrant. It is even uncertain that they
> were married. As I said at first, I don't belong here. I shall be leaving
> at once. This afternoon. Good morning."[36]

What Helga cannot stand throughout the novel is that her appearance and
education seem automatically to qualify her as a lady. Yet if the class that
extols her virtues knew the origins of her birth, it would, in all its bristling
hyprocrisy, condemn her. Like Laurentine in *The Chinaberry Tree*, Helga
could wrangle her way into comfort and class, but she hates the lie of the
situation.

She does leave Naxos, and the rest of her story is characterized by the
sudden starts and stops of her creator's own life. Because of her refinement
and education, Helga becomes the companion of a wealthy Negro woman
who works incessantly for the race. Because of her commitment to fairness,
Mrs. Hayes-Rore warns Helga, "By the way, I wouldn't mention that my
people are white if I were you. Colored people won't understand."[37]
Through her patron's beneficence, Helga becomes a part of a richly colored
upper-middle-class Harlem life and basks in the warmth of its comfort. But

as quickly as she is enamored of it, Helga becomes dissatisfied, this time because so many of her friends are "obsessed by the race problem." Helga gives us an illuminating description of the contradictions Harlem socialites nurtured when she analyzes her friend Anne's behavior:

> She hated white people with a deep and burning hatred with the kind of hatred which, finding itself held in sufficiently numerous groups, was capable some day, on some great provocation, of bursting into dangerously malignant flames.
>
> But she aped their clothing, their manners and their gracious way of living. While proclaiming loudly the undiluted good of all things Negro, she yet disliked the songs, the dances, and the softly blurred speech of the race. Toward these things she showed only a disdainful contempt, tinged sometimes with a faint amusement. Like the despised people of the white race, she preferred Pavlova to Florence Mills, John McCormack to Taylor Gordon, Walter Hampden to Paul Robeson. Theoretically, however, she stood for the immediate advancement of all things Negroid, and was in revolt against social inequality.[38]

Because Helga believes she is so deeply affected by this hypocrisy, she again experiences the feeling of suffocation she had so strongly felt at Naxos. Because Larsen gives us such an intense description of her restlessness, we are not completely sure that Anne's hyprocisy caused Helga's physical sensations or whether the mulatta is herself extremely neurotic. It is precisely at this moment that our heroine again encounters Dr. Anderson, the principal from Naxos. At this time, Larsen makes it clear that there is a strong physical attraction between the two. But upset with quivers of sensuality that Helga ascribes to her bad blood, and unlike Iola LeRoy or Laurentine Strange, Helga immediately puts off the good doctor and bottles up her troubled emotions.

Fortunately Helga receives an invitation from her mother's family in Denmark to come and live with them. At first she feels guilt at wanting to leave her people here in America. "She demanded in fierce rebellion—why should she be yoked to these despised blacks?" The sensation of being suffocated overcomes her and in a desperate attempt to breathe, she accepts the invitation.

A large part of the novel is set in Denmark where Larsen gives us the first in-depth description of a black woman living among the upper class in a European country.* Although preened and pampered by Danish society,

---

*Brown does give us a picture of Clotel living in Europe, but it lacks scope or depth for her European sojourn is completely restricted to her relationship with Jerome and with her estranged white father.

Helga again repeats her pattern of restlessness. She finds that here in this Nordic country she is seen as a "decoration, a curio, a peacock." Stereotypes precede her. Wooed by a flamboyant Danish painter, she comes to see that she is an exotic prize in his gallery of oddities. In a moment of clear panic, she tells her suitor:

> "But you see, Herr Olsen, I'm not for sale. Not to you. Not to any white man. I don't at all care to be owned. Even by you."[39]

Helga cannot avoid the insinuations that racial stereotypes inflict upon her. She hates Olsen's portrait of her. "It wasn't," she contended, "herself at all but some disgusting sensual creature with all her features." But what really disturbs her is that she believes she might indeed be that sensual creature, for she misses the music, the gaiety, of the Negro:

> "I'm homesick, not for America, but for Negroes. That's the trouble."
> For the first time Helga Crane felt sympathy rather than contempt and hatred for that father, who so often and so angrily she had blamed for his desertion of her mother. She understood now, his rejection, his repudiation, of the formal calm her mother had represented. She understood his yearning, his intolerable need for the inexhaustible humor and the incessant hope of his own kind, his need for those things, not material, indigenous to all Negro environments. She understood and could sympathize with his facile surrender to the irresistable ties of race, now that they dragged at her own heart. And as she attended parties, the theater, the opera, and mingled with the people on the streets, meeting only pale serious faces when she longed for brown laughing ones, she was able to forgive him. Also, it was as if in this understanding and forgiving she had come upon knowledge of almost sacred importance.[40]

One might think that Helga, armed with this new knowledge, might be able to free herself from her fear of suffocation, her fear of her own sensuality. But her return to upper-middle-class Harlem, where she must daily confront Dr. Anderson, now her friend Anne's husband, immediately reminds her why she left it in the first place. Life in America was "for Negroes too cramped, too uncertain, too cruel." Trapped by the denial of her own sensuality, she falls prey to a traveling minister whose passion and religion unleash her pent-up emotions. Possessed with the desire to do something with her life, she marries the Reverend Green and goes with him to work for the Lord in rural Alabama. But Helga finds out too painfully that she does not belong there either. The dinginess of her physical surroundings (poverty), the lack of intellectual stimulation, the petty hostility of the preacher's congregation, and the continual strain of childbearing finally succeed in suffocating her, drawing her into the quicksand from which she had been trying to escape all her life. The last lines of *Quicksand* are particularly effective. Held by the children she cannot leave, she falls into a sleepwalk:

> And hardly had she left her bed and become able to walk again without pain, hardly had the children returned home from the homes of neighbors, when she began to have her fifth child.[41]

I have discussed the events of *Quicksand* in detail because this novel so clearly reveals the hollowness of the upper-middle-class Negro society as well as the inappropriateness of the primitive motif. At the center of this morass is the figure of the pathetic mulatta who, because of increased social mobility as well as the circumstances of her birth, finds that she is seldom perceived as a person in either the black or the white world. Instead, she is an image. In this novel, the tragic mulattas of the abolitionist novels finally reach bitter fruition. Coupled with this devastating theme, Larsen's analysis of the small degree of sensuality that is allowed the lady deviates from the usual novel of upper-class convention, for Helga can be neither a lady nor a peasant resigned to "primal uncluttered feelings." Had Helga accepted the role of a lady in Harlem, or a peacock in Denmark, she would have lost part of herself. Yet she is unequipped to return to rural Negro life, which she at first believes is a return to the soil, to passion, to primitivism. She cannot accept the advice of one of her rural friends: "Laws, chile, we's all ti'ed. An' Ah reckons we's all gwine a be ti'ed till kingdom come. Jes' make de bes' of et, honey. Jes' make de bes' you can."[42] Like Knabis in Jean Toomer's *Cane*, the sophisticated Helga does not know how to survive in the rural South; yet her tragedy is specifically a female one. She is destroyed by her womb.

Although Larsen employs elements of both the novel of convention and the primitive motif in *Quicksand*, she uses them as a means of demonstrating their limitations. The urban, sensitive, light-skinned heroine of the twenties is not free either in conventional, urban, upper-class society or in "primitive," rural America. Given her options, she is doomed in Larsen's novels to become a self-centered, oppressed neurotic or a downtrodden, half-alive peasant.

Like *Quicksand*, Jean Toomer's *Cane* (1923) explored the psychological abuses inflicted upon the black woman. Toomer's *Cane* greatly affected the images of black women in literature, as Alice Walker so lyrically commemorated in her essay "In Our Mothers' Gardens." Although he published only one book-length piece, *Cane*, many critics consider Toomer the most important writer of the Harlem Renaissance. His structural uses of his material are so innovative, the effect of his characters so hauntingly memorable, and his grasp of the American cultural drama so integral, that his book charts a new direction in American literature.

Toomer was the grandson of P. B. S. Pinchback, the Reconstruction lieutenant governor and acting governor of Louisiana. Born in 1894 in Washington, D.C., he grew up in a rather exclusive environment peopled by the sons and daughters of ambassadors to the United States. From his early beginnings he had a sense of the larger world that lay beyond America. When his family's fortunes waned, he lived for awhile in a black Washington, D.C., neighborhood. Light enough to pass, his impacting experiences as a child seem to be more related to his extraordinary appreciation of nature rather than to the social realities that beset the turn-of-the-century black. As a young adult he drifted, like Nella Larsen, from one college to another, in his case from the University of Wisconsin to the Massachusetts College for Agriculture and finally to a physical training college in Chicago. For years he held many odd jobs, the most important one in terms of this discussion being his sojourn as a temporary superintendent of a small Negro industrial school in Georgia.[43]

Toomer had gone to Georgia to discover the roots of his father, a Georgian troubador who had disappeared not long after he married Toomer's mother. This perspective, along with Toomer's intense involvement in Gurdjieffian mysticism, gives *Cane* its lean intensity and penetrating insight. An enigmatic personality, Toomer had strong ties with many of the emerging Anglo-American writers of the day, as well as the Afro-American writers of the Harlem Renaissance. Knowing his genius, he was disappointed by the small quantity of *Cane*'s sales (it sold only five hundred copies), although it received the highest praise from both black and white critics. In 1931 Toomer, like Larsen, disappeared from public view. According to most chroniclers, he felt too restricted by upper-class, intellectual Negro mentality, too urban to become a Negro peasant, and yet too infused with an appreciation of black culture to become a white writer; others insist that it was Toomer's quest for singularity, his sense of his vision, that led him away from the materialistic world and deeper and deeper into himself.[44] He became a virtual hermit, living among the Quakers of Bucks County, Pennsylvania.

In spite of, or perhaps because of, his journey into self, Toomer's *Cane*, as Huggins so succinctly put it, was "more than other contemporary novels by black authors—a conscious exploration of Negro identity."[45] It was an exploration that marvelously succeeded because Toomer was courageous enough to discard the old conventions of language and form and attempt to create new ones. In so doing he was able in his work to accept and appreciate the past of black people as vital and rich, although it included the humiliation of slavery.

In conjunction with the search for the Negro's identity, Toomer expressed the essential qualities of America, rather than the ideals it purports to believe in. The soil of Georgia is an intense mingling of black and white culture, its cane a manifestation of the horror and beauty that is America. Miscegenation, the illicit union of black and white, is a dominant motif in the book and in many ways acts as a prism through which the observer might perceive the truth of the land. America is, in fact, a fusion of many races, many cultures, most of which are denied or maligned. In denying its own self-composition, it also evades a true definition of self. Although black, white, and Indian are constantly touching and affecting each other, this union, whether it is physical, spiritual, or emotional, is labeled illicit in the minds of the majority. In *Cane* this country's rejection of varied cultural composition results not only in self-deception but in the stunted growth of its people.

Toomer chose the essences of black women in the South to communicate this awesome truth. That they are mulattas of varying shades has more to do with his thesis than with any denial of darker-skinned black women. As a result of the touching of two cultures, their lives are painfully contained, their possibilities truncated, and their spirits abused and repressed. In his finely drawn, lean, but lyrical rendition of these mute, sometimes crazed women, Toomer deviated completely from the tradition of the upper-middle-class mulatta heroine. The black women of *Cane* had no outlet for their creative spirit. They could not even speak, so constrained were they by the society that denied them self.

It is precisely because the life-spirit of Toomer's peasant women and his urban women are so bereaved that his work belongs to neither the primitive nor the conventional school. He did not glorify either passion or refinement. Because his women *are* women in this society, their sexual experiences or lack of them gives flesh to their repressed spirit. Inevitably, their sexuality or their frigidity restricts them rather than frees them. So Karintha, "who carries beauty, perfect as dusk when the sun goes down, is a growing thing ripened too soon." Because her husband is away most of the time, "Carma has others." Fern's eyes "sought nothing, nothing that was obvious and tangible and that one could see. Nothing ever came to Fern." Restricted by her white complexion and her prissy social position in the town, Esther becomes a somnambulist. Louisa's mind snaps when her black lover is lynched by her white suitor. In the North, too, the repression continues. Middle-class Muriel is a locked house that can only be opened by the key of security. Avey, "Orphan Woman" of the North, lives in a daze of indolent sexuality:

> I described her own nature and temperament. Told how they needed
> a larger life for their expression. How incapable Washington was of

understanding that need. How it could not meet it. I pointed out that in lieu of proper channels, her emotions had overflowed into paths that dissipated them. I talked, I thought, about an art that would be born, an art that would open the way for women the likes of her. I asked her to hope, and build up an inner life against the coming of that day. I recited some of my own things to her. I sang, with a strange quiver in my voice, a promise song.[46]

It is no accident, however, that the black women in Toomer are primarily southern and rural. This setting is the root from which the tree of black American culture grows, for in the 1920s it had been a culture that was integrally linked to the land. It is in the South that one can see, flickering through the scent of the cane, the sting of its brakes, the essence of Afro-American culture:

> A girl in the yard of a whitewashed shack not much larger than the stack of worn ties piled before it sings. Her voice is loud. Echoes, like rain, sweep the valley. Dust takes the polish from the rails. Lights twinkle in scattered houses. From far away, a sad strong song. Pungent and composite, the smell of farmyards is the fragrance of the woman. She does not sing; her body is a song. She is in the forest, dancing. Torches flare . . . juju men . . . greegree witch doctors. . . . Torches go out. . . . The Dixie pike has grown from a goat path in Africa.[47]

Toomer's women are not only themselves, they are also the land. Without speaking, they sing its truth, that human beings are part of Nature. As they are abused, the land is abused. Karintha is associated with the dusk; Carma's face is a sunflower; Fern's eyes are a river. Besieged by the vortex of sexism and racism, many like Esther become "the color of the gray dust that dances with cotton leaves."

The sights, smells, and sounds of the rural South also permeate the novels of Zora Neale Hurston. Born in Eatonville, Florida, a black township, this flamboyant woman never lost her love for the rich folk culture that surrounded her as a child. At the center of her work as a folklorist, an anthropologist, and a writer was her desire to express the functional beauty of folk language, lore, and custom.[48]

Although a popular personality of the Harlem Renaissance, Hurston's major works were published during the thirties. In addition to short stories, plays, and scholarly articles, she published four novels: *Jonah's Gourd Vine* (1934), *Their Eyes Were Watching God* (1937), *Moses, Man of the Mountain* (1942), and *Seraph on the Suwannee* (1948). During that time she also published two books of folklore, *Mules and Men* (1935) and *Tell My Horse* (1938), as well as an autobiography, *Dust Tracks on a Road*

(1942). Despite many of her contemporaries' views that she was notable more for her wit and entertaining personality than for her books, she surpassed most of them, not only in her prolificity but in the quality of the work she published.

The style of her works is significantly different from most of the other Harlem Renaissance writers, for she knew intimately rather than talked about folk speech and folk images and used them as guides for her imagination.[49] Although New York was her home base during the Renaissance, she traveled throughout the South in her attempt to capture and preserve folk culture. In spite of her northern sojourn, she remained essentially a Southerner with a world view distinctly different from the major literary ideologies of that period.

While in New York City, Hurston studied anthropology at Columbia, under Franz Boas, the man who had dominated American anthropology for two decades and who had played a major role in changing the meaning of the word *culture* in anthropology. Boas had helped to discredit the stance of racial and biological determinism that early ethnologists such as Josiah Nott had taken.[50] He was also "particularly interested in the African survivals in Afro-American culture and Zora Hurston's field work would be part of the evidence documenting this unique Afro-American culture."[51] For Hurston, however, the folk tradition was not only a field of study, it was an essential part of her life.

I believe Hurston felt that scholarly articles were too restrictive in form for the vitality of her material. Instead, in her novels, Hurston incorporated the many aspects of folk culture into an artistic structure. Her novel *Their Eyes Were Watching God* is a classic example of the fusion of creative imagination with folk materials. It is also a significant novel, a transitional one, in the development of black woman images in literature. In it Hurston revised the mulatta images that had preceded her and led the way toward the presentation of more varied and complex women characters.

Their Eyes Were Watching God is a story within a story. Janie Stark tells the story of her childhood, her life, and her loves to her best friend, Phoebe, and to the community to which she has just returned. This aspect of the novel is critical to its substance, for Janie Stark is not an individual in a vacuum; she is an intrinsic part of a community, and she brings her life and its richness, joys, and sorrows back to it. As it has helped to form her, so she also helps to form it.

In Janie, Hurston creates a new black woman character. For the first time in black literature, we feel the growing up of a black girl, not from without but from within. We experience the first time she realizes she is black and therefore different from the white children on the plantation with whom she plays. We feel her young girl sensuality beginning to bloom as she sees the "love embrace and ecstatic shiver" of Nature. We hear philosophy that her grandmother gives her about the plight of the black woman:

"Honey, de white man is de ruler of everything as fur as Ah been able tuh find out. Maybe it's some place way off in de ocean where de black man is in power, but we don't know nothin' but what we see. So de white man throw down de load and tell de nigger man tuh pick it up because he have to, but he don't tote it. He hand it to his womenfolks. De nigger woman is de mule uh de world so fur as Ah can see. Ah been praying fuh it tuh be different wid you. Lawd, Lawd, Lawd!"[52]

The rest of her story is Janie's attempt to discover herself, to express her own being despite the opposition of nearly everyone she encounters. Because she is a mulatta, fair of complexion with long, straight hair, many see her as a prize, a definition of herself that she rejects.

In an effort to give her granddaughter security, her grandmother marries the sixteen-year-old Janie to old Logan Killicks. But Janie finds out that "marriage did not compel love like the sun the day." She is repulsed by his old flesh and by his envy of her youth and she is saved by Jody Stark, a black entrepreneur who takes her away from Logan and marries her. Stark develops a black town much like Eatonville, of which he is mayor. But he, too, does not see Janie. He sees only the mulatta image, the appropriate one for a man of his stature. He forcibly installs her as Queen of the Porch and cuts her off from any real contact with their community. She becomes his showpiece, his property.

Also, in this section, Hurston gives a wonderful picture of a small black town developing into a community. Through Hurston's language, the lying sessions, the whisperings, the music, the linguistic contests, and the communal celebrations as well as the misunderstandings are grandly preserved for everyone to see. Here is the speech that Jody Stark makes when the town is officially opened. Its richness and texture is Afro-American and its setting is most decidedly the community:

"Folkses, de sun is goin' down. De Sun-maker brings it up in de mornin' and de Sun-maker sends it tuh bed at night. Us poor weak humans can't do nothin tuh hurry it up nor to slow it down. All we can do, if we want any light after de settin' or befo' de risin' is tuh make some light ourselves. So dat's how come lamps was made. Dis evenin' we'se all assembled heah tuh light uh lamp. Dis occasion is something for us all tuh remember tuh our dyin' day. De first street lamp in uh colored town. Lift yo' eyes and gaze on it. And when Ah touch de match tuh dat lamp-wick let de light penetrate inside of yuh, and let it shine, let it shine, let it shine. Brother Davis lead us in a word uh prayer. Ask uh blessin' on dis town in uh most particular manner."[53]

Hurston sensitively traces the decline of Jody and Janie Stark's marriage.

Jody cannot understand Janie's dissatisfaction with her position of Queen of the Porch. He has given her status and material security; what else could she want? He bullies her until outwardly, at least, she submits:

> Times and scenes like that put Janie to thinking about the inside state of her marriage. Time came when she fought back with her tongue as best she could, but it didn't do her any good. It just made Joe do more. He wanted her submission and he'd keep on fighting until he felt he had it.
>
> So gradually, she pressed her teeth together and learned to hush. The spirit of the marriage left the bedroom and took to living in the parlor. It was there to shake hands whenever company came to visit, but it never went back inside the bedroom again. So she put something in there to represent the spirit like a Virgin Mary image in a church. The bed was no longer a daisy-field for her and Joe to play in. It was a place where she went and laid down when she was sleepy and tired.
>
> She wasn't petal-open anymore with him. She was twenty-four and seven years married when she knew.[54]

Janie is not only a mulatta who sees herself as a part of the folk, she is also resilient without the melancholy and tightness that previously marked that image. After twenty years of marriage, Stark dies and Janie falls in love with Teacake, a man many years younger than she and, by most people's estimations, far below her. Together they go to live in the Florida Everglades, rejecting the finery and status of the mayor's house because of their desire to know and love each other. This section of the novel emphasizes Janie's blossoming, her development of independence as well as sensuality. "Her soul crawled out of its hiding place."

Janie and Teacake's love affair ends tragically for Janie must kill her crazed lover because he has been bitten by a rabid dog. But Janie does not see her life as tragic; she sees it as full and rich. It is essentially this message that she brings back to her community, that self-fulfillment rather than security and status is the gift of life:

> She pulled in her horizon like a great fish-net. Pulled it from around the waist of the world and draped it over her shoulder. So much of life in its meshes. She called in her soul to come and see.[55]

Hurston's Janie not only revised the previously drawn images of the mulatta, the author's rendition of her major characters beautifully revealed the many dimensions of the black woman's soul as well as the restrictions imposed upon her by her own community—that she, like all others, seeks not only security but fulfillment. The pear tree with its leaves and blossoms becomes the image of Janie's sensuality as well as her desire for completeness: "Janie saw her life like a great tree in leaf with the things suffered things enjoyed, things done and undone. Dawn and doom was in the branches."[56]

Unlike most of the other writers of her time, Hurston emphasized the insular folk community as the setting for her works. Although emphatically imperfect, it somehow absorbs the many aspects of its individuals and continually recreates a world view that can sustain them and therefore itself. Hurston was so clearly concerned with the peculiar characteristics of the relationship between the black woman and her community that she rarely moved outside it. Perhaps the intensity of her view is related to the position the black woman holds within her community, for she has, since its beginnings, been entrusted with its survival and enrichment.

One of the first writers to use folk images and speech as well as the insular folk culture, Hurston anticipated future black women writers who would attempt to define themselves as persons within a specific culture rather than primarily through their relationships with whites. Fauset's characters, particularly in *The Chinaberry Tree*, also insulated themselves with a particular class, but Hurston's *Their Eyes Were Watching God* invokes not one class but the total community—its language, images, mores, and prejudices—as its context. In so doing, it articulates the Afro-American experience not only as a condition but as a culture. As a result, Janie Stark's cultural values, her sense of herself as a woman, is as far removed from Iola LeRoy as Zora Neale Hurston's language is from Frances Harper's.

In 1928 Hurston wrote in an essay, "How It Feels to Be Colored Me":

> I am not tragically colored. There is no great sorrow dammed up in my soul, nor lurking behind my eyes. I do not mind at all. I do not belong to the sobbing school of Negrohood who hold that nature somehow has given them a lowdown dirty deal and whose feelings are all hurt about it. . . . No, I do not weep at the world—I am too busy sharpening my oyster knife.[57]

Twenty years later this ebullient woman was accused of sodomy by a boy who was later found to be disturbed and whose mother had resented Hurston's advice that she take him for psychiatric testing. Although the case was dropped, and Hurston cleared, the Negro press made this incident into a major scandal.[58] Feeling that her race had tried to destroy her, and bitter over her fellow black intellectuals' rejection of the value of her folklore, Hurston again returned to the South. After a brief depression, she recovered her usual enthusiasm for life. However, as Hemenway, her biographer, reported:

> She was never again so belligerently independent as she had been
> earlier. . . . In her very last days Zora lived a difficult life, alone, proud,
> ill, obsessed with a final book she could not complete.[59]

She died in Eatonville, Florida, her birthplace, on January 28, 1960.

Today the works of Zora Neale Hurston are receiving much praise, especially from contemporary black women writers who see her as their spiritual
ancestor. However, both she and her works evoked much negative comment
during her lifetime and until the late 1960s. The moral charge of which she
was accused seems, particularly after one reads Hemenway's biography, the
dramatic climax of a series of innuendos that were leveled against her. Unlike Fauset, whose ladylike images were praised by Harlem Renaissance
intellectuals, both Hurston and her characters were often seen as irreverent.
Her sensuality, her ability to secure money from whites, her loud laughter,
her nonconformist behavior, her sometimes difficult and arrogant ways,
were an affront to the genteel spirit of the Renaissance.[60] At her funeral, a
black journalist who was her last employer made this fitting comment:

> Zora Neale went about and didn't care too much how she looked. Or
> what she said. Maybe people didn't think so much of that. But Zora
> Neale, everytime she went about had something to offer. She didn't
> come to you empty.[61]

One cannot help but note the similarities between Larsen and Hurston's
disappearances from the world. Although very different writers, they were
both assaulted by the prejudices of the other society. Larsen's writing ability
was challenged and Hurston's sex life was used, consciously or unconsciously, as a means of diminishing her effectiveness as a writer and as an
anthropologist. Both charges are indicative of the vulnerable position of
black women writers. Their sexual morality and intellectual capacity are
seen as tentative, not only by their fellow countrymen but by members of
their own race as well. Both writers fell prey to the racial and sexual stereotypes inflicted upon the black woman. If these stellar personalities could
be so wounded, one can imagine the many unknown and less protected who
suffered a similar fate. No wonder the New Negro Philosophy with its optimistic and genteel spirit gave way to the angry cries of the 1940s.

3
Ordinary Women:
The Tone
_____ of the Commonplace _____

"Lord, don't let this happen to me! I ain't done nothing
for this to come to me! I just work! I ain't had no happiness, no nothing. I just work. I'm black and I work
and don't bother nobody. . . ."[1]
　　　　　　　　—*Bessie to Bigger in* Native Son

When Zora Neale Hurston's *Their Eyes Were Watching God* (1937) was
published, it was reviewed both by Alain Locke, the philosopher of the
Harlem Renaissance, and by Richard Wright, an up-and-coming black
writer who was, at that time, a member of the Communist party. The judgments of these two very different men about Hurston's novel indicate some
major changes that occurred in black literature in the late 1930s. Locke,
who had been somewhat favorable toward Hurston's earlier work, said the
novel was "folklore fiction at its best," but asked when Hurston was going
"to come to grips with motive fiction and social document fiction."[2] Richard
Wright called the novel counterrevolutionary and a continuation of the min-
strel image.[3] By 1937 many of the voices of the Harlem Renaissance had
been effectively silenced by the Great Depression; both the novel of convention and the exploration of folk art were giving way, amidst the anguish
of the Depression, to social art. In white liberal circles as well, the image
of the Negro as "primitive" had been replaced by the "new image of the
Negro as a peculiarly oppressed proletarian."[4] During the next twenty years,
much of black literature concentrated on the black, who felt alienated and
cut off from his own community while confronted with a hostile white world.
　Richard Wright was the most important black literary spokesman of this
period. In his "Blueprint for Negro Writing," published in 1937, he summarized what was for him the weakness of past Negro literature and some

directions that new and conscious Negro writers should take. In the past Wright had asserted that "Negro writing assumed two general aspects: 1) It became a sort of conspicuous ornamentalization of the 'hallmark of achievement.' 2) It became the voice of the educated Negro pleading with white America for justice."[5] What Wright advocated for the New Negro writer was that he write for the Negro masses, "moulding the lives and consciousness of these masses toward new goals."[6]

Wright's *Native Son*, a novel that attempted to embody these principles, not only became the second novel by a black man to reach the best-seller list but also had enormous impact on the direction of the new black literature. In contrast to Hurston, Wright saw little beauty in black culture. Without avenues to power, black life was bleak, cut off from the possibilities of fulfillment and threatened by the ever-present hostile world. His novels and essays issued a cry of protest to a white audience that unless America recognize its native sons and give them their due, some blacks would rise up and destroy their oppressors.

This statement is perhaps too simplistic a rendering of Wright's works. His penetrating analysis of the effects of social deprivation upon the black man's personality and his use of the elements of protest within the black folkloric tradition are as important as his cry of protest. Nonetheless, many of his followers extracted certain elements from the fabric of his expansive works. The impact of the hostile urban environment, where one felt dislocated and cut off, and the inevitability of crime as the black person's only release from fear and alienation were two elements that Ann Petry used in her first novel, *The Street* (1946).

Born in Old Saybrook, Connecticut, Petry came to Harlem in 1938 to start a career as a journalist. During the early forties, she worked for *The Amsterdam News* and *The People's Voice* and got to know the social problems of Harlem. In 1944 she joined the New York Foundation to work on a sociological study of the effects of segregation on ghetto children. These experiences furnished the bases for her detailed description of a Harlem street.[7]

Petry's major concern in the novel was most emphatically the hostile environment of Harlem and its effects on the people who must endure it. The opening paragraph introduces us to her major character, The Street:

> There was a cold November wind blowing through 116th Street. It rattled tops of garbage cans, sucked windowshades out through the top of opened windows and set them flapping back against the windows; and it drove most of the people off the street in the block between Seventh and Eighth Avenues except for a few hurried pedestrians who bent double in an effort to offer the least possible exposed surface to its violent assault.[8]

In the following paragraphs Petry continued to set the mood for the novel. Even the natural elements are against the people who are forced to live in this environment. The book graphically presents the harshness of life: the dim hallways, the dank smells, the congestion, the closed nature of this promised land. Petry's novel presents Harlem as a jail where the people are locked in and are only allowed to come out when they go to work.

Gone is the glamorous Harlem of the twenties. Nowhere is there relief from bleakness—not in the personalities of the people or the institutions of the community. Even the spiritualists have turned commercial, and the bars have become dangerous. In *The Street* Harlem does not emerge as a community, for everyone is competing with everyone else for whatever each can get. Cut off from each other, the people merely pass one another, touching only when they must or when it is to their advantage.

One of the major differences between Wright's novel and Petry's is her voluminous use of external detail. Wright's novel is more about Bigger Thomas's psychological state, his reaction to his condition, than the presentation of the external condition itself. Bigger's fate is presented as revealing deeper levels of man's soul rather than being the record of another unfortunate's defeat. While Wright endows his material with psychological overtones, Petry employs the tone of the commonplace. She is particularly effective in selecting the many details and seemingly trivial struggles that poor women can seldom avoid.

> The butcher shop that she entered on Eighth Avenue was crowded with customers, so that she had ample time to study the meat in the case in front of her before she was waited on. There wasn't, she saw, very much choice—ham hocks, lamb culls, bright-red beef. Someone had told Granny once that the butchers in Harlem used embalming fluid on the beef they sold in order to give it a nice fresh color. Lutie didn't believe it, but like a lot of things she didn't believe, it cropped up suddenly out of nowhere to leave her wondering and staring at the brilliant scarlet color of the meat. It made her examine the contents of the case with care in order to determine whether there was something else that would do for dinner. No, she decided, hamburger would be the best thing to get. It cooked quickly, and a half-pound of it mixed with breadcrumbs would go a long way.[9]

The Street is different from most novels by Afro-American women in that its female characters are so cut off by everyone and everything. In almost all of the other novels that focus on the black woman, there is some hint of companionship, some human interaction, and some contact with a social institution—through the church, a tight circle of friends, or the family—that may ultimately fail to change her fate but nonetheless tries. In this sense, Petry stays close to the tendency of many protest writers to see black culture as nonfunctional. Perhaps that is because Petry's purpose in the novel is to heighten intensely the overwhelming odds that her heroine, Lutie Johnson, must face. In addition to persistently rendering a hostile environment, Petry obviously understood the stereotypes that were inflicted on black women, for her female characters are decidedly intended to counteract them. She sets up characters with particular physical characteristics that match specific stereotypes and then proceeds to show how they are not quite what they seem. In so doing she both adheres to and deviates from the standard images.

Lutie Johnson, the heroine of *The Street*, is a good-looking, brown-skinned girl. Brought up by her grandmother and a depressed father, she has come to believe fervently that if you are a good girl, and if you work hard and live right, you can make it. *The Street*, a devastating account of the falseness of that myth, strikes a heavy blow at one of the major tenets of many Renaissance writers— that you can make it if you try.

To make her point as unassailable as possible, Petry creates an impeccable heroine. Although she is brown-skinned, Lutie fits the stereotype of the tragic mulatta. She seems to be cut off from any community, and although she is a beautiful woman, she refuses to use her charms to further her advancement. Petry presents Lutie Johnson as having the soul of Iola LeRoy to counteract the prevailing image that lower-class black women are whores. But since Lutie Johnson is black and poor, no one else relates to her as a decent woman. She is coveted by all the men in the novel, both black and white. Her beauty, in the final analysis, helps, as much as any other factor, to defeat her.

Lutie Johnson is also a mother. *The Street* is one of the first novels, if not the first, in which a woman novelist presents a struggling, urban black mother attempting to create a better life for herself. Irene in Larsen's *Passing* is also a mother, but her comfortable economic position allows her to relegate much of the childrearing to a nanny. She may be able to evade her young son's questions about lynchings, but Lutie must confront Bub's questions about why blacks are treated the way they are.

In addition, during the course of the novel, Lutie Johnson works as a domestic, the urban counterpart of the mammy. But she does not fit the stereotype of the mammy either physically or psychologically. She is not content to have her mistress cry on her shoulder; she wants the good things that her employer takes for granted. This section of the novel is particularly effective, for Petry combines the theme of cultural transference along with an analysis of why so many black marriages break up. Lutie Johnson learns much about American values from the wealthy Chandlers:

It was a world of strange values where the price of something called

Tell and Tell and American Nickel and United States Steel had a
direct effect on emotions. When the price went up everybody's spirits
soared; if it went down they were plunged in gloom.

After a year of listening to their talk, she absorbed some of the same
spirit. The belief that anybody could be rich if they wanted to and
worked hard enough and figured it out carefully enough.[10]

In trying to approximate their values, Lutie works as much as possible. In
staying away from home too long and too often, she loses her unemployed
husband to another woman. Increasingly, he feels his lack of power as she
takes on the Chandlers' values until he must find an outlet for his frustration. Yet Lutie cannot figure out what else she can do. He cannot find work
and she can. Petry clearly indicts the white society for the failure of many
black marriages and implies that it consciously is seeking the fragmentation
of the black family.

It is not long before Lutie realizes that no amount of saving from the
small salary she receives will get her out of her condition. So she tries to
break into the entertainment world. Petry invokes a developing stereotype
—that of the black woman singer. But again Lutie finds that talent is not
enough and that her only saleable commodity is sex. Although Lutie refuses
to give in to this temptation, Petry suggests that many others were forced
into this compromise and that that is the only way they were able to survive. As such, Lutie's insistence on her moral standards results in her destruction. She kills Boots, her potential employer, when he tries to rape her.

The murder scene is skillfully constructed to illustrate Petry's thesis that
crime is inevitable, given the hostility of the environment. In revenge for
Lutie's rejection of him, the superintendent of her apartment house tricks
her son Bub into committing a petty crime. Lutie needs money desperately
to get her son out of juvenile hall. Her mother's love forces her to ask Boots,
the head of a band, for the money she needs. But he has been instructed
by his white boss, Junto, that Lutie must belong to him. Boots strikes out
at Junto by trying to force Lutie to sleep with him, and she, already tense
and upset, hits him. After that first blow, Lutie cannot turn back. If she does
not continue to hit Boots, he will kill her. But if she kills him, she will be
accused of murder, for who ever heard of a black woman, especially a
beautiful black woman, being raped? She releases all her frustration in this
act, the only deviation she has allowed herself from the straight and righ-
teous path:

A lifetime of pent-up resentment went into the blows. Even after he
lay motionless, she kept striking him, not thinking about him, not even
seeing him. First she was venting her rage against the dirty, crowded
street. She saw the rows of dilapidated old houses; the small dark

rooms; the long steep flights of stairs; the narrow dingy hallways; the little lost girls in Mrs. Hedges' apartment, the smashed homes where the women did drudgery because their men had deserted them. She saw all of these things and struck at them.

Then the limp figure on the sofa became in turn, Jim and the slender girl she'd found him with; became the insult in the moist-eyed glances of white men on the subway; became the greasy, lecherous man at the Crosse School for Singers; became the gaunt Super pulling her down down into the basement.

Finally, and the blows were heavier, faster, now, she was striking at the white world which thrust black people into a walled enclosure from which there was no escape; and at the turn of events which had forced her to leave Bub alone while she was working so that he now faced reform school, now had a police record.

She saw the face and the head of the man on the sofa through waves of anger in which he represented all these things and she was destroying them.[11]

As Lutie flees the snow-covered world, leaving her son to reform school, she remembers one of her teachers saying, "Really, I don't know why they have us bother to teach your people to write."[12] She concludes that her teacher had been correct. Why teach people to write, why give them the illusion that they are free when they are actually imprisoned? The Street, Petry concludes, is no different from the plantation, except that many of the slaves do not understand that they are slaves.

It is significant that Wright's novel begins with Bigger Thomas' accidental murder of a white woman and his subsequent understanding of that act, and that Petry's novel ends with a black woman's murder of a black man in self-defense. Petry is more concerned with proving her thesis that no matter how conventional and no matter how American a poor black person may be, she will be defeated by her environment. Bigger Thomas's considerable reflection upon his "crime" gives him insight into the free will and choice he exercises as well as the conditions that have helped to create him. At the end of *Native Son*, Wright has Bigger accept the responsibility of his own actions, but Petry's Lutie never has any opportunity for choice. Perhaps that is why her novel is so unrelentingly grim and its effect so depressing. She effectively refutes the argument that the black woman will be awarded her humanity if she only becomes a "lady," while coming dangerously close to denying an essential characteristic of humanness, the responsibility for one's actions. Her novel poses a perennial question of contemporary black literature: given the harshness of racism, to what extent can each individual control his or her fate?

Petry wrote two other novels, *Country Place* (1947) and *The Narrows*

(1953); one work for children, *The Drugstore Cat* (1949); and two books for young adults, *Harriet Tubman: Conductor on the Underground Railroad* (1955) and *Tituba of Salem Village* (1964). But except for her excellent short stories of the late forties, she never published another work that would be similar to the naturalistic quality of *The Street*. After 1953 she emphatically turned to the writing of children's literature. In so doing she anticipated the trend of many contemporary black women writers, like Lucille Clifton, Gwendolyn Brooks, and Alice Walker, who feel the urgency to create imaginative and relevant works for black children.

From the late forties to the sixties the plight of the black male was the dominant subject of the black novel. The works of Wright, Chester Himes, James Baldwin, and Ralph W. Ellison created controversy and comment not only in their own circles, or even America, but all over the world. During that period, no black woman emerged as a significant novelist. Instead, black women writers prevailed in poetry. Gwendolyn Brooks and Margaret Walker are two such poets; nonetheless, each of these women has written one memorable novel that further develops the images of black women in literature.

Poet Laureate of Chicago, Gwendolyn Brooks is one of America's finest and most often praised poets. She has published seven volumes of poetry: *A Street in Bronzeville* (1943), *Annie Allen* (1949), *The Bean Eaters* (1960), *Selected Poems* (1963), *In the Mecca* (1968), *Riot* (1969), and *Family Pictures* (1970). She also has published two children's books, *Bronzeville Boys and Girls* (1956) and *The Tiger Who Wore White Gloves* (1974); an autobiography, *Report from Part One* (1972); a short novel, *Maud Martha* (1953); and a collection of all her works, *The World of Gwendolyn Brooks* (1976).

Set in Chicago during the late thirties and forties, *Maud Martha* is a series of lyrical, perhaps autobiographical, vignettes about a black girl growing up in a closely knit family. Unlike *The Street*, this work emphasizes the sensitivity of the black girl-woman in an urban community. Maud Martha is not alone; she is loved by her family and nurtured by their communal rituals. We hear through her mind's voice the sounds of her family, her community, and the unknown outer white world. Her world is a cocoon in which she has sufficient protection and nourishment to find her own self. The novel begins:

> What she liked was candy buttons, and books, and painted music (deep blue or delicate silver) and the west sky, so altering, viewed from the steps of the back porch; and dandelions.
>
> She would have liked a lotus, or China asters or the Japanese iris, or meadow lilies—yes, she would have liked meadow lilies, because the very word meadow made her breathe more deeply, and either fling her arms or want to fling her arms, depending on who was by, raptur-

ously up to whatever was watching in the sky. But dandelions was what she chiefly saw. Yellow jewels for everyday, studding the patched green dress of her back yard. She liked their demure prettiness second to their everydayness; for in that latter quality she thought she saw a picture of herself, and it was comforting to find that what was common could also be a flower.[13]

But Maud Martha's life is not all candy buttons. She wants to be as lovely as her older sister; her pensive soul must venture out to school past the "nasty boys", "the sharp boys," and with her family she must face the possibility that they might not be able to keep their home.

In this novel, as in many of her poems, Brooks also presents the problems that many black women encounter about distinctions in shade. As Maud Martha grows older she must accept the fact that her dark complexion and her untameable hair are not desirable in her own community:

"I am what he would call—sweet. But I am certainly not what he would call pretty. Even with all this hair (which I have just assured him, in response to his question, is not 'natural,' is not good grade or anything like good grade) even with whatever I have that puts a dimple in his heart, even with these nice ears, I am still definitely, not what he can call pretty if he remains true to what his idea of pretty has always been. Pretty would be a little creame-colored thing with curly hair. Or at the very lowest pretty would be a little curly-haired thing the color of cocoa with a lot of milk in it. Whereas, I am the color of cocoa straight, if you can be even that 'kind' to me.

He wonders, as we walk in the street, about the thoughts of the people who look at us. Are they thinking that he could do no better than . . . me? Then he thinks, Well, Hmph! Well, Huh!—all the little good-looking dolls that have wanted *him*—all the little sweet high-yellows that have ambled slowly past *his* front door—What he would like to tell those secretly snickering ones!—That any day out of the week he can do better than this black gal."[14]

Maud Martha is no beautiful heroine. She is, like so many of Brooks's poetic characterizations, an ordinary person. Yet like all ordinary people, she is herself, a marvel. That ultimately is Brooks's major theme: she heightens our awareness of the wonderfulness of the commonplace. Like Petry, then, Brooks pays special attention to the seemingly trivial details of life, details that are the daily fare of most women. But in contrast to the naturalistic writer of *The Street*, Brooks's details include the wonder as well as the limitedness of the commonplace.

Nevertheless, as an an ordinary black woman, Maud Martha not only has a rich family life and cultural roots, she must also wrestle with the prejudices of the black and white world. She must encounter the snobbishness of upper-class Negro society. When her husband cannot get a job, she must suffer the ordinary racism of the white woman who hires her to be her maid. She must try to explain to her child why Santa Claus does not like her.

Yet Maud Martha's world, like Janie Stark's, is essentially the world of her community. Like other women, she has a child to whom she gives the gift of imagination as well as physical care; she listens to the gossip about the many characters who live in her apartment building; she worries about the bills and the war. Like everyone else, she has her bad days when she thinks about the vulnerability of life:

> People have to choose something decently constant to depend on, thought Maud Martha. People must have something to lean on.
>
> But the love of a single person was not enough. Not only was personal love itself, however good, a thing that varied from week to week, from second to second, but the parties to it were likely, for example, to die any minute, or otherwise be parted, or destroyed. At any time.
>
> Not alone was the romantic love of a man fallible, but the breadier love between parents and children; brothers; animals; friend and friend. Those too could not be heavily depended on.
>
> Could be nature, which had a seed, or root, or an element (what do you want to call it) of constancy, under all that system of change. Of course, to say "system" at all implied arrangement, and therefore some order of constancy.
>
> Could be, she mused, a marriage. The marriage shell, not the romance, or love it might contain. A marriage, the plainer, the more plateaulike, the better. A marriage made up of Sunday papers and shoeless feet, baking powder biscuits, baby baths, and matinees and laundry men, and potato plants in the kitchen window.
>
> Was, perhaps, the whole life of a man a dedication to this search for something to lean upon, and was, to a great degree, his "happiness" or "unhappiness" written up for him by the demands or limitations of what he chose for that work?
>
> For work it was. Leaning was a work.[15]

Clearly, Brooks' Maud Martha could not have been the focal character of a black novel in 1892. Although she has her romantic fantasies, she is no Iola LeRoy. Nor is she, like Fauset's heroines, merely conventional. She knows the value of intangibles and certainly does not qualify as an upper-class heroine. Nor is Maud Martha a beautiful Lutie Johnson, tragically destroyed by her environment. Maud Martha is quite ordinary, which is not to say that she is patterned after a white ideal or that she is dull. It is just that she is not reduced to a stereotype either in the grand heroic style or the mean downtrodden mode. Nor does she perceive herself as a deviant, for she does not define her humanity as merely being the sum and substance of social problems. In *Maud Martha*, Brooks deflated the mystique of heroism and grand defeat by illuminating the commonplace and thus created a new type of black woman character.

In contrast to Brooks's tightly structured novel, Margaret Walker's *Jubilee* (1966) is a massive historical book. Her literary reputation is primarily based on her two collections of poetry, *For My People* (1942) and *Prophets for a New Day* (1970), while her novel has been seen by critics as a popular novel.

The novel tells us the story of Vyry, first as a slave before the Civil War and then as a freedwoman after Emancipation. It is based on the stories Walker's grandmother told her about her great-grandmother, buttressed by twenty years of research. In *How I Wrote Jubilee*, Walker discussed the major elements of her novel and told us the story of her long years of research. She intended her novel to be essentially different from the usual Civil War romance in that she was telling the story from a slave's point of view rather than from the master's. She wanted the story not only to be the tale of one slave's life but of an entire culture. To achieve these two things, she used folklore as her major structural element.[16] At times, then, Walker's novel is reminiscent of the novels of Zora Neale Hurston. *Jubilee* is saturated with many of the various aspects of folk culture: the songs, sayings, customs, food, medicinal remedies, language, and of course the double-leveled styles of behavior through which the slaves managed to survive.

One of the major problems in writing a historical novel from the slave's point of view was Walker's awareness that most slaves who lived on plantations knew very little about what was happening in the outside world. Unable to read and write, and restricted in their movements, they could not tell us themselves the important historical events that were affecting the pre-Civil War South. Since Walker did not find a solution to this structural problem, the novel seems split. On the one hand, we experience the drama of Vyry's life through the action of the novel, and on the other hand, the novelist often intrudes upon this drama with historical facts about the period. At such points, the novel does not jell into a whole.

Walker did include in her rendition of Vyry's life the many images of black women that persisted throughout slavery. But although she used stereotypical characteristics of the mammy, the conjure woman, the concubine, and the mulatta, she did revise them sufficiently to correct many of the false myths attached to them.

Like Hurston's Janie, Vyry is a mulatta who does not view herself as caught between two worlds. She is a black woman, a slave who is the cook of her master's household and must work long hard hours. The fact that the master is her father has very little impact on her life. Nor does Vyry have angelic pretensions; her mixed blood does not inspire the slaves around her. In addition, she is a mother whose love for her children precludes any extraordinary feats of heroism. She is primarily a practical woman, imbued with the caution and common sense that the slave had to have to survive.

The same is true of the other women images we find in the novel. Although Vyry's mother, Sis Hettie, is the concubine of the master, her life is painful. She dies at age twenty-eight, killed by constant childbearing. Granny Ticey, the midwife who tends to Sis Hattie on her deathbed, is no conjure woman, at least not in the tradition of the pre-Civil War novel. She is a no-nonsense herbalist and the closest thing to medical personnel available to the slaves. Aunt Sally, the cook that precedes Vyry, who is the young girl's substitute mother for awhile, is no typical mammy. She steals food, has little respect for her mistress, and teaches Vyry the tricks of survival in Missy's kitchen. Even the stereotypical view of the white mistress is somewhat revised. Big Missy is no pining alabaster lady. She is the thrifty manager of her husband's estate who is bitter at being cut off from the rest of the world.

In *Jubilee* Walker presented the slave culture that Frances Harper could hardly acknowledge. Instead of dramatizing the shame and humiliation of slaves or the extraordinary feats of heroism that slaves performed during that period, Walker's novel emphasizes the practical slave culture without which black people as an abused race would not have been able to survive. Further, this culture, she insisted, helped the slave to retain some measure of his own self-respect. Although flawed, then, the novel does what many antebellum, abolitionist, and Renaissance novels did not do. It not only revises the stereotypes of the past, it also eulogizes the past of the ordinary black person whose ancestors might not have been a Gabriel Prosser or an Ellen Craft, but who nevertheless together created a folk culture that was complex and practical.

Jubilee takes us back, at least in subject matter, full circle to the antebellum and abolitionist novels of the nineteenth century. One hundred years later, however, the stereotypes of the contented mammy, the loose woman, the heathen conjure woman, and the lady-mulatta have been greatly revised, their images transformed not only by the historical appreciation of the realities of slavery, but also by an acknowledgment of and a respect for black culture. The content and style of Walker's novel reflect the many stages in the development of a tradition of black women novelists. She was able to present Vyry as a black woman within a culture rather than as a proper mulatta, partially because the novels of Frances Harper, Jessie Fauset, and Nella Larsen revealed the limits of that type, both from a historical and literary perspective. She could use folklore as a structural element because of the life and work of Zora Neale Hurston, and she was able to employ both the elements of protest that characterize *The Street* and the tone of the commonplace that is an essential part of *Maud Martha*. In applying these lessons, with some success, to the historical period when the negative images of Afro-American women took hold, she went to the root of the old stereotypes, making space for younger novelists to create character rather than type, and to explore the many dimensions of their consciousness and craft.

Book II

A Promise Song

INTRODUCTION

Although *Jubilee* was published in 1966, Margaret Walker actually started writing it in 1947. She tells us in her essay on how she wrote *Jubilee* why it took her twenty years to complete it:

> People ask me how I find time to write with a family and a teaching job. I don't. That is one reason I was so long with *Jubilee*. A writer needs time to write a certain number of hours every day. This is particularly true with prose fiction and absolutely necessary with the novel. Writing poetry may be different, but the novel demands long hours every day at a steady pace until the thing is done. It is humanly impossible for a woman who is a wife and mother to work on a regular teaching job and write. Weekends and nights and vacations are all right for reading but not enough for writing. This is a full-time job, but for me such full attention has only been possible during the three Depression years I was on the Writers Project and during that one school year in which I finished *Jubilee* I enjoyed the luxury.[1]

Walker's explanation elaborates on a little commented on but obvious explanation about why there are not more black women novelists. It also points up why, until recently, the images of black women that occur in most of these novelists' works are so much related to the upper middle class. In addition to the social and educational restrictions imposed on the majority of black women, the prevailing societal stereotypes suggest that they have little creativity, little intelligence.

During the 1950s, even the upper-middle-class stereotype of the black woman prevalent during the first half of this century seemed shrouded in silence, for there were few focal black women characters either in the Afro-American or Anglo-American novel. On the societal level, however, various aspects of nineteenth-century literary stereotypes continued to have currency. Two variations on the mammy image are worth mentioning as a backdrop to the emergence of black women novelists in the sixties and seventies: the sapphire and the matriarch.

The Sapphire heightens one aspect of the mammy image, her domineering characteristic. Loud-mouthed, strong-willed, and practical, this image is based on a woman character called Sapphire of the "Amos 'n' Andy" show, a television program that was popular during the fifties. Sapphire's most salient quality is her ability to make black men look like fools, partly because she is unfeminine, that is, strong and independent, and partly because she is, by nature, emasculating. Although similar to the mammy, Sapphire is not so much maternal toward white folks as she is unfeminine in relation to black men. To them, she is cold, hard, and evil.

During the sixties, the Sapphire image was reinforced by the image of the matriarch. Probably the study that gave the greatest credence to this image was the Moynihan Report of 1965:

> According to Moynihan, white society has forced the Black community into a matriarchal structure which, because it is so out of line with white America's patriarchal family system, retards the progress of the Black community as a whole. It is this black female dominance— asserts Moynihan—that will lead to a host of pathologies in the next generation of black children.[2]

The myth of the black matriarch, which received much publicity in the mid-sixties, is particularly insidious, since ironically it is based on the concept of woman from a patriarchal perspective. A detailed analysis of the sociological and psychological research related to this myth is beyond the scope of this work.[3] Suffice it to say that the matriarch is another variation of the image of the mammy, and that in this modern version, the notion of deviance is heightened, so black women, rather than society, are blamed for "pathologies" in the black community.

Contemporary black women novelists have responded to these stereotypes, both the nineteenth- and twentieth-century versions, not so much by creating countertypes as was done in the past but by attempting to create their own definition of woman within the scope of their particular milieu. As an essential part of this attempt, they have incorporated the theme of the black woman's frustrated creative spirit into their works. What all of these stereotypes omit—in fact, refute—are qualities of creativity and conscious self-definition essential to humanness.

The three writers I discuss in detail—Paule Marshall, Toni Morrison, and Alice Walker—portray in their novels women whose creativity is repressed either as a result of their coming to believe these stereotypes or because they cannot escape the images society has created for them. In addition, their works dramatize the effects of women's repressed creativity on the fabric of their communities—their men, their children, their social and political lives, their communal expression. Paradoxically, even as these writers express this story of frustration, they also sing the struggles of the black woman to express herself in whatever way she can.

I have chosen these three novelists to discuss for particular reasons. Each has written at least two novels; each has grown from one novel to the next; each has begun to form a unique vision or philosophy of life in her creation of her world; and each represents distinct trends in American literature.

Few contemporary black women have published two or more novels. Beyond the question of numbers, most novelists need the opportunity to write more than one novel to know and form their own unique worlds, as well as to develop the characteristics of craft that they feel to be their own. More importantly, perhaps, in their first two novels, Marshall, Morrison, and Walker based the making of their worlds on their characterizations of black women. In so doing, however, they not only attempt to define woman within the context of their own vision but are also searching for values they perceive as essential.

Paule Marshall, the oldest of these writers and a pioneer in her own right, not only concentrates on sculpting complex Afro-American and West Indian women characters, she does this within the context of the rituals of these societies. In recreating these rituals, she dramatically reiterates the lessons of history and culture. Through her experimentation with language and structure, Toni Morrison not only weaves fables about the meaning of the terrors imposed on the black woman by both Anglo- and Afro-American society, she also begins to develop a unique mythological system. While creating visions of the black woman within the beauty and horror of southern culture, Alice Walker emphasizes the value of fusing the personal and the political into a whole. The works of these three women are part of the tradition I have just articulated and are in fact possible because that tradition existed. Yet in keeping with the character of that tradition, they are transforming it, for they are not only expressing their own creativity, they are also telling the stories their mothers and grandmothers, aunts and great-aunts, were not allowed to write.

I am also continuing my discussion of the tradition of black women novelists with a detailed discussion of their novels not only because of the reasons just mentioned, but because the works of black women writers, their substance and craft, are seldom noted. I offer these essays on their works in the light of the tradition just discussed and in the hope that we will not have to recoup these novels for later generations, for they will be a part of an articulated tradition.

4
Sculpture and Space:
The Interdependency of
Character and Culture in
—— the Novels of Paule Marshall ——

Paule Marshall is supremely devoted to the creation of character. She has written a collection of novellas, *Soul Clap Hands and Sing* (1961); many short stories; and two novels, *Browngirl, Brownstones* (1959) and *The Chosen Place, The Timeless People* (1969). In her works, and in talks she has given about the craft of novel writing, she emphasized her need to create distinct human beings who are affected by culture and society, and who also affect these two important elements. Her works are pieces of sculpture; the shape and rhythm of her characters can scarcely be detached from the space around them.

Perhaps her keen insights into the interrelationship between character and culture stems from her own background. As a first-generation American of West Indian descent, she lived and dramatically experienced the merging of, sometimes the conflict of, two distinct cultures within the same psyche. That experience is valid not only in itself but also in the subtle shades of light it casts upon the unique drama of Afro-Americans. The Afro-American experience, as W. E. B. Du Bois so elegantly stated, is just that—the interface of two cultures within the same collective body, whether or not each individual within the body consciously knows it.

This concern, the need somehow to separate, analyze, and then bring together these varying influences, is one of Marshall's concentrated thrusts. Coupled with her discussion of this dilemma, particularly in her novels, is her sculpting of women characters who at first glance might seem to be the stereotypical contours of the black woman. Under her careful, tender, yet incisive hands, these outlines are transformed into distinct women. She shows us that if we glance too quickly, we might see only the outline of the domineering mother, the black prostitute, the martyred mother. But if we follow closely the contours of these forms, we will see how we have not perceived their essences as they move within the space of their culture.

PART I

Browngirl, Brownstones: Self-Consciousness and the Rituals of Survival

In her first novel, *Browngirl, Brownstones*, these two concerns, the interface of two distinct cultures and the creation of distinct women characters, are embodied in the growing up of Selina Boyce, a first-generation American girl of Barbadian descent. Selina intensely loves her imaginative, seemingly carefree father who wants to return to the land he inherited in Barbados, where he fantasizes that he will live like a king. She tries to protect her father and his dream from her strong-willed mother, Silla, who is obsessed with owning a Brooklyn brownstone. Within the context of this family struggle, character and culture interact and continually transform each other, as the community to which Selina Boyce belongs tries to adjust to its new American setting without losing its own integrity.

Browngirl, Brownstones is an American novel, for it records the immigrant's experience, which gives America so much of its uniqueness. In this novel, though, the immigrant experience is thrice heightened in that these newcomers are black, subject to the racism of this society as well as to America's hesitation to accept anything "alien" into its body. Also, these black immigrants cannot even easily merge into the Afro-American social fabric, for they themselves are not sure they can be or want to be a part of that tradition. The novel, then, is not only about the conflict within the Boyce family, it is also about the process of redefinition that this immigrant community must, by necessity, be engaged in.

The West Indian immigrants, as was true of other immigrants, had come to America, not because they desired different cultural values, but because they wanted to make a better living. They were different from other European immigrants, however, in that their land had never been truly theirs. Brought there as slaves, they had already had to develop a hybrid culture, based on their African origins but very much affected by the British system that held them in bondage. In addition to the feudalism European immigrants were fleeing from, West Indians also had to contend with racism and colonialism in their own land. But because black people were the majority culture in the West Indies, the land seemed to be theirs and their cultural habits seemed to be predominant. Oppressed at home by colonial feudalism, racism, and starvation—forces that seemed insurmountable, they fled to America, the land of plenty. But they quickly learned that a better living was not guaranteed even by working like a slave, and that to improve their economic status, they might have to adjust their cultural values, for in

America they were the minority rather than the majority. The novel *Brown-girl, Brownstones* measures the spiritual prices that many of them paid to advance economically or even to survive—a primary one being their need to expel or destroy any one of them who did not pursue their common goal. As Suggie, one of the minor characters in the novel, puts it:

> "Yuh mother! Them so! My people! I's hiding from them with tears in my eyes," she raged, unheeding. "Y'know what they want me to do?" She spun around. "I must put on a piece of black hat pull down over my face and go out here working day in and day out and save every penny. That's what. I mustn't think 'bout spreeing or loving-up or anything so. . . . Be-Jees, I ain' gon be like them, all cut out of the same piece of cloth."[1]

They want, *they* think, *they* do: the *they* in this novel is the Barbadian community, as much a character in its impact as any of the individuals who people the novel. Through its rituals, which are dedicated to its own continuity, the immigrant community assumes a power greater than the sum of its parts, compelling, urging, insisting that every one of its parts bend to the common goal: the owning of a brownstone, the possession of property, as a bulwark against poverty, racism, failure.

The brownstones, then, are not just buildings or even homes. They are the embodiment of the community's will to overcome all obstacles, to create a protective barrier between it and the hostile world. Like Ann Petry in *The Street*, Marshall begins her novel with an imagistic description of its setting, in her case the line of brownstones on the street. But unlike Petry's street, Marshall's brownstones are not a hostile environment; they embody the community's means of survival and defense:

> In the somnolent July afternoon the unbroken line of brownstone houses down the long Brooklyn street resembled an army massed at attention. They were all one uniform red-brown stone. All with high massive stone stoops and black iron-grille fences staving off the sun. All draped in ivy as though mourning. Their somber facades, indifferent to the summer's heat and passion, faced a park while their backs reared dark against the sky. They were only three or four stories tall—squat—yet they gave the impression of formidable height.[2]

Within the context of a determined immigrant community, the conflict between Silla and Deighton Boyce takes on cultural dimensions—dimensions that help to explain some of the causes for their individual war without diminishing the specificity of their particular personalities. Their war with each other emanates, in part, from their definitions of woman and man, definitions that are often in conflict with the reality of their life in America, but are related to the process of self-definition that their community is going through. Yet Marshall does not make her Silla and her Deighton stereotypes. They do not become all Barbadian-American women and men who are in a similar predicament. The structure of the novel, at every turn, expresses Marshall's concern both to sculpt her characters in all their uniqueness and to probe the space of their cultural dimensions.

The novel is divided into four books: "A Long Day and a Long Night," "Pastorale," "The War," and "Selina," the titles indicating mood, as well as time sequence. The central event from which all else ripples is Deighton's inheritance of a small piece of land in Barbados, Silla's determination to sell it against his will and to use the money as a down payment for the brownstone, and Selina's attempt to prevent her mother from culminating this deed. So the individual books trace the development of this war within the family. The first book is set off by the proximate cause of this internal war. When Deighton receives the news of his inheritance, all hell breaks loose. In the second book, "Pastorale," the storm within the family seems to calm, as Silla regroups, allowing us to concentrate on Selina's development as a girl-woman. In the third book, the longest and most pivotal of the novel, the war actually breaks out as Silla sells the land without Deighton's knowledge. Deighton responds by spending the money on extravagant clothes for the family and is ostracized by the community for his foolishness. Struck down by all but Selina and injured on his job, he retreats into a religious haven. Renouncing his family, *the* mortal sin in the Barbadian community, he in turn is renounced by Silla who turns him over to the immigration authorities as an illegal alien. He is sent back to Barbados but falls or jumps to his death in sight of port. The war seems to be over, but actually it has just begun. In the fourth book, Selina continues to fight her mother and the Barbadian community in her father's name, only to find in her affair with Clive that she is much like her mother. The novel ends as Selina begins to understand her own complexity, as well as her mother and her father's character, through her own struggle for independence in a world both dangerous and exciting.

That is the plot of the novel, a substantial *Bildungsroman*, as we experience the development of a young naive girl into an unfinished but complex woman. The novel is able to generate the great power it has precisely because Marshall goes beyond the plot, penetrating each character within the family and sculpting in careful shapes the world in which they live. In each book there is an interrelationship drawn between four elements: the development of the girl Selina into a complex woman, the love and conflict between Silla and Deighton Boyce, the pervasive influence of the Barbadian culture and community through its distinctive beliefs and rituals, and the hostilities of the outer American world.

Marshall begins her design of interrelatedness in the first scene of this novel, for "A Long Day and a Long Night" starts not with the movement of the plot, but with the description of the brownstone houses and the history of their various inhabitants up to 1939 when the dark sea of West Indians slowly begins to edge its way in. For these brownstones have served other communities in their attempts to realize the American dream.

Then we are introduced to one person within the many brownstones. The girl-woman Selina immediately becomes the novel's point of view character. Symbolically, she first introduces us to her brownstone. Pretending to be an elegant lady, like the previous inhabitants of the brownstones, she takes us on a tour of her house. In the process she studies an old family photograph, contrasting the past images of her sister, mother, and father with their present forms. Our introduction to Silla and Deighton, then, is in terms of Selina's assessment of their youthful images, an assessment that alerts us immediately to the conflict between them that will be the focus of much of this novel:

> The young woman in the 1920s dress with a headband around her forehead could not be the mother. This mother had a shy beauty, there was a girlish expectancy in her smile. . . .

> Her father was the only one she believed in the picture. Despite the old fashioned suit and the spats, it was her father. The angle at which he held the cane, his detached air, the teasing smile proclaimed him. For her, he was the one constant in the flux and unreality of life. The day was suddenly bright with the thought of him upstairs in the sun parlor, and slamming down the photograph she bounded from the room, taking the steps two at a time.[3]

Deighton's conversation with Selina also helps to prepare us for the war that will erupt in the family, for not only does he inform us of the letter of inheritance he has just received, he also impresses upon us the superiority of his upbringing to that of his wife, Silla. Although his youth had been filled with gaiety and fun, his wife's youth was one of hardship and servitude. Significantly, although Deighton sees himself as an individual, he characterizes Silla as one among many. As a result, Selina's mental picture of her mother's, and hence her father's, past cannot stand by itself. Even as she listens to her father she sees in her mind's eye her own image of the Barbadian immigrant community, an image of the "watchful wrathful women" whose only thought is to "buy house." Paradoxically, although she does not yet understand this, the awesome strength of these women, and hence the Barbadian community, comes not from the possession of power but from their lack of it. The contrast between Selina's perception of "the mothers" and the reality of these women's lives is buttressed by our first glimpse of Silla, as she comes home from work, her entrance becoming even the more dramatic since it ends the first scene in the novel:

> Silla Boyce brought the theme of winter into the park with her dark dress amid the summer green and the bright-figured housedresses of the women lounging in the benches there. Not only that, every line of her strong-made body seemed to reprimand the women for their idleness and the park for its senseless summer display. Her lips, set in a permanent protest against life, implied that there was not time for gaiety. And the park, the women, the sun even gave way to her dark force; the flushed summer colors ran together and faded, as she passed.[4]

Throughout much of this novel, Selina associates Deighton with the sun —with freedom and warmth—while her mother is, for her, the epitome of winter—cold, unrelenting, and restrictive. The contrasting forms of the wintery Silla and the sunny Deighton may at first seem to be reminiscent of the stereotypical images of the domineering black matriarch and the irresponsible black father. But the imprint the old photograph of Silla has left on our minds, as well as Marshall's description of Deighton as a man "whose face was like his eyelids—a closed blind over the man beneath," guards against any immediate judgments we might make. Much of this novel is a tender reconstruction of how the young mother with the shy beauty assumes the characteristics of the wintery Silla and of how the dapper Deighton becomes a man well hidden behind his sunny laughter.

Not only does Marshall, in this first scene of the book, immediately signal us that neither Silla nor Deighton are the stereotypes they appear to be, she also shapes the contours of the dominant elements of the novel. She introduces us to the Boyce family in its specificity and in its context, that of the Barbadian community struggling against a hostile world. Central to this shaping is the young Selina, ageless in her insistence on understanding and having some control over the elements that affect her.

Underscoring the microcosm of the family as it relates to the larger Barbadian culture and the even larger world, this initial scene is followed by a potpourri of introductions to the folk who rent rooms in the Boyce brownstone—folk who are representatives of the outer world. Marshall masterfully shows us the peculiar light that is illuminating these shapes by beginning the description of each character analysis with Silla's fusion of Barbadian language and wit into a pithy synopsis of that individual. Thus we are introduced to Suggie Skeete, the Barbadian woman "who gives herself without guile and with a full free passion," but of whom Silla, along, we are sure, with the rest of the Barbadian community, says:

> "That concubine don know shame. Here it tis she just come to this
> man country and every time you look she got a different man ringing
> down the bell."[5]

So it goes with the other folk. Silla's synopsis of their characters illuminates not so much Suggie, or Mrs. Thompson, the kindhearted Afro-American woman, or Miss Mary, the old white woman of another era, as the
particular consciousness of Silla and her community. Also, Silla's view
of Deighton, in this section, is most revealing as it is truth coupled with
cynicism:

> "But look at he. That's one man don know his own mind. He's always
> looking for something big and praying hard not to find it."[6]

Silla's assessment of Deighton begins the scene in which they have their
first conversation in the novel; appropriately, their exchange is a heated
quarrel about the land. This topic is of course crucial to the developing plot
of the book, but what strikes us most about their conversation is the inner
conflicts between them that have been brewing for years. We also sense the
tension of unrelieved sexual desire that hangs between them, a tension
caused by their contrasting philosophies of life.

The scene is drawn in careful detail to accentuate this contrast. As man,
Deighton is dapper, dressed for his Saturday night stroll down the avenue
(like Gwendolyn Brooks's Satin Legs Smith, Deighton becomes a king when
he dresses up and goes out on the town); as woman, Silla is working in the
kitchen, her hands smeared with dough. She also is dreaming of relief, her
version being the owning of a house. They stand there in their apparent
disguises, the man needing mobility for his outlet, the woman needing stability for survival. Their disguises, inbred and overgrown, have long prevented any true and sympathetic communication between them. Having
learned long ago to hold Deighton's big words in suspect, Silla does not
believe him when he tells her of his inheritance; she must see the letter.
Even then, she insists: "It can't be true. This is all some forge up something," thus diminishing his delight about his good fortune. As she continues
to assail Deighton, we come to see that it is not only that she doubts his
word, but that she resents his luck for he has not worked for or desired
advancement as intensely as she has.

Their particular stances within their community are also illuminated by
their hassle over the land. Silla takes all of her resentment of Deighton's
good fortune to her particular group, the community of Barbadian women
who gather around her kitchen table. United in their common sex, background, and goals, their talk seasons the coconut bread Silla is baking to
make extra money; their taunts strengthen her desire to own a house. Like

their African ancestors, they constitute a female society that protects and supports its members, as it acknowledges the dangers inherent in being female. Appropriately, this section is headed by an old proverb:

> Of all things upon the earth that bleed and grow, a herb most bruised is woman.[7]

In contrast, Deighton stands alone outside his community. After talking to Silla, Deighton strolls down Fulton Street, delighting in the outside world as the lights and neon signs regenerate him. But his spirits dip when he is accosted by Seifert Yearwood, one of his own. Their conversation is revealing. Seifert reminds Deighton that the outside world will assault him because he is a black man and a foreigner and that his only protection is to own property. Deighton cannot stand to be reminded that he is seen by anyone as less than a man. The pain is too deep, too searing. Such knowledge must be hidden, pushed down:

> That touch recalled things thrust deep into forgottenness: those white English faces mottled red by the sun in the big stores in Bridgetown and himself as a young man, facing them in his first pair of long pants and his coarse hair brushed flat, asking them for a job as a clerk— the incredulity, the disdain and indignation that flushed their faces as they said no. . . . He broke from Seifert Yearwood's hold and before Seifert could recover he was hurrying away, calling back "I gone."[8]

In the first book, then, we are introduced to the outward poses that Silla and Deighton present to the world while we are given some indications that their poses are only part of what they are, adaptations that they have created to retain some part of themselves and yet exist in the alien world. Marshall, though, is interested in revealing the complexity of these two characters' personalities rather than their disguises and why they respond to the hostile world in the way that they do.

To help us understand their responses, she gives us an insight into their past, how the differences between their backgrounds create blocks in their relationship, and how their sense of themselves as man and woman influences their behavior. Deighton remembers Barbados with fondness, for his childhood there was carefree and happy. As a man, it had become increasingly difficult for him to retain his self-respect, even in this home of his, but still, he had his childhood memories to ignite his imagination and give him hope. To him, the land he inherited is symbolic as well as physical. It is the dream of his youth, a time when he still had hopes that he could be someone. Silla, however, does not see Barbados as the solution to her problems; she remembers it with bitterness. During a discussion with her women friends about sending their children to war, she explosively expresses her feelings about Barbados; we know that she can never return there:

> "Iris, you know what it is to work hard and still never make a headway? That's Bimshire. One crop. People having to work for next skin to nothing. The white people treating we like slaves still and we taking it. The rum shop and the church join together to keep we pacify and in ignorance. That's Barbados. It's a terrible thing to know that you gon be poor all yuh life, no matter how hard you work. You does stop trying after a time. People does see you so and call you lazy. But it ain laziness. It just that you does give up. You does kind of die inside. . . .[9]

It is because of this desire to avoid such a fate, for she understands it so well, that Silla will do battle with Deighton, that she will, if necessary, destroy him. The threat not only of poverty but of the spiritual death that often accompanies it is ever present in her mind. Barbados is not the only place where such a death might take place; she is always aware of the terror and hostility of the world. Nor does she feel herself exempt from cruelty and greed. People, she seems to say, over and over, must struggle and fight for what they want, even to the point of violating their own sense of self. They must always be prepared, regardless of hard work or good planning, for the worst.

Yet we sense that Silla has taken this harsh view of the world and her place in it because her womanly expectations were never fulfilled. Part of her nature, too, is a tender softness that she cannot always hide, a softness that emerges particularly when she encounters vitality and strength in another person. Of course, we are aware of Selina's perceptions of her mother's image in the old photograph. Her perceptions are corroborated by Deighton, when he recalls the youthful Silla, a Silla who awaits promises, without knowing the price that she will have to pay to have them fulfilled. We know then that Silla used to be soft and tender. What we come to see, as the book progresses, is that the softness is still there and that it is precisely because she feels she cannot appear to be soft that she must be doubly hard. Her softness, she believes, has been betrayed. Many scenes in Book Three illuminate these seemingly opposite qualities: her toughness and her softness, and how they are related to each other.

Such a scene occurs when Selina, on her own, leaves home and goes to meet her mother at work in an attempt to stop her from selling the land. The interrelatedness of design is masterfully sculpted, for to meet Silla, Selina must leave the cocoon of her Barbadian world and venture out into that snow-covered, hostile world in which her mother works. To do such a deed, Selina must believe that her mother is strong—strong enough to defeat her father, so strong in fact that drastic action is needed. What Selina discovers as she looks at her mother work is that Silla is even stronger than she thought. Appropriately, Silla is making shells for the war:

> Watching her, Selina felt the grudging affection seep under her amazement. Only the mother's own formidable force could match that of the machines. Only the mother could remain indifferent to the brutal noise.[10]

Silla is shocked that Selina has come through the dark streets to meet her. But she is touched by her daughter's concern for her, so underneath her rage, an odd softness peeks out. Just as Selina admires Silla's strength, the mother cherishes the daughter's spunk and initiative.

> "But look at my crosses. Curls and all now. And take trolley this time of night by sheself. Oh God, a force-ripe woman."[11]

Selina has come, however, not to see her mother, but to plead for her father. Yet as she watches her mother gaze at the store windows with their beautiful clothes and their promise of gracious living, she remembers the shy, soft mother in the photograph who had been promised everything and had received, it seemed, so little. Not surprisingly, when Silla discovers that Selina has come to plead for her father rather than to meet her, her toughness immediately reappears:

> "Love! Give me a dollar in my hand any day!" she cried in a voice that was too loud to be convincing. "Oh, I can see what you gon give, I can see from the way you think now that you ain gon amount to much. Scorning work and money like the father before you."[12]

Deighton does not see the old country as a place of death. True, he might be able to make more money in America, but he feels he will have to give some essential part of himself. He will have to become a petty drudge, a pawn instead of a man. Through Marshall's careful characterization of Deighton's personality, we come to see that behind the dapper, carefree manner is the form of a man both afraid and angry—afraid that he is not what he wants to be and angry that so many obstacles stand in his way. His solution is to pretend disdain for concerns such as money and status. His solution is to be proud, too proud to desire the mundane. But perhaps even more than Silla, he covets status, prestige, money, some acknowledgment of his manhood. The fear and anger in him erupts, particularly when he must confront the white world. For example, after studying an accounting course for two years, he goes to look for a job. Silla asks him:

"Which places you going?"

"The three places offering the best salary."

With a look both cruel and pitying she said, "You don want no job," and turned to the children. "Instead of him going to some small office where he might have a chance—no, he got to play like he's white."

"Silla, lemma tell you something," he interrupted, his smile gone and annoyance darkening his face. "I ain been studying this course off and on for near two years to take no small job. That the trouble with wunna colored people. Wunna is satisfy with next skin to nothing. Please Mr. White-man, gimma little bit. Please Mr. White-man, le' the boy go to Harrison College so he can be a schoolmaster making $10.00 a month. Please, Mr. White-man, lemma buy one of these old house you don want no more. No I ain with wunna. It got to be something big for me 'cause I got big plans or nothing a-tall. That the way a man does do things!"[13]

Thus it seems that Silla has accepted the way of the white world, while Deighton is insistent on receiving his due, on being a man. But ironically, Deighton's desire to have everything or nothing results so often in his having nothing that his insistence turns into self-deprecation. Of course he does not get the job. Now the anger gives way to fear and acceptance:

Despite his bitterness, there was a nuance, a shading of something else. A frightening acceptance, it seemed to be, which sprang, perhaps from a conviction hidden deep within him that it was only right that he should be rejected. . . . He said nothing more after that, and two weeks later he brought home the trumpet and a beginner's book in music and was soon his affable teasing self again.[14]

It is this difference in their responses to material gain, to America, a difference that has to do partly with their contrasting backgrounds and partly with their order of priorities, that forces them into battle against one another. Marshall analyzes the reasons why they respond as they do. Their respective responses are what they are because of their definition of what a man and a woman should be, and because these definitions are threatened by their confusion about what America is and what it promises. In this land of plenty, Deighton's manhood may be at stake, but Silla feels that her sense of herself as a woman is already beyond her reach; now her survival is at stake.

On the surface, it appears as if they have exchanged positions, poses within their patriarchal community. But on a deeper level, their behavior is intimately connected to that view of life. Unwilling to accept too little, Deighton cannot allow his manhood, the basis of his identity, to be tested. He fears it will be blown away and, unable to safeguard it, he will get what he deserves; he will be nothing. Silla is angry and tough, because to survive she must sacrifice so much of what she considers her womanliness, her desire to be dependent and soft, to Deighton's pride and fear. "Watchful and wrathful," her destiny is irrevocably connected to Deighton's choices.

Their modes of behavior then are intertwined. In effect, Deighton needs Silla's fire to relieve him of the guilt he feels in not being able to conquer this hostile world. Silla needs Deighton's acceptance of his fate to energize her, to make her angry enough to keep on struggling.

Their mode of interaction is marked, underscored, in one of the most pivotal scenes of the novel, the moment when Silla tells Deighton she has succeeded in selling the land behind his back. It is as if a vendetta has been accomplished:

> "Cry Silla," she said. "Yes, Silla has done it. She has lied and feigned and forged. She has *damned* her soul but she did it."[15]

> Suddenly he halted. His head dropped and he may have been inspecting his polished shoes, the crease in his trousers or the linoleum's gay pattern. But really he was watching the slow dissolution of his dream: the white house with Grecian columns and stained glass bathroom windows crumbling before it was even built, the flamboyant tree withering before it could take root. He moaned, breaking inside as the dream broke. Yet, as the moan tapered into a sigh, something else emerged. That sigh expressed a profound relief. It was as though Silla, by selling the land, had unwittingly spared him the terrible onus of wresting a place in life. The pretense was over. He was broken, stripped, but *delivered*.[16]

Obviously, Deighton believes that he has already failed himself and his family; yet his acknowledgment of that belief *delivers* him from the responsibility to struggle. Ironically, Silla plays a major role in his deliverance from struggle, but only because she is willing to *damn* her soul, that is, to go against her sense of self to survive. She knows this, and that is why she is so angry with Deighton, as well as herself, for she feels she must take on the dirty struggle to survive because Deighton will not. Her anger, in turn, triggers an even deeper sense of failure and guilt in Deighton. He feels compelled to strike back at her to reaffirm his manhood in some way. On this occasion, he strikes at Silla's most vulnerable point, her desire for him, her desire to be soft with him. Using his one weapon, charm, Deighton seduces his wife, gets from her the money she has acquired from the sale of the land, and then uses it to buy extravagant clothing for the family, thus underscoring the pettiness and futility of her "victory." Silla, realizing the price she has again paid for her softness, her weakness, assumes an even more terrible hardness. It is precisely because these two people characteristically interact in this way that they cannot go beyond their own mutilated definitions of themselves as man and woman.

In analyzing the complexity of her two antagonists as they struggle to retain some semblance of themselves as man and woman and still manage to survive as a unit, Marshall does not let us forget that Selina, their young daughter, is trying to discover herself as a woman. The second book, "Pastorale," is a lyrical interlude between the dramatic action of the first book and the war that breaks out in the third book. Whatever changes may be going on in her parents' lives, the eternal process of "becoming" continues. "Pastorale" distills the mad sweetness of prepubescent Selina as she struggles into womanhood, looking back and peering forward at the same time, bewildered and elated by the changes that are taking place in her body. The author savors Selina's simultaneous fear of and desire for womanhood: menstruation, budding breasts, and the possibilities of sex. As her body develops, so does Selina's consciousness about whom she might become and what specifically she wants to become. So the war between her parents is not only their war. As an observer she is also a participant, for her parents' struggles affect her own developing consciousness.

But not only is she being shaped by her parents, she also is being affected by her community, for it possesses a strict code of behavior as well as a particular style of expression so it might survive. Selina learns quite dramatically that when one of its members threatens its order, the community does not hesitate to step into his or her personal life. Infuriated by her father's lack of tenacity and prudence, it rejects him, casting him outside its protective walls to be devoured by the outside world.

The scene in which the community ostracizes Deighton is, as it must be, one of ritual and form, a moment when it is present in its totality and in its essence. Such occasions occur for a community when it is celebrating life, death, or renewal. In this novel, the occasion is the biggest Barbadian wedding of that year. Ironically, the Boyce family wears the extravagant clothes Deighton had bought in his attempt to pay Silla back. Marshall carefully prepares us for the community's judgment of him by meticulously presenting the nuances of the ritual. The mask is arranged, the ceremonial robes donned, and the gestures and facial expressions are carefully, although spontaneously, enacted. Even as the ritual begins, Marshall underlines the concept of woman and man that is crucial to the struggle between Silla and Deighton as part of their community:

Silla swept into the room and the sunlight leaped toward her, sheening her blue satin gown, and it was like sunlight striking a blue sea. The gown fell to a swirl at her feet and curved low around her full breasts. Blue glass earbobs glinted; blue satin gloves sheathed her oil-stained hands. She paused, calm almost pensive, buttoning the gloves—framed by the dark oak doors, her reflection held in the tall mirror. But she did not even glance in the mirror. Perhaps she needed no reassurance of her beauty.

For she was handsome, as the women from the hills of Barbados sometimes are, a dark disquieting beauty, which broods in their eyes and flashes in their gestures, which underscores their atonal speech.

Silla had learned its expressions early from her mother and the other women as they paused in the cane fields and lifted their sun-blackened enigmatic faces to the sea, as they walked down the white marl roads with the heavy baskets poised lightly on their heads and their bodies flowing forward in grace and restraint. They seemed to use their beauty not to attract but to stave off all that might lessen their strength. When a man looked at them he did not immediately feel the stir in his groin, but uneasiness first and then the challenge to prove himself between those thighs, to rise from them when he was spent and see respect and not contempt in their faces. For somehow their respect would mean his mastery of all of life; their contempt his failure. . . . Such was Silla's beauty today, heightened by the blue gown.[17]

Marshall also prepares us for the tone of this ritual, for not only will it be a union of woman and man, it will be a point of separation. We know, even before we get to the wedding, that every Barbadian already scoffs at Deighton for his foolish action. Also, Marshall underlines the community's power by creating this wedding around a bride who is being forced by her mother's love of status to marry the groom, "a sad bride who walked toward her bridegroom like Iphegenia to her death at Aulis."

The ritual begins to unfold. As the community wishes happiness to the sad bride, it consoles Silla for the abuses she has received from Deighton, so much so that Selina begins to see that the wedding is not for the bride but for Silla. Finally this litany of lamentation and praise reaches its climax as Silla's friends propose a toast to her and her house. Silla does not accept the toast. Like the sad bride, she is overwhelmed by the community's weight and impressed by her own loneliness. Her responses heighten the tension in this scene, for although the ritual is being done in her name, the community does not care so much about her as an individual as it does about its own principles of survival and continuity.

As the dancing and merriment erupt, the talk of houses succumbs to the community's reaffirmation of its vitality and strength. Marshall again introduces another element that will heighten the contradictory pulls within Silla as well as the community itself. An old man, a reminder of the old culture, asks Silla to dance, and when she insists she does not know how he exclaims:

> "I know what?" he cried, angering. "But what wrong with you Silla, that you change up so since you come to these people New York? You don does dance! You must think I forget how you used to be wucking up yourself every Sat'day night when the Brumlee Band played on the pasture. You must think I forget how I see you dance once till you fall out for dead right there on the grass. You must think I forget, but girl, I ain forget."[18]

We gasp with Selina as we confront the gap between the scheming Silla and the younger Silla who gave herself to such ecstacy, an ecstacy that is at the essence of the Barbadian culture, an ecstacy that somehow seems opposed to the inordinate emphasis she and her community now place on property.

As their communal ecstatic throb reaches its peak, as the dancers pointedly sing. "Small Island, go back where you come from." Deighton enters. This moment is perhaps the most dramatic one in the book, for the community does not judge him in a legalistic manner. They combine their old values with the new values they now espouse. Dancing, they turn their backs on him; dancing, they bar him from the ecstacy, the pleasure that is at the core of the culture. As a member of the community, Silla is compelled to follow suit:

> Silla had seen him and as he opened his eyes, she lifted her head to stun him again with her beauty. Strangely, the same passion lanced her eyes—stronger, more urgent than his even. It reached out across the hall to claim him to confess that despite what they had both done, despite their silence, they were joined always. Her hand half lifted as though to beckon him close, a gesture that said she would, with her hand in his, declare all this to the others. But even as he took the first tentative step forward, her hand dropped and her derisive laugh drove him back.[19]

The community's judgment is final. Closing protectively around Silla, Selina, and Selina's sister Ina, it dances, simultaneously shutting his family in while shutting Deighton out, until he is forced to flee, as the song, "Small Island, go back where you come from," collectively announces its sentence.

As a result of its judgment, Selina not only learns about one important characteristic of her community, she also peers into the complexity of her father's nature. Although she sides with her poetic father in his rebellion against the community, she is puzzled by his response. For he now turns to another community in which he is again a subordinate. His immersion in the religion of Father Peace is only a logical continuation of his need to be part of some grand design without being able to create the design for himself. In his last-ditch effort to maintain some sense of himself, he gives up. It is in this searching section of the novel that Selina begins to scrutinize the complexity of her father's seemingly affable nature and the extent of his feeling of impotence:

> Deighton leaped up from his seat of recognition, trembling, the perspiration coursing past his blind eyes. "So true, I am nothing!" And his arms flew out in a gesture that did, indeed, cancel his entire self. "God is everything. Need you, Father need you." And others leaped up, shouting their happiness and their need; their feet pounded out their joy.

> Selina's head ached and she felt the tears rising. She did not understand. She was no longer wise or old, but confounded by life still. She thought suddenly of Percy Challenor presiding like a threatening god at the head of his table on Sundays. They were alike, he and Father Peace. They ruled. What was it that made her father unfit to do the same? Why was he the seduced follower and not the god. . .?[20]

In renouncing not just material possessions but his role as a father, Deighton commits the unforgivable sin within his community. By renouncing his blood ties, he threatens the community's basic value: continuity. It is this act of renunciation that drives the mother, Silla, to the depths of torment.

In her agony, Silla expresses her side of the argument, her inability to understand what Deighton is doing or what his values are. She emphasizes two areas, for her the kernel of her life with him. Not surprisingly, she cannot understand why he came to America, if it is not for "self-improvement," and by that she means material gain. Her line of reasoning echoes the major principle of the Barbadian immigrant community, and her conclusion is much the same as theirs, "You don belong here mahn." Her second area is more personal, although just as connected to their cultural milieu. When she asks him, "Who should they call Daddy then?" she is not asking him about his role as a man, but also about hers as a woman. Throughout the novel, Silla is referred to as "the mother." For her the drive for material success is as much bound up with her children as it is with her community. She cannot understand how it could be otherwise for Deighton She knows that he defines his manhood so much as doing something extraordinary that he seems to fail before he even begins. As in their struggle over the land,

though, she is so appalled by his resignation to failure that she reinforces
it all the more:

> She could not stop. The wall she had built against the thoughts during
> their long silence had cracked, the words streaming through, and she
> was powerless to stop them. Then, too she did not want to stop. For
> his humility galled her. His quick assent to all she said goaded her on.
> Why didn't he leap up and shout her down, or lean across the table
> and smash the words from her mouth? But no, instead he exulted in
> the pain each word brought and repaid her abuse with compassion.
> It was his wish to suffer that suddenly spurred in her the need to make
> that suffering full. She rose, her eyes groping through the shadows to
> the family photograph. Gazing at it, she said with dread emphasis,
> "Then years back, it was the car. The piece of old car you had to have
> even though it was the depression, just to make like a big sport in
> front the boy. That piece of old junk that made his heart worse and
> killed him before his time."[21]

As her words take shape, as Silla reiterates her position as the abused
and vengeful mother, she achieves the opposite of what she had intended.
In heightening Deighton's failure as a father, in giving it extraordinary character, he is able to embrace it. Again, she delivers him from the struggle,
for now she has located for him an act of monumental failure, an act that
gives meaning to his suffering. Knowing his crime, he can suffer willingly
for it. Knowing his crime, he can leave his family for Father Peace, renouncing his role as father even as he atones for the sin of causing his son's death.

What we come to see as we near the end of the war is that a dominant
stroke in Deighton's character is his need to suffer for a crime that he cannot
remember committing but that he feels he must have, since the world insists
on punishing him. This stroke is even more clearly marked in his final appearance in the book when Silla brings the authorities to take him away as
an illegal alien.

Again, Marshall sculpts the space with precise strokes, carves her characters in relation to their space. Again, her design is an interrelated whole.
First, we are shown an almost ascetic, peaceful space. In his monk's cell
behind Father Peace's restaurant, Selina, as if taking Silla's place, is washing Deighton's socks. The outside hostile world does not exist. This inner
world is small, spare, uncomplicated. Then suddenly Silla intrudes. As she
points Deighton out to the immigration officers, her loud voice is not only
hers but that of the Barbadian immigrant community that believes it cannot
afford such deviance from its principles. It is all there: Selina trying to
understand her parents' conflict; Deighton resigning himself to his fate as
an impotent man; Silla caught between pity and anger toward her destroyed

man; the threatening outside world; Barbados the hope, Barbados the fear. It is in this scene, a scene in which Deighton must play the role of the sunlit martyr and Silla the role of the avenging wintery woman-devil, that these two people acknowledge the truth:

> They might have been alone with the world around them stilled and the years rubbed away like smoke from a glass. For the look they shared must have been the same as when they first met; shy yet curious and at its core the stir of love. Silently they asked each other what had gone wrong, what it was that had ruined them for each other, and their mutual bewilderment confessed that they did not know.[22]

Thus the war between Silla and Deighton ends. But it is a war in which there are no spoils, no victors. Both have tormented each other. Neither can understand the causes that have brought them to the turning when their essential natures were betrayed by each other. Both are intertwined in their defeat of each other. Although Silla does not die physically as does Deighton, she carries with her the knowledge that she has delivered him to the outside world, that she had to, like Judas, bring his death upon him. Their respective punishments are fitted to their personalities. Deighton probably commits suicide rather than face the image of his failure in the eyes of folk he knows in Barbados, and Silla must continue on, remembering throughout her life her act of betrayal.

Although the war might be over for Deighton, Silla must now confront Selina as her next opponent, an opponent who has witnessed her act of betrayal, an opponent as strong-willed as she. For in her development of her own self-consciousness, Selina chooses to be a rebel like her father against the restrictions her mother and the Barbadian community represent. The shift in battle personnel is beautifully executed by Marshall, for the book "The War" ends with a climactic battle between Silla and Selina. Again, all of the elements of this writer's design are fused into a kinetic whole. Even as we catch our last glimpse of Deighton, Selina throws the word *Hitler* at her mother. We are reminded that the war within this family has taken place in the context of a larger world war. Even as Selina begins her rhythmic chant, Ina comments about her mother and sister: "What is it with you two? Why're you always at each other's throats? You're alike, you know that! The same." As if acknowledging that fact, Silla allows herself to be beaten by Selina, until the daughter finally clings to the mother. As if acknowledging that they are kindred spirits, Silla

> sat quietly holding her on the sofa under the brilliant light. Then, almost reverently, she touched the tears that had dried white on her dark skin, traced with her finger the fragile outline of her face and

rested her hand soothingly on her brow. She smoothed her snarled hair. Yet, despite the tenderness and wonder and admiration of her touch, there was a frightening possessiveness. Each caress declared that she was touching something which was finally hers alone.[23]

So even though the world war ends on the day the Boyce family hears of Deighton's death, the war within the family continues, as Selina, who sees herself only as her father's daughter, becomes the angry one and takes on the responsibility of avenging the betrayal of his dreams.

Throughout the first three books of *Browngirl, Brownstones*, the emphasis is on the complex characters of Silla and Deighton as illuminated by their struggle over the land. Except for "Pastorale," Selina is focal only in terms of their effect on her. As girl-woman, her personality is being formed, her character sculpted in relation to her parents' strong shapes. She does not choose her form in these first three books; rather, her evolution is subordinated to their context.

In Book Four, appropriately called "Selina," the focus of the novel shifts from the parents to the daughter, for Selina begins choosing her own space. As she grows older, she must encounter the many forces that in fact have helped to shape her parents; she must discover the space that is the context for their characters; she must assess, with knowledge rather than naiveté, her judgment of them. This book is the culmination of the novel, for it is during her adolescence that Selina begins to make herself, begins to choose what that self as woman will be. Given the elements available for her composition, elements that we have experienced in the first three books, we are prepared to immerse ourselves in her creative process.

Nonetheless, although the focus of the book changes, the elements of Marshall's design do not. Deighton and Silla's struggle still continues in the person of Selina, for she cannot yet understand its complexity or bring it to some resolution. Always present is the Barbadian society, persistently reaching out to claim her, not only as her mother's daughter but as an adult member of the tribe. Also, the outer world issues challenges to her as she begins to move beyond the boundaries of her family. Structurally Book Four is not a separate entity but a necessary part of this design.

The opening section of "Selina" reaffirms Marshall's design. Immediately we are presented with the images of Winter and Spring associated respectively with Silla and Deighton. Only now these images are united in the person of Selina:

Selina carried what seemed the weight of winter in her body, which felt sear, numb and as though laid in some chill place until spring would come.[24]

Clearly Deighton, or at least his dream, is still alive to Selina; clearly she must, in her father's name, reckon with her mother. Marshall uses this beginning section on Selina's budding womanhood to reinforce our sense of Deighton's values, lest we construe his death only as defeat. As Selina listens to her friends talk about the material things their fathers are giving them, she tells us of his legacy to her, a legacy without price:

> But she would have liked to turn and tell Beryl very quietly, there in the dim hall with the others gathered apprehensively on the landing above, what he had given her. How one cold March afternoon long ago she had found him stretched on the cot in the sun parlor in his shirt sleeves, his head cradled in his arms and humming. "Is it spring?" she had asked, her breath coming in cold wisps. He had drawn her down beside him, loosened her arms and said, "Yes." And suddenly she had sensed spring in the air, seen it forming beyond the glass walls and had not been cold any more.
>
> How could Beryl understand that this was what he had given her? and its worth?[25]

Her father had given her the gift of wonder, of imagination. An artist without a form, he had bestowed his sensibility on his daughter in images so lucid, so indelible, that she would never forget them. But even as Selina defines for us the magic in Deighton's character, an opposing view—the need and desire for material things—flickers through her mind. So the conflict between the two views continues as Selina begins to feel for the other side of the issue. Perhaps such a sensibility as Deighton's demands another kind of sensibility to keep it warm and comfortable, just as a sensibility that is essentially practical is deadening without the touch of magic. Perhaps Silla and Deighton at one time shared so much of the same sensibility that the one in having to become solely practical is enraged, while the other in being only magical is razed by guilt.

Silla has always had to bear the responsibility of making a future for her children. In this section, even as Selina contemplates her father's gift to her, "the mother" is plotting to send her to college. Once Silla decides that Selina deserves this opportunity, she moves in her usual decisive and forceful manner, even to the point of commanding Miss Mary, the old white tenant, to die. This scene manifests one side of Silla's character, her ruthlessness, coupled with her strong mother's will to do whatever is necessary for her children. Unable to live herself, she will make it possible for them to do so.

In spite of her strength of will, though, Silla has been weakened by Deighton's absence, as well as by her own knowledge that she has betrayed her husband, and that Selina has witnessed her betrayal. She has sacrificed her husband to her children and in so doing has alienated herself from her children. She is as tragic in life as Deighton is in death:

> Every morning she found her mother at the table, sometimes asleep or simply staring down into a cup that had long since been emptied. For days the bed upstairs remained untouched, dust sown like fine seeds on the rose satin bedspread. Instead of sleeping she cleaned at night—Selina would hear the vacuum cleaner's whine in her sleep— and studied a course in practical nursing, since she worked in a hospital now that the war plant had closed. She would be studying in the kitchen, yet the lights in all the rooms, the halls even the chandelier in the parlor would be burning, giving the high-ceilinged rooms with their gilt and rich wood a festive air. Often she fell asleep amid the books on the table or stumbled with exhaustion into the dining room and slept, fully clothed in one of the stiff-backed chairs, her body braced.[26]

Because Selina sees herself as her father's daughter, she resists not only her mother's attempts to possess her but the Barbadian community's as well. She takes her father's place as the individual who stands outside the community. As foil for Selina's resistance, her sister Ina will take her rightful place within the Barbadian-American world, but Selina does not want to be cut out of the same piece of cloth as everyone else. So she resents the community's attempt to close in on itself, even as it imitates American society. From her point of view, their desire to disassociate themselves from other blacks, as well as whites, is "clannish," "narrow-minded," "selfish," and "provincial." Fleeing from what she feels to be unbearable restrictions to her development as a person, restrictions that will not allow her to experiment or to be creative, she opposes her tribe even as she seeks herself.

Selina's affair with Clive Davis becomes the fulcrum through which she begins to shape her own contours. Through the space she creates with him she begins to clarify her understanding of her mother and her father, her own definition of herself as a woman, as well as her relationship with the tribe. Marshall uses their relationship in the same way that she uses the struggle over the land in the first three books as a means of structuring the characters within their cultural context without diminishing personality distinctions.

From Selina and Clive's first meeting, Marshall sets up the ingredients of their relationship, ingredients that will give cohesiveness to this section. From the beginning, Selina is the active one, the one who must rebel, must experience, must experiment, and Clive is the knowing observer and teacher rather than an intense participant. All of Selina's anger, confusion, and vitality are compressed into this first meeting so we feel that Selina was destined to discover someone like Clive.

Appropriately, Selina's dramatic rebellious act against her community is done in its presence and in the midst of one of its rituals. Moved by her anger at the Barbadian Association, she rushes out of the meeting, but cannot get out, cannot open the door to the street. So she asks a figure in the shadows to help her. That is how these two meet. Selina is actively trying to get out, but cannot: Clive is a shadow in the darkness standing between the inside and the outside. On this occasion as on many others he is waiting to take his mother home, but he does not come inside to the meeting. He, like Deighton, stands apart from his community but not too far away from it. But unlike Deighton, he can articulate his position and the wherefores that have brought him to it.

Thus their first encounter illuminates their positions, their distinct stances in relation to the community, as well as the strong differences in their personalities. Her anger mitigating her usual caution, Selina reveals, "I don't know what I am." Clive queries, "What do you do that you like?" Selina responds, "Nothing, not a thing which I suppose makes me nothing." Having made her admit her confusion, Clive opens the door for her, not only to the street, but to the beginning of her sexual life. Yet even as he thrusts himself into her openness, Selina wishes that her mother and the Barbadian Association could see her, could see that she was indeed Deighton's Selina. As if sensing her need to rebel, to experience, Clive suggests: "Look, how would you like to take lessons from me—so that when you're my age you won't be like me."

Why does Clive see himself as a flawed man? As a little colored boy who is trying to make it on the strength of a nonexistent talent? Like Deighton, Clive possesses the sensibilities of an artist without a form or discipline necessary to transform his inclinations into crafted activity. He thinks, he talks, but he lacks passion or will. As a more articulate Deighton, he sardonically ridicules the clay out of which he feels he has been created, sneering at the efforts he has made to break out of the mold. He talks continually as a block against action, treating his life lightly because he takes it too seriously. He treats his own state of mind as an object so often he cannot forget himself enough to commit spontaneous action.

His inability to renew himself is drained by the love-hate he feels for his mother, whom he describes as "the small hard dry type of West Indian who lives endlessly and endures all." Like Deighton's mother, she has cuddled her son, sacrificed for him, and expected everything from him. Like Deighton, he resents, yet needs, the pull of "the mother." In his inimitable way, he verbalizes the threat that many men have felt about their original home:

"Mothers? Hell, they seldom say die! Fathers perhaps. Like my poor
father. He just acts like I don't exist. But not mothers. They form you
in that dark place inside them and you're theirs. For giving life they
exact life. The cord remains uncut, the blood joined, and all that that
implies. They hold you by their weakness, their whining, their sickness, their long-suffering, their tears and their money. . . . We're all
caught within a circle of women, I'm afraid, and we move from one
to the next in a kind of blind dance."[27]

The mothers are magnified and become for Clive as they have for Selina
the entirety of Barbadian society, the ones who see art and the artist as an
expensive luxury. The immigrant society had to sacrifice much of its own
magic and imagination to survive, had to be ruthless and practical. Like the
mothers, it expects payment for its sacrifice, or the pain, the work, the agony,
would not have been worth it. Clive knows their side of the story well and
has in some way internalized it. In contrast, Selina's way is clear; she will
not allow the others to restrict her. But Clive believes that his mother
and his tribe have a point. So he is caught between the two value systems,
his own sensibility, what he cannot help being, and the world that has fed
and nurtured him. His emotional conflict is heightened by his belief that he
is not a great creative genius but a man of minor talent. His articulation of
his plight illuminates the weakness of character that can come from a community's inability to perceive the individual differences among its members.
Marshall carefully stresses each line of Clive's portrait, completing not only
his shape but the shapes of so many others as well.

"Oh and then there's my unhappy breed. Far below the gods and a
little above the slobs and worse off than either. We languish in our
own special kind of limbo, gaining for ourselves the slob's ridicule
and the artist's contempt. We're the men of minor talent, the Pre-
tenders. What's wrong with us?" He glanced at her intent face as though
she had asked the question. "Any number of things. We're not bold
enough. We think and talk too much, and don't really feel. We were
born the wrong color. We despaired before our time. We have the
forms, the techniques but no substance. We're not really driven. . . .
Oh, there are any number of things upon which we can conveniently
hang the blame. Christ, my kind knows what they should do— call it
quits and high-tail it back to the herd. But we hold out. Hoping.
Hoping for what?" He bent his harsh gaze on her and then muttered.
"We're the least among the apostles."[28]

Since Clive knows his disease so well, why can't he cure it? Knowledge does not seem to be enough—in fact it sometimes paralyzes. Paralysis of the will is his disease, whatever his particular dilemma. That is the difference between Selina and Clive. Selina does not have the knowledge he has gained; in fact, she is ignorant of the subtle distinctions within her own Barbadian community and not yet exposed to the covert dangers of the outside world. But she has spirit, passion, willfulness. Clive recognizes these qualities in her from their first meeting. Lacking passion himself, he is drawn to it, basking in its radiance and warmth. Leaning on her spirit, he tells her what he knows. Perhaps that is why Selina is studying dance, art in motion, while Clive is playing at painting.

The two villains that occupy these lovers' space, that will not let them be, are of course the monolithic thrust of the Barbadian community and the racism of the white world. Through Clive, Selina begins to see the savage nibblings inherent in prejudice, as well as the complexity of her parents' characters. Clive does not have answers, but he has cultivated the art of analysis. As a teacher he helps her to develop what she needs most in her character, the ability to see around corners as well as straight ahead.

Two incidents in the book illustrate the nature and relatedness of these villains. Selina begins to grasp her community's need for everlasting defense when she meets one of her white classmate's mother. Their conversation is a familiar one to any West Indian who has lived in these United States. As her girl friend's mother insists that American Negroes are somehow different from West Indians, Selina realizes that although she did not want to be cut out of the same cloth as every Barbadian, she will be seen by the white world not as Selina but as a blurred black figure with an accent.

Selina's rude realization is connected, in the novel, to her plans to defeat her own community to save Clive and herself. Angered by the white woman's insensitivity, she flees to Clive for solace, only to find that his mother wants him to pick her up. Desperately, Selina tries to force Clive to break away from this maternal dependence, but he cannot or will not. In his final act of instruction, Clive shows Selina the passivity that is at his core. More important, in his last act, he emphasizes Selina's inability to accept resignation or inaction. In discovering this truth, she knows herself to be her mother's child. She knows, too, that unlike Deighton or Clive, she can be part of her community and yet not be controlled by it for she is willing to both understand and challenge it. As if to prove this, she refuses the scholarship the Barbadian Association gives her, for she knows she has feigned allegiance to their code. Willful, but honest, she attacks the community even as she pays them the respect of telling them of her deception.

Having experienced the racism of the outer world, having suffered the beauty and hopelessness of a man much like her father, and having respectfully challenged her community, Selina is able to face her mother as a complex human being and is able to give the aging Silla her due:

"Mother," she said gently, "I have to disappoint you. Maybe it's as you once said: that in making your own way you always hurt someone. I don't know. . . ." Then remembering something Clive had said, she added with a thin smile, "Everybody used to call me Deighton's Selina but they were wrong. Because you see I am truly your child. Remember how you used to talk about how you left home and came here alone as a girl of eighteen and was your own woman? I used to love hearing that. And that's what I want. I want it!"

Silla's pained eyes searched the adamant face, and after a long time a wistfulness softened her mouth. It was as if she somehow glimpsed in Selina the girl she had once been. For that moment, as the softness pervaded her and her hands lay open like a girl's on her lap, she became the girl who had stood, alone and innocent, at the ship's rail, watching the city rise glittering with promise from the sea.[29]

As the mother lets the daughter go, we see the completion of Marshall's design. The shapes of Silla, Deighton, and Selina intersect each other, for each is a part of the other and yet distinct. In creating such a design, Marshall dramatizes for us, as well as for Selina, the reasons why Silla had to assume the guise of the domineering mother and Deighton the pose of the carefree father. Selina now understands what her mother and father did not, "what it was that had ruined them [as man and as woman] for each other," and that given their personalities, and the oppressiveness of their situation, it could hardly be otherwise. We feel, because of the daughter's self-knowledge, she may be able to sustain what the mother could not—her own independence and wholeness, as well as an appreciation for others who might be different.

As Selina throws one of her silver bracelets, the symbol of West Indian ancestry, onto the landscape of Brooklyn, we know that she is part of this immigrant community forever. But she must leave it; she must go backward and forward in time, in her own personal revolution. Indelibly touched by her mother's fire, her father's grace, she must go to the islands, must confront the sound of the Caribbean sea, the source of the dreams, fears, and rituals that were the raw materials for her own self-consciousness.

PART II

The Chosen Place, The Timeless People: A Lesson in History

In *Browngirl, Brownstones*, Paule Marshall's analysis of Selina's development reiterates the interdependency of character and culture. Because this story focuses on an immigrant family within a changing culture, the novel not only traces Selina's adolescence but also the manner in which a people adapt to a new environment while trying to keep their roots. At the core of the characters' significant actions, in this case their sense of the essence of man and woman, is an ambivalence, an emotional confusion that this hybrid culture feels about both the old and the new country.

In her second novel, *The Chosen Place, The Timeless People* (1969), the culture that Marshall so graphically depicts is rooted firmly in the past, a past so much a part of the present that time or change seems irrelevant, almost deceptive. Like *Browngirl, Brownstones*, this panoramic novel is marked by Marshall's sculpting of characters within the space of a culture. But in *The Chosen Place, The Timeless People*, the culture in its depth and timelessness becomes the major character in the novel to which the individual personalities are subordinated. In Marshall's first novel, the development of Selina's character delineates the process of flux within New York Barbadian culture; in her second novel, the major actors have already become themselves. Instead, the development of the novel consists of the characters' recognition of themselves because of their unwitting confrontation with its dominant character, the Chosen Place: Bournehills.

However, although there is a difference in the scope of her world between her first novel and her second, Marshall uses similar techniques in both, techniques that we begin to realize are central to her vision. In *The Chosen Place, The Timeless People*, as well as in *Browngirl, Brownstones*, the characters' concepts of themselves as woman or man and as members of a culture are related to the rituals of their particular community. In addition, in her second novel, Marshall dramatizes how the rituals of the members of an oppressed society affect and are affected by the culture of the ruling society.

Overtly, this story consists of the interrelationship between the team members of the Center for Applied Social Research (CASR) and the people of Bournehills, the agricultural section of Bourne Island, a small dot in the Caribbean. Like so many agencies of its type, CASR is an offshoot of several business corporations that want to uplift the impoverished of the world while they save on government taxes. The practice of philanthropic enterprise has become increasingly an earmark of American corporate structure. In choosing this line of development, the author employs a major theme of black literature, the process of struggle between the controllers of the world and those who are controlled. CASR could stand for any number of abbreviated agencies whose wealth is based on exploitation but whose ostensible purpose is the uplifting of the world's unfortunate. To underscore the tenuous nature of CASR, Marshall carefully traces its beginnings. This philanthropic agency has its roots in the trading of staples, such as salted meat, fish, flour, and of course slaves, between Africa, the islands, and Philadelphia. CASR comes to Bournehills, then, not only because of its philanthropic mission but also because their respective histories are intertwined. The salt fish that made CASR's parent corporation wealthy has also been for generations the only protein food Bournehills folk were allowed.

Just as CASR could be any one of many philanthropic offshoots of major United States corporations, so Bournehills becomes a symbol for "every place that had been wantonly used, its substance stripped away, and then abandoned," but that through its tenacity and traditions stays alive if only to expose the wrongs done to it. The novel begins with this epithet:

> Once a great wrong has been done, it never dies. People speak the words of peace, but their hearts do not forgive. Generations perform ceremonies of reconciliation but there is no end.[30]

That this saying comes from the Tiv of West Africa is crucial to the novel's design, for the people of Bournehills are descendants of West Africans brought over by force to be slaves in a land that, like them, is used and finally abandoned.

This story about the relationship between CASR and Bournehills, then, is not only local. Wherever there are those wealthy enough to plan help projects for those from whose labor their wealth is derived, we will find the same elements of arrogance and tenacity, obtuseness and revelation. What Marshall does is to analyze the contour of this relationship so we may perceive more intensely why a great wrong cannot be righted by goodwill, money, new ideas—by ceremonies of reconciliation. Such an analysis cannot be effective if it is general or rhetorical. The relationship between the controllers and the controlled is all pervasive, not because it is history, sociology, or anthropology, but because it affects the lives of people at both ends of the spectrum. Once begun, such a relationship is like a snake biting its own tail. The particularity of CASR and Bournehills' relationship is the prism through which we feel the depths of the more general phenomena. It is through our experiencing of the specific individuals as they compositely make up history or culture that we become immersed in the complexity of social morality. In this novel, then, as in *Browngirl, Brownstones*, character and culture shape each other. Here, though, the shapes of Marshall's characters are sculpted on a grander scale as a people's history is reiterated in the present. Even before CASR was created, its ancestors had been formed by, and had helped to form, Bournehills, in a relationship so deep, so intense, that this contemporary encounter is but part of a seemingly timeless drift, a drift that surely can be changed only by acts more powerful than ceremonies of reconciliation.

THE DESIGN
In writing such an ambitious analysis, Marshall had to construct a care-

fully shaped design, or the analysis itself would become incohesive or tedious. She divided her novel into four books: "Heirs and Descendants," "Bourne-hills," "Carnival," and "Whitsun." The content of the first two books flow from an analysis of the major actors of the book, and central to "Carnival" and "Whitsun" are touchstone times in the rhythmic process of the Bourne-hills year. The foci of these four parts reflect the novel's two major build-ing blocks: the delineation of character as it is shaped by ethnic and personal culture and the ritualistic flow of time. Paradoxically, the flow of time is used to evoke a feeling of timelessness; the seasonal cycles of Bournehills compositely make up its timeless rhythm, its rituals; the delineation of per-sonal characters is used to show how individuals are distinctive features of the seemingly impersonal face of history. Time and timelessness and char-acter and culture exist in a continual movement. Neither element can be changed without affecting the other. Marshall gives flesh to these general principles of hers by carving lines and crevices in her characters that reveal both their own person and culture and by creating a sense of tradition through painstaking presentation of the Bournehills' rhythm. Structurally, such a technique banishes disorder or tedium, for time gives the novel its own cohesiveness, and the delineation of character keeps us emotionally involved in her analysis.

The design of the novel encompasses three types of characters. These characters illuminate and are illuminated by the Chosen Place. Some like Merle, Lyle, and Vere are Bournehills natives who have journeyed to other places only to return home; others like Saul Amron, Harriet Amron, and Allan Fuso are outsiders who have come to Bournehills, they think, to right some of the wrongs done to it. Then, of course, there are the Timeless People, like Stinger and Gwen, Ferguson and Delbert, Leasy and Carring-ton, for whom Bournehills is "the world." Their existence appears at first glance to be defined by the conditions of the land, by the planting and harvesting of sugar cane, and by the rigid class system that has been im-posed on them.

Within these three groups, we meet a range of characters covering the class and sex distinctions that are important in Bournehills society and in the Euro-American world that has affected the island. Merle, as a Bourne-hills woman, has had a chance to go to school in England and has had quite different experiences from Vere, who left Bournehills for the States where he worked as a laborer. Saul and Harriet, although married, come from dif-ferent traditions; Saul is a mixture of various Jewish traditions and Harriet is a descendant of the American founding fathers. The characters, in fact, are a microcosm of the West, both black and white, as they meet and mingle in Bournehills.

In the first book, "Heirs and Descendants," we are introduced to the newcomers and returners in terms of their sex, class, and culture, through

Merle, the crossroads character of this book. The second book, appropriately called "Bournehills," describes the beginning of the relationship among
the newcomers, the returners, and the Bournehills folk. In "Carnival," the
third book, the newcomers are put to the test by Bournehills culture. It is in
this book that we begin to sense those individuals who will accept the truth
of the land and act on it and those who will not. "Whitsun," the fourth book,
completes the cycle, as the regeneration or deterioration of the newcomers
moves toward its climax.

In addition to these two major structural elements, time and delineation
of character, Merle Kimbona is the unifying force throughout the novel. As
a crossroads character,* Merle represents both the tradition of Bournehills
and that of Europe. Biologically, she is a descendant of an English planter,
Duncan Vaughn, and West Africans who were brought to Bournehills. Born
and reared on this small West Indian island, she also had spent many years
in England. Marshall's initial description of Merle emphasizes all of these
cultural strains in her:

> And she was dressed like a much younger woman, in the open-back
> shoes which featured some rather fanciful, embroidered scroll-work
> across the instep and raised heels to give her height, and a flared print
> dress made from cloth of a vivid abstract tribal motif: cloth from the
> sun, from another cosmos, which could have been found draped in
> offhand grace around a West African woman. Pendant silver earrings
> carved in the form of those saints to be found on certain European
> churches adorned her ears. The saints, their tiny faces gaunt with
> piety, their eyes closed in prayer, were trembling anxiously from the
> force of her annoyance. Numerous bracelets, also of silver, bound her
> wrists. But these, unlike the earrings, were heavy, crudely made, and
> noisy. They lent a clangorous, unsettling note to her every move.[31]

Merle, though, like so many blacks in the West, has not found a way to fuse
these different traditions that she has experienced into a harmonious whole:

> She had donned this somewhat bizarre outfit, each item of which stood
> opposed to, at war even, with the other, to express rather a diversity
> and disunity within herself, and her attempt, unconsciously probably,
> to reconcile these opposing parts, to make of them a whole. Moreover,
> in dressing in this manner she appeared to be trying (and this was
> suggested by those unabashedly feminine shoes) to recover something

---

*Crossroads here as in Legba, the Voodoo loa of the crossroad, which combines opposites.

in herself that had been lost: the sense and certainty of herself as a woman perhaps.[32]

Like many crossroads characters, Merle's sense of disunity is epitomized in her lack of surety about her own sexuality. An essential part of her despoilment was her affair with the rich English woman who had given her those saint earrings, the woman who had turned from a benefactress into a vindictive curse when Merle gave her up for Ketu. Like Bournehills, Merle has been used, stripped, and abandoned, for she has had many losses in her life. At two, she had seen her mother killed before her eyes by one of her father's other women. In spite of this, her "aristocratic" mulatto father had never acknowledged her even when he provided her with money to go to school in England. Motherless, fatherless, she gets involved with a flighty crowd in England, through which she meets the wealthy woman who keeps her. When she meets her African husband, Ketu, she has already broken with her benefactress but in a moment of vindictiveness, the English woman lets Ketu know of his wife's previous sordid relationship. Unable to stomach it, and without warning, Ketu takes their daughter to Africa, leaving Merle a lonely, broken woman. She has returned to Bournehills, the land of her birth, where her life is only partially known, to somehow resolve her fate. But the result of her personal losses is an occasional but serious lapse into silence when she can neither speak nor hear. Like Bournehills, she seems defeated by the world; yet her eyes have retained their vitality, just as Bournchills tenaciously clings to its traditions. Throughout the novel, in fact, Merle is identified with Bournehills. She becomes a living symbol of its plight and its strength. She is one of its people and has been used as it has by the conquering world.

In practical terms, the newcomers are personally tied to Bournehills through Merle, for she owns the only guesthouse on that part of the island. Ironically, it is the house left to her by the father who never acknowledged her. In fact, when we first meet her in the book, she is going to meet Saul, Harriet, Allan, and Vere's plane but is prevented from doing so because of the usually washed away Bournehills roads. When they do meet her for the first time at Lyle Hutson's house, the black upper middle class of the island has been discussing Bournehills as a "place out of the dark ages" that refuses to be changed. Merle walks in, changing the tone of the correct gathering with her vital eyes and never-ceasing talk. She immediately becomes the newcomers' guide through the complexity of this island that defies definition.

We first meet our other focal characters—Vere, Allan, Harriet, and Saul —as their plane approaches Bourne Island. It is in the author's description of their cultural and social background, their definition of themselves as man or woman, and their reaction to Bournehills' landscape that she plants the seeds for their respective ordeals. Marshall uses the technique of graphic description to unravel the layers of each character's personality throughout the novel, for the psychology of these persons will affect the way in which they are changed by Bournehills.

Vere is the first traveler we meet, since he knows the terrain of the island of his birth and can identify its parts correctly. Through his mind's eye we see the town of New Bristol, Cane Vale sugar factory, and the stripped hills and valleys. Weighted down by the immutability of Bournehills and the inevitability of his return to it, Vere reflects upon his need for escape from that lot that befalls the men of his land. Their lives lack excitement or any avenue to power, for him the characteristics of masculinity. His antidote to this fate is his dream of car racing, a vehicle that he feels will give his life meaning and drama.

In contrast, Allan Fuso, the statistician, is returning to the island to work for CASR because it means for him some reprieve from the boring academic life he feels destined to lead. His background is crucial to his sense of himself:

> All the various strings that had gone into making him (and between his parents these included the whole of Europe from Ireland to Italy) might have been thrown into one of those high-speed American blenders, a giant Mixmaster perhaps, which reduces everything to the same bland amalgam beneath its whirring blades.[33]

The most thorough of these initial descriptions is that of Harriet Amron:

> Out of the four on the plane only Harriet had kept watch. She had been the first, in fact, to sight Bourne Island when it had been nothing more than a small green wen on the absolutely smooth, stretched skin of the sea. Long before it was even due to appear, when all that could be seen down through the deep cloudless well of air that was the sea, she had been quietly waiting and watching for it, her head with its disciplined cowl of wheat-colored hair framed by the oval-shaped window, her trim, tall, pleasantly angular body poised lightly on the seat. Despite the long flight, her beige linen dress looked as if it had just been put on fresh. A slender wedding band was her sole jewelry.[34]

We discover, as we listen to her think, how she had grown up as a sheltered child of an old and wealthy Philadelphia family, how she dreads becoming like her helpless and useless southern mother, why she divorced her first husband, a nuclear scientist, and how she met and married Saul Amron, her present husband whom she got to head CASR, a project of the institute with which she is intricately connected. We immediately perceive from these reflections that Harriet's sense of herself as a woman is that of being a helpmate to a man, and that it is because of her influence that both she and her husband are going to Bournehills. We discover, too, that she is a descendant of Widow Sheppen, the old Philadelphia widow who had in the seventeenth century built her wealth on salt fish, staples, and slaves, and that Harriet's relationship to this island predates her marriage to Saul. What is most revealing about her section, though, is her first reaction to Bournehills, a reaction that will be the basis for her relationship with its people, a reaction that is as much a part of her ethnic as well as her personal history.

> It struck her as being another world altogether, one that stood in profound contradistinction to the pleasant reassuring green plain directly below; and she wondered gazing intently out toward those scarred hills, how an island this small could sustain such a dangerous division. To add to matters, the hills were filled with shadows even though it was noon and the sun stood at its zenith. Because of the shadows Bournehills scarcely seemed a physical place to her, but some mysterious and obscured region of the mind which ordinary consciousness did not dare admit to light. Suddenly, for a single unnerving moment, she had the sensation of being borne backward in time rather than forward in space. The plane by some perverse plan might have been taking her away from the present, which included Saul and the new life she was about to begin with him, back to the past which she had always sought to avoid.[35]

Her husband, Saul Amron, is the only major character on the plane from whose mind we are barred in our initial meeting with him. Marshall introduces him through the thoughts of the others, rather than his own, since, because he is a Jew, others immediately notice him:

> He was asleep in the aisle seat, or appeared to be—Allan wasn't sure —his loose, oversized body in which no two bones seemed to fit properly, propped up beside his wife, Harriet, whose face was toward the window. Allan's gaze took in the nose, rising like the curved blade of a scimitar out of the pale, somewhat fleshy face, the forehead that in its breadth and height looked vaguely hydrocephalic, the hair, coarse and rust-colored (nigger hair, Allan's mother would have called it) which was beginning to recede at the temples.

> He had lain like this, shamelessly on view, offering without apology, himself and all his physical flaws to anyone who cared to look. . . .[36]

BOURNEHILLS AS SYMBOL

As different as these characters are, what is the quality of Bournehills that will so gravely test them? When we see this tiny island from the plane,

Marshall describes it as another small island that seems expendable; yet she continues her description by saying that because it stood off by itself from the rest of the islands, "it might have been put there by the giants to mark the eastern boundary of the entire continent, to serve as its bourn." In essential ways, then, this small, seemingly expendable island is a prototype of other Caribbean islands, precisely because of its location and the characteristics that underscore the European's perception of the Caribbean, that of being a gateway to the New World.

Even before Merle drives the CASR team from New Bristol to this forsaken section of the island, we are told that various types of people have strong feelings about Bournehills. To Vere, it is his fate of monotony and powerlessness; to Allan, it is a reprieve from nothingness; to the up-and-coming professionals of New Bristol, it is a place that, for some perverse reason, chooses to be backward; to Harriet, it appears as a dark region of the mind; and to Merle, it is a refuge, "Sweet Beulah Land." When we see the land up close for the first time with Saul Amron, the anthropologist, it seems familiar to him, since it is like all the other field locations he had worked in all over the world, places that held unresolved conflict for him.

To the people of Bournehills, their home is unique because of its history and traditions. It was in Bournehills that Cuffee Ned, the great slave rebellion leader, had started his revolt, had struck a grave blow against the slavemasters of Bourne Island. It was in Bournehills that the people of the island had at one time worked as one to free themselves from bondage. Cuffee Ned was one of them and they were part of him. This revolt was their one significant act of unity and strength, an act that is alive to them despite the passage of time. The Cuffee Ned Rebellion is chiseled into the sculpture of this land, shaping everyone and everything on it. Their collective act is living history, an acknowledgment that the present and past are fused.

Merle, his guide, is the one who announces this reality to Saul as he stands on Bournehills soil for the first time. Beginning with the book called "Bournehills," Cuffee Ned and his rebellion are as much a part of the present as any of the living characters. The people's awareness of this unity of past and present is symbolized by the Bournehills ritual greeting:

> . . . they would slowly raise their right arm like someone about to give evidence in court, the elbows at a sharp ninety-degree angle, the hand held stiff, the fingers straight. It was a strange, solemn greeting, encompassing both hail and farewell, past and present.[37]

Cuffee Ned's great feat is the perpetual subject of the men at the local rum shop, as if in recalling the great leader they could bring meaning to their grating lives. As vivid as the present-day sun, every detail of his brave deed is discussed and argued about. The rebellion itself is ritualistically reenacted every Carnival Day by the entire population of Bournehills, when for one day in the year, they become a people in control of their own lives; they become one.

In contrast to the glorious feat of Cuffee Ned, Bournehills people work day in and day out, without any respite or reward. They barely manage to survive, despite their unceasing labor. One of the most memorable scenes in the novel occurs when Saul, in his anthropological pursuits, goes to see Stinger and his wife, Gwen, work in the cane fields. He is stunned at how their labor daily transforms them from vital people into zombielike bodies.

> Then even as he watched Stinger succumb, Gwen passed him on her way down to the lorry. All along she had been carrying on a lively exchange with the other headers, joking and calling out to them as they bent over their work, but now that the morning had crept into afternoon to which there seemed no end, she had fallen silent. And suddenly, she appeared less certain of her footing on the steep grade. The almost offhand confidence of the morning was gone, and like Stinger, who remained absorbed in his cutting to the exclusion of everything else, she was only conscious of the dangerous footing down the hill. The set of her back, the way she stepped—first carefully feeling the ground ahead with her foot before placing her weight on it—said she had marshalled her slender forces to see her down.
>
> She passed, and under the waving green forest on her head, Saul saw her face, a face which when she laughed proved she was still a young woman. But in the short time since he had last glanced her way it had aged beyond recognition. A hot gust of wind lifted the overhanging leaves a little higher and he glimpsed her eyes. . . . He tried describing them to himself some days later when he could bring himself to think of them. But he could not, except to say they had had the same slightly turned up, fixed flat stare that you find upon drawing back the lids of someone asleep or dead.[38]

Saul reels from the transformation he has seen, for he knows that this daily descent into death barely puts food on Gwen and Stinger's table. They continue to be, as their ancestors had been for hundreds of years, yoked to a system that literally works them to death while it steals the fruits of their labor. So it has been from time immemorial, not only in Bournehills but in much of the "underdeveloped" world.

In Bournehills, the past is vivid, refusing to be hidden by an illusory present. There is no pretense as there is in other areas of the world that things have changed for the better. The characters cannot assert that the great wrong committed centuries before has been remedied or even ameliorated;

rather Bournehills society is clearly based on a feudal slave model. As Ferguson, one of the natives, puts it: "Why Bournehills come like a nation God has forgot."

The many development schemes plotted on Bournehills had been done without the consent or consultation of its people and without any respect for their traditions. Nor have these projects changed the hierarchy of power on which the island's poverty is based, for the schemes in the final analysis seem always to benefit the landlords. In fact, their only result has been to give the impression to those naive or willing enough to accept them that something in fact was being done. Two scenes are juxtaposed in the novel to accentuate the fact that the schemes to move Bournehills into the twentieth century are camouflage rather than reality.

One such scene occurs when Lyle Hutson, the successful Bournehills barrister and politician, tells Merle and her guests about the new development plan. Unfortunately it is a common plan in the Caribbean. The boys in New Bristol had decided that the only way to improve the economy of Bourne Island is to bring in more foreign investors and to expand the tourist trade. To draw in more investors, the local government intends to give new business a tax-free period from five to fifteen years and to waive their custom duties. Omitted from the plan is any mention of agriculture, the main industry of the "little fella." No provisions are made to change the agricultural base from a cash crop industry to crops that would feed the residents, for then Bournehills would not have to import most of its food, and major United States companies would be unhappy about that. In addition, the landowners would be ruined, for there would be no profit from the sugar industry. Merle explodes at Lyle after hearing the plan. Her reaction coalesces the feeling of Bournehills people about these schemes:

> "Signed, sealed and delivered. The whole bloody place. And to the lowest bidder. Who says the auction block isn't still with us. . . . And then you wonder why Bournehills is the way it is. Why with all the improvements you try out down here it still won't change, get into 'the modern swing of things'?" She uttered a dark weighted laugh that Saul had occasionally heard from others in the district, and which always left him vaguely disturbed, wondering. Then, in an even lower voice, and speaking almost as if she herself was not conscious of what she was saying, she added. "Bo, you don't know it, but Bournehills is the way it is for a reason—that people in town are too blind to see. And it will stay so, no matter what, for a reason."[39]

The new development plan is the politicians' scheme to improve the conditions of life on Bourne Island. Doubtless there will be more shopping centers and more air pollution. But the "little fella" will still be subordinated

to the landowners, be they British or American. To reinforce this crucial
point in her analysis, Marshall follows Lyle and Merle's discussion of this
new plan with the visit of Sir John Stokes to his property, Cane Vale Factory.
This lord comes to visit his subjects as his ancestors have done for centuries.
Marshall's description of him, a man dressed as if he is going on a safari, takes
us back into a period that we may have thought was past but is very much a
part of the present of Bournehills and much of the world. As feudal over-
lord, he inspects the factory, with no regard for its workers or how crucial
the sugar cane crop is to them. His final comment, as he leaves the factory,
reveals the arrogance and callousness of his tribe: "It's always a bit of a
shock, don't you know, to realize that the thing that sweetens your tea comes
from all this muck."

During the inspection tour, Ferguson, one of the more articulate of the
workers, tries to speak to Sir John about the old rollers that will not hold
up much longer. Ferguson, as we have come to know him in the novel, is a
spirited community leader who loves to brag about Cuffee Ned and who can
outtalk anyone. But when he is confronted with Sir John's stiff superiority,
he is struck dumb. The relationship between the lord and the serf has been
ingrained in him for so long that emotionally Ferguson cannot suddenly
strip off this long tradition of habit. He cannot speak to Sir John. Saul, who
has watched their interaction, sums it up in a talk with Merle:

> "You mean the white-hunter outfit? Yep. Complete with swagger stick.
> You should have seen him waving the damn thing around, lord of all
> he surveyed. I think the outfit got me more than anything else. Maybe
> because in most of the places I've worked—in South and Central
> America—the Sir Johns—those from outside who've come in and
> taken over—were Americans in business suits or those they kept in
> power: the patrons with three or four times the size of Bourne Island
> or strong-arm generals in uniform. So, for me, Sir John in his safari
> suit took a little adjusting to. But dress aside, they're the same, all of
> them. Out to own and control the world, and determined to hold on
> no matter what means they have to employ. And they behave the same,
> the arrogant bastards, towards the people they feel they own. Yes,"
> he said, his voice dropping, "perhaps worst of all is the effect their
> mere presence has on people."[40]

Why then should Bournehills accept some new-fangled, good-intentioned
plan to bring it into the twentieth century if the hierarchy of power will remain the same? Why should it camouflage the truth? At least, it can hold
onto its substance, even as it suffers. As old, staunch Leesy says about Saul
Amron and *his* project:

"Change Bournehills! Improve conditions! Ha!" Her laugh was full of a secret knowing. "The only way you could maybe change things around here would be to take one of Bryce-Parker's bulldozers from the conservation scheme and lay the whole place flat flat flat and then start fresh."[41]

BOURNEHILLS AS PROCESS

Bournehills' refusal to camouflage reality has tremendous impact on the characters in the novel, as they rediscover their past and try to merge it with what they believe to be their present. For Vere, Allan Fuso, and Harriet and Saul Amron, the discrepancy between what their cultural and personal past has been and how they conceive of the present begins to surface more and more in the face of Bournehills' tenacious hold on history. This discrepancy becomes larger and larger throughout the book "Bournehills," until in "Carnival," the fears and falsehoods they carry within them can no longer be ignored. The last book, "Whitsun," describes how they are affected by having their illusions stripped away, and what actions they commit or refuse to commit to regenerate themselves. Each one of the characters' passage from illusion to truth is necessary to Marshall's design, for each one represents a facet of the panorama of Bourne Island society that Marshall is analyzing.

A native Bourne Islander, Vere knows what his life will be like when he returns to Leesy, his grandmother, in Bournehills. The contrast between their differing views on life illustrates the effects of the Western world on Vere's generation. For Leesy, life is ordered and ritualized; she lives as her ancestors have always lived. The tiny half-acre of canes that she owns outright is her pride and her rock: all of her acts are centered on keeping and taking care of it. Her relatives, whether they are dead or in England, remain alive to her, their spirits remembered in the photographs that line the walls of her house. The canes are for them as much as they are for her. To keep a piece of land so her descendants or relatives might never starve is the belief that has always ordered her life.

To Vere, on the other hand, Leesy's life is a heavy weight that threatens to take his manhood away and crush him. He wants a life that has some excitement, for he knows the cultivation of the cane brings only hard work, a little food, and no glamour. Before he left for the States, he had sought this excitement in a woman, a light-skinned red girl from town who Leesy declared had color but no personality. As Leesy predicted, this Canterbury girl had his baby, took his money, and betrayed him. It is even said she neglected the child, causing it to die. Having learned the fickleness of high-colored women, he decides to seek excitement in some process he can have total control over—building a car and racing it in the Whitmonday car race. Thus he will become a local hero. But before he can accomplish his dream, he feels compelled to avenge himself on the red girl from Canterbury. Only then, he believes in his soul, can he truly assert himself as a man.

Much of the focus on Vere in the book "Bournehills" consists of his own personal rituals, of his preparations for revenge on the Canterbury girl, and of the construction of his car. In a straightforward, absolutely confident manner, without any talk or fuss, Vere sets about looking for the right kind of vehicle. He takes his time, for he will know the car when he sees it. During this period of incubation, he becomes friends with Allan Fuso who listens to his dreams of a car while others scoff. The friendship between Vere and Allan will be crucial, as we discover later, to Allan's recognition of his past, for Allan does not realize that the young machinist is holding back the masculine aspects of his personality until he accomplishes his goals. When Vere does find the right car, he systematically rebuilds it despite the taunts of the Bournehills community. His first moment of glory comes when he is finally able to make the rebuilt Opel run. Of course, Vere, accompanied by Allan, drives the rebuilt car, the symbol of his mastery over matter, to Merle's house where, like a presiding priestess, she pours libations over it. In front of the Bournehills community who had gathered at the sight of the newly moving car, in front of the barrister Lyle Hutson, who is visiting from New Bristol, Merle praises and regales the conquering hero. Leaving his site of triumph, Vere tells Allan what color he will paint his new idol. We understand how much this car symbolizes accomplishment and power to him:

> "Red," Vere said without hesitation. "She'll really look like new then, like a car just out of a store, not one I made myself. And I don't want just any old red. Oh no." He shook his head strongly. "It's got to be fire red, so when people see me coming they'll know for certain it's me."[42]

Leesy's reaction to Vere's obsession with a car epitomizes their philosophical differences. Her Bournehills resistance to modern things is cast in a religious form:

> It was as though she believed beyond question that all such things as cars, all machines, had human properties, minds and wills of their own, and that these were constantly plotting against those whom they served. They were for her, the new gods who in a far more tyrannical fashion than the old, demanded their sacrifices. Something in her gaze as she stood there peering out, her face as reamed and eaten away by time as the wood of the door, said she feared and detested the Opel straddling Vere as much as she did the rollers at Cane Vale which had crushed and killed her husband years ago.[43]

But in typical Bournehills fashion, she holds her tongue, knowing that whatever she says will whet Vere's appetite for the car even more. He will have to experience this god's sacrifice. "Those who don't hear will feel," her attitude seems to say.

While he is rebuilding his car, Vere has not neglected his other task, revenge on the girl from Canterbury. His mode of carrying out this necessary act, laced as it is with patience and cunning, has the tonal quality of any number of folk ballads. Instead of confronting the girl immediately, he goes twice a week to town where he follows her from her home to a club and back home again. His back straightened by a cane he has pressed against his spine, his patience intensified by the knowledge of the inevitability of his revenge, he never talks to her. Like an animal stalking its prey, he watches and waits, refusing to answer her even when she verbally assaults him.

During this period of watching and waiting, he does not have anything to do with other women, for his final act of revenge demands a chasteness, an unswerving directness, so he will not be diverted. His ritual continues until the appointed day, Carnival, when all illusions are stripped away, when all wrongs are righted. On the day of Bacchanal, Vere takes his new red car, the symbol of his renewed masculinity, to town. He goes to the girl's house, but this time he does not wait, he enters. The moment for honor restored has been carefully prepared. In her room filled with boudoir dolls, he whips the red girl with the old cane.

> And Vere, for his part, was wielding the cane with a dispassion that was in keeping with her stoicism. The two of them might have been carefully following the rules and practices of a strict code which they accepted without question. So that there was nothing vengeful or even angry about the blows he dealt her, which was odd, given the wrongs she had done him. Rather, he struck her—the cane coming down with slow regularity across her hard neck, his face closed and impassive— in the same puritanical manner a father might a child, to chasten and reform it. It was the way the girl's father had probably chastised her as a child, and the way Leesy had thrashed him with the same Malacca cane when he was a boy.[44]

But his restraint does not last; the sight of the dolls, her most valued possession, with their painted blue eyes and blond hair, their white skin and elaborate dresses, infuriates this young black man, for the inanimate objects are symptoms of this Canterbury girl's weakness. In her search for glamour, for her femininity, she wants to become them. Even her Carnival costume is a replica of one of the doll's dresses. So he strikes out against this particular image, this false idol. It is only then that he can be avenged, for in destroying the doll he has found the only way really to hurt her:

It is then that her cry broke—and it began at a high, with no buildup whatsoever: a sudden shrill atonal scream which rose and fell with the regularity of a siren in the tiny room, and which called to mind, in its almost ritualistic fluting, the high-pitched, tremolant keening of Arab women mourning their dead. It was a cry expressive of such sorrow and loss it could not have been simply the doll she was mourning, but all the things she had ever wanted and been denied.[45]

The scene is a magnificent one, not only because of the ritualized waiting that has led up to it, but because the girl's identification with the boudoir dolls, like Vere's obsession with his car, reveals both the need to have some drama in their lives and the deep wound that has been inflicted upon their psyches by a culture more seductive than their own. To be a woman, the Canterbury girl wants to be beautiful and glamorous, qualities, she has been taught, that reside in blond hair, blue eyes, and expensive clothes, not in the hard life black women of Bournehills are forced to lead. In the same way, Vere identifies power and masculinity with having control over a fine car, rather than being controlled by the grating hard demands of the sugar cane fields. These two, the man and the woman, are alike in their desires and in the way they have chosen new gods to appease them.

Vere may see the Canterbury girl's vanity, but he does not perceive his own. As soon as he has completed his act of revenge, he finds another woman. That is not difficult for him, for the red car makes him the most desirable man at Carnival. But owning and riding the car is not enough glory for him. He intends to win the race on Whitmonday so everyone will acknowledge the superiority of his creation.

Marshall graphically describes the race with meticulous care; each of her strokes heightens Vere's quest for power. First we are told about the origins of the race, how specifically masculine it is, how it began as the taxi drivers' way of impressing the girls. Then we hear the cheering lines of spectators not only from Bournehills but from the town as well. The Whitmonday race is, like Carnival, a national event. The tension builds as the procession of cars moves toward the starting line. Then we learn that only that morning, Milly, Vere's new girl friend, has announced that she is pregnant. We feel Vere's virility and assurance heightened by this news as he comes close to the fruition of his dreams. We experience the power of the Opel as the conquering hero takes the lead; we hear the hosannas of the crowd acknowledging Vere as the undisputed winner.

Then it happens. The dream breaks, as the new gods demand their sacrifice. Suddenly, the brakes will not hold. In his moment of victory, the car masters the man, Vere, crushing him beneath its heavy weight just as he feared life in the cane fields would do.

Leesy, Vere's grandmother, never comes to the Whitmonday race. On this particular occasion, she waits at home, waits for the news of her grandson's death. Leaving the show of grief to Merle, she stoically stays alive to bury her grandson and to harvest the canes from the field that would have been his legacy. She does not understand, as Allan does, Vere's need to take a chance and risk everything to show that he is a man. All she knows is that her men have been crushed by monstrous machines, the gods of the new world, which human beings arrogantly believe they control.

Allan, on the other hand, respects and envies Vere, his masculinity, his courage in risking everything for glory. In keeping with his immigrant ancestry, with the fear of being an alien in his own country, Allan has been bred to pursue security and safety. A likeable, bright young man, he becomes a competent statistician rather than enter a profession that might invite challenge. When he becomes friends with Vere in the book "Bournehills," he feels his spirit renewed, as if he has been given back his adolescent friend Jerry Kislak, who died in the marines. But when he witnesses Vere's mastery over the new car, he experiences mixed feelings:

> Vere had succeeded where everyone, including himself, had been convinced he would fail. He had taken a chance, risked everything, and done it. Out of the corner of his eye, Allan studied the dark profile outlined against the slow-moving frieze of bedraggled houses and shops lining the road, and seeing the pleased, proud, utterly self-confident expression on Vere's face, he was suddenly swept by a host of feelings that had begun their slow build-up the moment he had arrived in the yard and had seen the Opel standing ready and waiting. And which he couldn't understand. Because in the midst of the admiration and relief he felt he was seized at the same time by an unreasonable envy, even a kind of anger that, for a split second, before he struck it from his mind, made him wonder whether some secret part of himself wanted Vere to succeed with the car.[46]

Allan's confusion about his feelings for Vere is clarified during Carnival. The self-confidence and virility that Allan had glimpsed during that ride emerges full-blown in Vere after this Bournehills man's revenge on the Canterbury girl. As if to underscore Allan's self-recognition on that night, Marshall has him lose his glasses, causing his vision to be painfully enlarged. In keeping with the spirit of the night, Vere has found two girls, one for himself and one for Allan, and Allan's nightmare begins.

Vere takes one of the girls, Milly, to bed and leaves Allan to the other girl. As the girl, Elvira, tries to seduce Allan, he remembers his other encounters with women. What Allan experiences during this night reveals that Bournehills is not his reprieve, but his unmasking:

In the place to which he had fled, far from the surface of his body, out of her reach, Allan scarcely felt the mouth against his or the hand on his shoulder. Rather, he was remembering the small portion of his mind that was still functioning (the memories coming in little fitful snatches that were like part of the continuing nightmare of the evening), other encounters such as this, all of which had ended badly as this one would. Because greater than any desire he had ever felt for them (and not even desire so much as a passing curiosity) had been, first of all, his distaste: their bodies, it had always struck him, lacked purity of line with the up-jutting breasts and buttocks, the suffocating softness; and secondly, his fear, borne of a recurrent phantasy of his as a boy that once he entered that dark place hidden away at the base of their bodies, he would not be able to extricate himself but would be caught, trapped, condemned to a life-and-death struggle there for which he sensed he was ill-equipped.[47]

What he comes to realize that night is that his fear of women is in fact his fear of life.

He articulates this truth about himself in the book "Whitsun," after Merle prods him. Believing that Allan is grieving over Vere's death, Merle tries to comfort him. Instead, she opens him up. Vere's death had brought back memories to Allan that he wanted to forget: the guilt he felt when Jerry Kislak, a real man, died while he, Allan Fuso, stayed alive. Knowing that he is afraid of challenge, knowing that he lacks "guts," Allan Fuso retreats behind his statistics and accepts his fate. He refuses to leave Bournehills. Since he has no land with which to identify, this abandoned land, the land of his self-recognition, becomes his hideout from life.

In contrast, Harriet's journey to Bournehills is no retreat; rather it is, she believes, the beginning of her involvement with life. By becoming Saul's rock, she hopes to rescue him from the limits of a teaching job, for more than anything she wants to be useful, indispensable to a man whom she helps to create. Like Allan, her major attribute is orderliness, but unlike the immigrant man from New Jersey, Harriet's ancestry has vested her with implacable confidence in her philosophy of life. She keeps this sterling quality intact by dispelling any confusion from her mind. Her order, she believes, always triumphs, for she has not grasped, as Allan has, the limitations of a monolithic view. Knowing Harriet's tendency to impose her order on reality, Saul warns her never to interfere in the CASR team work. His warning is justified. Central to Harriet's character is her need to help someone, so she will not be like her useless mother. In keeping with her unruffled confidence, she gives that help only on her own terms and according to her own counsel.

Her activities in Bournehills flow from her need for order and her obsessive desire to be useful. She establishes her own personal rituals that have little to do with Bournehills life, for she is resolved to ignore the " dark" powers she glimpsed in her first view of the land, powers she experiences again when Lyle Hutson first touches her:

> And she had remembered then Lyle Hutson placing his hand on her arm in the bar to detain her, and how when she had glanced down somewhat disconcertedly (she was not used to having comparative strangers touch her) at that black hand, she had had the impression, strange and fleeting and scarcely conscious, that it was not his hand resting on her, or any part of him, but rather some dark and unknown part of herself which had suddenly, for the first ever, surfaced, appearing like stigmata or an ugly black-and-blue mark at the place he had touched her.[48]

Order, linear organization, is used as the antidote to this and any other emotional intrusion in Bournehills. Her life here, as in Philadelphia, is carefully manicured.

Essential to Harriet's maintenance of order and composure is secretiveness; she always keeps a part of herself from others so she can retain self-control. This characteristic of hers is structurally as well as substantively significant to the novel, for to elucidate this contained woman's character, Marshall must show her in reflection more than any other character in the book. Also, the author must spend more time on delineating Harriet's personality, for unlike the other major actors, she does not engage in intimate dialogue. Allan has a sense of apartness, too, but he does become good friends with Merle and then with Vere. Harriet, however, does not risk opening herself to anyone, even to the point of never discussing her past with her husband, Saul, partly because she feels somewhat guilty about her background. Her one confidante is Chester Heald, a person from her own class. Although she dismisses her immediate family from her life, she wields power through Uncle Chessie, the head of an important Philadelphia law firm and member of the institute's Board of Directors. She sees him as her surrogate father, the one to whom she appeals when she wants or needs something. He is the continuing thread in her life, and her letters to him get as close as Harriet, the person, ever gets to true communication.

Only one person from Bournehills tries to peer beyond Harriet's composure and that is Merle. When she sees this Philadelphia lady for the first time, Merle associates her with the Englishwoman who had destroyed her life. Merle, the seer, is correct in her initial assessment, although she does not understand why, until the last book of the novel. For most of the novel, however, Harriet easily keeps Merle and everyone else at arm's length by mentally erasing even the smallest detail that does not reinforce her sense of order. The assurance she exudes proves to be effective unless she allows alien lines into her established design. So we find in the book "Bournehills" that whenever she comes close to another person or situation, her unwitting insistence on maintaining her order of things causes problems. Since Bourne-hills is such a tenacious entity, its order tries her sorely, although at first she does not feel the strain; in fact, she welcomes the challenge:

> "Yesterday, while you and Allan were out, I walked a little way into the village, just to look around. I managed to get a peek inside some of the houses on what they call the main road." She paused; then, "They were awful, Saul; worse, I think, than anything I ever saw in North Philadelphia. I don't see how they can bear living in them."

> He stiffened perceptibly, and then slowly, in the dimness he turned to her with the look he sometimes gave her—which said that even after their long affair and the year and more of marriage he still didn't know her well enough to know how to take some of the things she said.

> "It's not as if they have any choice in the matter," he said. "They don't choose to live as they do." His voice was quiet.

> "Of course not. Oh Saul,"—she swung toward him—"did I seem to be implying that?"

> "I'm afraid it sounded like it," he said. His pale eyes with the numb centers had hardened.

> "Oh no! But you know I didn't mean anything like that, don't you?" He looked at her for another long moment, then finally gave her an uncertain nod.

> Reaching across she touched the corner of his mouth as if hoping to evoke a forgiving smile. "Darling, you're going to have to," she said, "teach me how to say these things so they don't come out sounding wrong."

> He smiled faintly, in response perhaps to her touch, then, with a sigh turned away. "I don't know how much of it can be taught, Hatt. There's some things you have to come to on your own, if it's in you to do."[49]

It is Harriet's inability to learn from Bournehills—it is her insistence on being useful on her own terms—that finally leads to her undoing.

Throughout the book "Bournehills," she commits errors that betray her inability to understand another culture. Her lack of perception, though, is what strikes us more than any other of her misdemeanors. She is incapable of seeing beyond her order of things because she sees Bournehills—every-thing, in fact—in terms of her relationship with Saul. Marshall uses the character of Harriet to show how devastating this concept of a woman can be, not only for herself, but for those around her. Since Harriet sees Saul as the only important thing in life, as the only principle by which she abides, she cannot grasp the complexity of his or her life in Bournehills. So when he begins to immerse himself in Bournehills life, when he begins to become emotionally involved in its people's needs and desires, she feels rejected. She cannot understand why Saul is not as detached as she is from this island.

But although she does not realize it, Harriet is not really detached from Bournehills. The island society threatens her order of things and she begins to remember childhood events that she had pushed into her unconscious, especially her mother's relationship with Alberta, her black maid. As if to dispel this uncomfortable memory, Harriet asks Uncle Chessie, in one of her letters, to increase Alberta's pension; in effect, she tries to assuage her guilt-sore with monetary salve. The unruffled lady from Philadelphia is be-ginning to feel Bournehills' truth without, of course, acknowledging it. She does not recognize, or does not want to recognize, the connection between her memories of black Alberta and the oppressed Bournehills society.

Because of her carefully devised detachment from Bournehills society, Harriet is able to hold her own until the book "Carnival." She becomes a member of the Bournehills troupe partly because she sees her participation in Carnival as a challenge. But she does not understand that the nature of the challenge is spiritual rather than physical. The essence of Carnival is "all o' we is one," a truth that is too common for Harriet to embrace. So when she finds herself enveloped by the black dancers, she has the most horrifying vision of her life. The dancers, as if in a trance, seem to her to be heading toward the bay. She believes they need direction or this mentally unbalanced black mass will destroy itself and her, for to her, this lack of conscious control means chaos. She does not understand that Carnival is a ritualized outpouring of energy of the life-force common to all human beings so they might be regenerated. Marshall uses all her powers of perception and craft to give this scene energy and magnificence:

> "This way!" She was pointing almost angrily now. For they had reached the small side lane and were about to surge past it, their helmets with the silly camouflage of leaves bobbing away. "Where are you going? Turn here! Turn here! You, can't you hear me? I said turn here!" she shouted up at a tall black-bearded youth, older than most of the others, whom she had been thrown against. The youth's gaze, fixed on the invisible goal, shifted briefly and he saw her: her white annoyed face,

the imperious hand pointing. And he remained strangely unimpressed. He heard and understood her order, but paid no heed. Instead, planting himself in front of her, his arms holding off the crowd molling and tumbling around them, he moved his body from the waist down in a slow lewd grind. She sprang back and he laughed, his mouth and tongue very pink within the black circle of beard and the lesser blackness of his face. Then he was gone, bullying his way through the mob ahead. . . .

. . . And in her slowly drowning mind there appeared to be no end of them. She would never have believed there were so many—all with the same young, set black faces and farseeing eyes—on the island, in the world. Moreover, she suddenly realized, the thought occurring just seconds before a saving numbness came over her and her head dropped, that they wouldn't end, as she had believed, in the bay. There would be accidents, yes. In the crush, some of them would lose their balance and fall in the water and have to be rescued. One or two might even drown before the wild march to the Oval had ended. But the vast body of them would reach the goal they had set for themselves: the thing she had seen in their eyes. . . .[50]

Harriet's composure is completely disrupted by the dark powers she fears, that is, by the flow and energy of life not yet fixed. She rejects the spirits and forces within human beings, within her, that are not known, that are not completely rational or ordered. She cannot give herself up to the flow, the energy that binds all human beings together. The touch of Lyle Hutson's black hand, which had terrified her so, is magnified into a thousand black hands who see beyond her order, can experience ecstacy (can stand outside their own consciousness), and still do not lose their direction. Blackness for her becomes identified with the abyss of irrationality that might swallow her up. Her psyche's protective barrier is cracked by this traumatic tearing of her order, and thereafter she cannot stop all of the memories she had pushed back, all of her own disorders she thought she had quelled, from spilling into her consciousness. Because she refuses to acknowledge her own irrational energy and its positive qualities, she is overcome by chaos.

By the time we get to the book "Whitsun," Harriet has begun to splinter, but her fixed composure prevents her from acknowledging her grave condition to herself or anyone else. After Carnival she returns to her closed rhythm, although she is not sure that her order will triumph this time. In a revealing letter to Chessie, she allows herself, for a moment, to see the truth: "You have no idea, Chessie, nor did I until I came here what life is like in the Bournehills Valley of the world. I don't think I will ever recover from the experience of these past six months." But her response to the truth of Bournehills is to get away, to get back to Philadelphia, the city of order, light, and, paradoxically, brotherhood, as soon as possible. Still, she will not go back without Saul, for her leaving alone would be an admission of defeat, an acknowledgment that she is no longer indispensable to him. So she waits.

While she is waiting, the nightmarish vision she had at Carnival begins to take over her consciousness; she begins to feel that the black faces surrounding her are conspiring against her, for even her friends do not pay attention to her advice, nor do they seem to benefit from the juices, aspirins, and medicines she so good-naturedly hands out to them. Because Harriet will not go beyond ceremonial acts of reconciliation, she asks, as so many others have:

> *What was it they wanted?* She could not have said. But it was too much, of that she was certain. She could not give it, whatever it was, without being herself deprived, diminished; and worse, without undergoing a profound transformation to which she would be called upon to relinquish some high place she had always occupied and to become other than she had always been [author's emphasis].[51]

She wants to make Bournehills in her own image, her own order. But Bournehills cannot change for the better unless she changes, and she refuses to do that. The descendant of the Widow Shippen, Harriet refuses to give of herself, refuses to give up her sense of superiority.

Marshall organizes the deterioration of Harriet's character by showing that she is both victim and oppressor. As a woman, she has been taught to live for and through her husband, so she has little sense of her own nature and sees her relationship to him as paramount. Yet as a member of the upper class, she not only feels superior to others, she has access to money and power and thus the capacity to destroy.

When Harriet learns of Saul's affair with Merle, these two themes merge. As a woman who lives through her husband, Harriet is unable to accept Saul's assertion that the affair, although over, was meaningful. His refusal to call it trivial is joined in his wife's mind to the fact that Merle is black, that "the other woman" is part of the dark forces aligned against her and her order. In an instant of self-revelation, she lashes out at Saul: "I think of your touching someone like that and I can't stand it." Now Harriet Amron is sure that everyone in the island is set against her.

Such a myopic view could be dismissed as neurotic. But because Harriet has access to money and power, she can attempt to destroy those who threaten her order. First, with the arrogance of her class, she tries to buy Merle off by offering her money to leave Bournehills. When that fails, this Philadelphia lady appeals to her Uncle Chessie to take her husband off the project. Because she cannot see anything but their life together as having significance, she does not care about the work Saul has put into the project, or what will happen to Bournehills. She reasons that in the final analysis, he will see that she, as always, is right.

When Harriet's plan misfires, when Saul tells her that they are finished and that he will not leave the island, the basic principles upon which her identity is based, her womanhood and the power of her status, receive a fatal blow. Splintered by her failure to remake Saul in her own image, her unconscious yields to her private disorders. The patterns underlying her order are revealed to her in snatches of memories she has previously dismissed as chaotic. But although her own irrationality confronts her, she still will not accept the truth of the Bournehills dawn:

> Dawn came but she couldn't see it because of the boarded-over windows. She felt its coolness, though, through the thin walls, and she could tell the moment the first light appeared. She sensed it, that dawn light, blossoming with the opalescence of a pearl and moving slowly, with all the stateliness of a royal barge, into the heart of the darkness outside. They embraced—the darkness and the light, so that when she finally rose and opened out the shutters she had the impression that night, bedding down in the great folds of the hills, contained the dawn, and the dawn the darkness. It was as though they were really, after all one and the same, two parts of a whole, and that together they stood to acquaint her with an essential truth.[52]

Harriet's final act of the novel beautifully reveals the rigidity of her order. Following her personal ritual, she goes for her early morning swim and is never seen again. Her suicide, however, accomplishes what money, access to power, and her role as helpmate could not, for in the face of her death, Saul must leave Bournehills and Merle. Paradoxically, Saul, at the height of his last argument with Harriet, had spoken her eulogy:

> "*What is it with you and your kind anyway?*" The question, hurled at her across the intervening space, jarred the room and everything in it but had no effect on her. "If you can't have things your way, if you can't run the show, there's to be no show, is that it?" His voice shook and the face thrust her way across the desk was quivering. "You'd prefer to see everything, including yourselves come down in ruins rather than 'take-down,' rather than not have everything your way, is that it. . . .?" [author's emphasis][53]

Saul Amron, as the head of the CASR project, obviously believes, when he comes to Bournehills, that ceremonies of reconciliation can set a great wrong right. Like Harriet, he wants to be useful. But in contrast to his wife, he has personally endured suffering because of historical wrongs. As a Jew, he knows how immoral history can be, and as an anthropologist, his previous field work has impressed upon him the difficulty of effecting real change. More enlightened than Harriet, he easily becomes a part of the Bournehills fabric. Subordinating himself to its order, Saul becomes friends with Delbert, Stinger, and Ferguson, the "little fellas" of the village. Of all the newcomers, this Jewish anthropologist is the most sensitive, both personally, culturally, and intellectually, to nuances of power and powerlessness in Bournehills.

Before he comes to Bournehills, however, Saul's sensitivity takes the form of personal guilt rather than action. He uses his belief that he has failed in his personal relationships and in his profession as an anthropologist as blocks against the painful actions he must commit to effect change in the warped world. Since life in Bournehills is so undisguisedly harsh, he must reassess his own personal morality. The Bournehills landscape, which reminds him of the other raped lands he has worked in, brings back memories of his own Jewish ancestry and of life with his first wife, Sasha.

The memories and the swirling mental disorders they cause will not subside. Marshall pointedly has Saul confront his own personal confusion much earlier in the novel than do the other newcomers. His nightmarish visions begin in the book "Bournehills," rather than in "Carnival," because he is culturally and personally closer to the truth of the island. His struggle with the past is initially triggered by watching Gwen and Stinger transformed daily through arduous labor from living beings to zombielike creatures.

Like the biblical Saul on the road to Damascus, he has a vision, the substance of which is his mother's recitation of her people's suffering. As Shepardic Jews, they had wandered the two continents of America, from South America through the Caribbean to New York. Her tale becomes the crucible for the suffering her son would see in the world:

> But although her story had been suspect and had even ceased to impress him after a time (what difference did it make being an aristocrat among Jews if one were still a Jew, he had wondered at age eight, thus committing his first heresy and beginning in his life-long apostasy), it nonetheless came to stand in his child's mind for the entire two-thousand-year history of exile and trial, including the Nazi horror which was still to come when he was a boy. Moreover, her tale, in assuming the proportions of an archetype, a paradigm, in his youthful imagination, also came to embody, without his realizing it (the story working its powerful alchemy on him when he had been most vulnerable), all that any other people had had to endure. It became the means by which he understood the sufferings of others. It encompassed them all. It had even, suddenly, reached across the years to include within its wide meaning what he had just witnessed on the hill.[54]

That vivid familial memory is coupled with another, the image of the old Jewish man he knew in his childhood who turned every day into Yom Kippur, who tried to atone for the world's sins by beating his chest with his frail fists.

As Saul pursues his own personal salvation, he tries to penetrate the nature of existence in this abused land, and because of his culture, he is humble enough to admit that something about Bournehills is eluding him, something that Merle refers to when she explodes about the new redevelopment plan. Of all the newcomers, Saul is the only one who asks the critical questions: Why won't Bournehills change? Why doesn't it take advantage of the few modern amenities that come its way? Why does it cling to the past with such vehemence? These questions are not merely academic to this Jewish anthropologist, for Bournehills' tenacity touches some unhealed wound in his psyche. He moves closer to the truth when he witnesses Sir John's visit to Cane Vale and the effect this "lord" has on Ferguson. Faced with his friends' fixed position in the hierarchy, Saul begins to question the efficacy of the project. Again, it is Merle who pushes toward the inescapable conclusion. Saul admits to her that his work as an anthropologist might not only be ineffectual but harmful, for "all these projects, no matter how ambitious, are committed to change things gradually and within the old framework." Having acknowledged his own complicity in this historical crime, he muses that he has always felt he ought to try to bring about real change but that he has never really tried.

In answer to his question about Bournehills' stubbornness, the land continually thrusts this question in his face. Why can't he commit himself to real change rather than half steps? What we discover is that Saul's creative energy seems to be blocked by the guilt he feels about his own personal history, for he believes that he caused his first wife's death. Like a plant stunted in its early years, he refuses to blossom. He confronts his guilt on Carnival night, the night of irrationality and revelation. Again, it is Merle who guides him toward confession and absolution. Marshall structures this scene beautifully as she gradually unveils the compelling interaction between our personal lives and history. While having a drink with Saul, Merle asks him what he thought of the Bournehills troupe's reenactment of the Cuffee Ned Rebellion. In that moment almost all of the pieces of the Bournehills puzzle come together for Saul:

> "It said it all. . . . It's that people," he began, moving forward again, "who've truly been wronged—like yours, like mine all those thousands of years—must at some point, if they mean to come into their own, start using their history to their advantage. Turn it to their own good. You begin, I believe, by first acknowledging it, all of it, the bad as well as the good, those things you can be proud of such as, for instance,

Cuffee's brilliant coup, and the ones most people would rather forget, like the shame and ignominy of that long forced march. But that's part of it, too. And then, of course, you have to try and learn from all that's gone before—and again from both the good and the bad—especially that! Use your history as a guide, in other words. Because many times what one needs to know for the present—the action that must be taken if a people are to win their right to live, the methods to be used: some of them unpalatable, true, but again there's usually no other way—has been spelled out in past events. That it's all there if only they would look. . . ."[55]

Saul has seen the link that Bournehills as a place represents between the past and the present. He has grasped the continuum between our own personal lives and the composition of history. But Merle is not satisfied; she wants to move him not only to acknowledgment but to action. Saul, she knows, cannot act until he feels his own positive energy. In an effort to cleanse him, Merle, the crossroads figure, uses both African and Western images. Pronouncing herself an African juju woman, she jokingly suggests that they exchange roles. She will be the anthropologist and he the subject. She will interview him from her frame of reference just as he has done with so many of the oppressed from his own viewpoint. During the course of her examination, Merle pierces Saul's unconscious—the memory of his guilt is put into words, is looked at, so it, like history, can be a regenerative force. He recreates his crime. His first wife, Sasha, had survived the concentration camps only to die most horribly in Honduras of childbirth, because Saul felt that he had become so involved in work he could not see her needs. Her ghost is resurrected and with it the question Saul, as a Jew and an anthropologist, has asked all his life: what is the meaning of futile suffering? As if to heighten that already vulnerable spot, Sasha had cursed him with her last breath, as she asked, "Why had she been made to suffer so? What had she done?" What Saul had concluded from his own personal and cultural experiences is that it is impossible to change a world in which senseless and unjust suffering could continuously recur. He is paralyzed by his own impotency and therefore his own guilt.

Merle, in turn, does what few anthropologists would do. She reveals to her subject the events that caused her husband to leave her and take their child with him to Africa. Merle, though, is angry at Ketu's inability to understand and forgive her, rather than guilty about her youthful affair with the rich English benefactress. Steeped in rage, the West Indian woman cries:

"Damn him for not understanding. Damn him for not giving me a chance. Damn him for leaving me standing here all this time waiting for them to come back."[56]

Although Merle is outraged rather than guilt-ridden, she is like Saul, restricted by a moment of the past. For years she has been standing in that empty London street, abandoned by husband and child, just as for years, Saul has been anguishing at his first wife's deathbed. Until they transcend these moments of the past, they cannot act in the present. On this Carnival night, each penetrates the other's part; each knows the other's need for wholeness. They become lovers and from this point on in the novel, Saul and Merle's ordeals merge.

In coming together each is reliving a crucial element of their past tragedies. To sleep with Saul, a white man, Merle must trust him, in spite of the memory of her English benefactress' betrayal. Although uncomfortable about his whiteness, she calls him her juju doctor, one to whom she can lay bare her soul. Through physically knowing Merle and Bournehills, Saul is freeing himself for action. But in loving Merle and Bournehills, he is hurting his second wife. It is fitting, then, that in the book "Whitsun," both Merle and Saul must use the remnants of their past to move into the present. The plight of Bournehills puts them to the test. A crucial incident brings their personal lives together with the making of Bournehills history. They have the chance to become actors in, rather than victims of, history.

Bournehills society is shaken when, immediately after Vere's death, Sir John closes Cane Vale, the only sugar mill in Bournehills, because one of the machines falls apart. Bournehills' very existence is threatened by this act. Merle's reaction to the closing of the mill reconciles the opposing tendencies in her past. She fights the closing with what she has, her powerful voice, her feeling for Bournehills, and her knowledge of the West. She publicly curses Saul, challenging him to act against his own as she dramatically recalls the great wrong that the West has committed and continues to commit against her people: "Kill! Destroy!" she yells, "That's all your science and big-time technology is good for." Exhausted by her inability to control her outrage, she sinks, as she has in the past, into a catatonic state.

But this time Merle's paralyzing anger and subsequent silence has an effect. While she is withdrawn from the world, the people of Bournehills, if only for a moment, move beyond the past into the present. Together, Delbert, Stinger, Ferguson, and Saul devise a plan to haul the canes from their village to another district. For the first time since Cuffee Ned's Rebellion, all of the people of Bournehills work together as one. However, Marshall refuses to let us believe that one single gesture, although significant, will change the face of Bournehills. While the canes are being hauled, Saul goes to visit the catatonic Merle. Although silent, Merle through her disharmonious room reveals the truth of this abused land to the worn anthropologist. Her room is not only an expression of her struggle for harmony but also a microcosm of Bournehills. Surrounded by sketches of past life in

Bournehills as well as Merle's moments of her own curious history, Saul sees that:

> Only an act on the scale of Cuffee's could redeem them. And only then would Bournehills itself, its mission fulfilled, perhaps forego that wounding past and take on the present, the future. But it would hold out until then, resisting, defying all efforts, all the halfway measures, including his, to reclaim it; refusing to settle for anything less than what Cuffee had demanded in his time.[57]

Even Saul's practical recommendations to the institute, such as the running of a water pipeline into Bournehills, could be meaningful only, he realizes, if these steps are preludes to the really significant one: Is he willing to go beyond halfway measures?

Of course, before Saul can wrestle with that question, his own personal alliances intervene. Harriet's letter to Chester, Saul's subsequent dismissal from the project, and Harriet's suicide exclude any possibility of action. Saul is defeated by his own personal extension, for the institute, as well as his wife whom he chose, after all, for her order and helpfulness, are not interested in Bournehills' redemption. Saul is not strong enough to change his own personal patterns. He again allows grief and remorse to block action.

His sojourn in Bournehills has not been in vain, though, for he has helped Merle to go beyond the past. Merle takes the one act necessary to live in the present; she leaves Bournehills to look for her child in Africa. On her return to the island she plans to use her knowledge of her birthplace and the West to rouse her people to action. In assisting Merle in her regenerative process, Saul learns that he does not fail everyone that is close to him. He may have, in his mind, failed his first wife, Sasha, his second wife, Harriet, and the folk of Honduras and Bournehills. In attempting to straddle so many cultures, in always being in the middle, he has given himself to none. But he has helped Merle to reconcile the conflicting traditions in her own composition. He has helped her move toward wholeness.

In cyclical fashion, the novel ends on the same road on which it began; Delbert, Stinger, Ferguson, and Allan accompany Saul to meet his plane. In reflecting upon the interaction between Bournehills, the Chosen Place, one image connects all the major characters of the novel, the image of a lost child. Neither Vere, Allan, Harriet, Saul, nor Merle have been able either to produce life or to maintain it. Although they are unable to regenerate themselves for different reasons, the image of the lost child stands as a result rather than cause of their respective flaws. Vere loses his first child because the Canterbury girl will not give up her dreams of glamour for the hardships of motherhood. She has been seduced by Western culture. Similarly, Vere destroys himself in an attempt to become a hero, but not before he has conceived another child. Perhaps his unborn child will have a chance to be whole rather than split if the young of Bournehills learn to distinguish between the illusion of Western culture and its reality. Because of his fear of life, Allan is unable to unite with a woman. His life will not result in others. Harriet was not able to conceive any children with her first husband, the nuclear scientist, and does not think she will have any with Saul. She believes her womb has been polluted by the death weapons her first husband helped to build. Saul's child died at childbirth, killing its mother, Sasha, Saul believes, because of his wanderings and his neglect, although Sasha might have been unable to produce a child because of the technological experiments practiced on her by the Nazis. His lost child is a symbol to this wandering Jew of his personal guilt. For most of the novel, Merle is resigned to the loss of her child. In going to find her daughter, she commits *the* significant action in the novel toward self-renewal.

The most striking of all the child images, though, is the swollen belly of Gwen, for the child within it, if child it is, refuses to be born. Long past its time, its insistence on remaining in the womb reminds us that Bournehills, too, refuses to live unless it can truly be whole and free. Until the great wrong is set right, until the land is cleansed by fire and brimstone as it was in the time of Cuffee Ned, until generations of the island and the West go beyond ceremonies of reconciliation, Bournehills may, as Gwen's baby, declare its potential in harshly recognizable terms but will refuse life unless it can truly have it.

"Who ever heard of making such a big to-do over a child that's not born yet. It'll come when it has a mind to."[58]

PART III

The Development of a Novelist: **The World of Paule Marshall**

Paule Marshall's growth from her first to her second novel dramatizes specific tasks that a writer, if she wishes to become a novelist, must attempt. In her first novel, *Browngirl, Brownstones,* the emphasis is on development itself, as a young girl struggles to create a self that is tuned to her own personality as well as to the outer world. It is a typical first novel in that Marshall as a young writer is consciously seeking the forms that suit her. Like James Baldwin's *Go Tell It on the Mountain,* or James Joyce's *Portrait of the Artist as a Young Man,* the novel *Browngirl, Brownstones* is about *becoming* rather than *being.* Because these novels try to define the specific potential of both the protagonist and the writer, they are psychologically searching in theme and tone. Both protagonist and writer, however, must reckon with the world. Although primarily subjective, Selina cannot discover herself in a bell jar just as Marshall cannot express her themes unless she finds a form that is communicative. In her search for self and form, Marshall, like most first novelists, relies heavily on her own background. This is not to say that *Browngirl, Brownstones* as a first novel about growing up is an autobiography. Selina is not Paule Marshall; rather Selina is Marshall's creation as her writer's intuition crafts her own experience. Since most of us, when we are young adults, are preoccupied with defining ourselves, so our creations about adolescence reveal the particular knots we are trying to untie.

Marshall, as the creator of a first novel, is also trying to become a person who writes. Part of the underlying struggle in *Browngirl, Brownstones* is the solving of basic novelistic problems. Her first novel explores areas in the world of technique with the enthusiasm of a novitiate and the carefulness of a serious student. Plot, narrative, imagery, setting, character development, interrelatedness of design, can be done in any number of ways. *Browngirl, Brownstones* for Marshall, like *Go Tell It on the Mountain* for Baldwin or *Portrait of the Artist as a Young Man* for Joyce, poses a basic question: which way is my way?

Browngirl, Brownstones establishes Marshall as a relentless analyst of character within the context of a particular culture. All else—setting, plot, imagery, narrative—is subordinated to this end. Because she sees characters in a context rather than isolated from society, she uses setting as a major indicator of character. Her lucid descriptions of the spatial environment permeate her prose, not as elegant fillers but as substantive to the theme. Her prose, usually profuse and lush, is sensual not for its own sake but as signals of her characters' composition.

Even Marshall's book titles emphasize spatial relationship as a major indicator of character. The words, *browngirl* and *brownstones* set up a relationship between Selina and the vortex of forces represented by the brownstones. The title *The Chosen Place, The Timeless People* is a concentrated outline of her second novel. The book titles also succinctly indicate the enlargement of theme from the first novel to the second. *Browngirl* is a singular although generic word; *The Chosen Place, The Timeless People* obviously proclaims a land and its people as unique. So, too, the spatial term in her second book, *The Chosen Place, The Timeless People*, in contrast to *Browngirl, Brownstones*, points to a greater theme.

The interrelatedness of complex shapes and settings is so fused in Marshall that her books are verbal sculptures. Form and space and humanity and culture cannot be separated. Her words chisel features, crevices, lines, into the grand, seemingly formless mass of history. Certainly marked in *Browngirl, Brownstones*, this sculpted effect is the dominant formal characteristic of *The Chosen Place, The Timeless People*. The land is the people, the people the land. Yet complexity and individuality of character are not sacrificed to largeness of theme. The intricacy of detail is maintained, even extended, in Marshall's panoramic novel. Paradoxically, Bournehills shares with Selina the process of *becoming*; neither have realized themselves. But *Browngirl, Brownstones* is determined by one point of view character, Selina; *The Chosen Place, The Timeless People*, as seen from varied points of view, presents Bournehills as a symbol for the tenacity of oppressed lands. The second novel encompasses the theme of the first—becoming— and moves it to a sociopolitical and mythological sphere. Although its spatial dimensions are larger, *The Chosen Place*'s many characters are as thoroughly explored as Selina. Marshall's analysis is powerful because she so profoundly loves her characters, and she insists, throughout her work, that social themes are distorted if not fused with the complexity of individual human beings.

Because she believes this fundamental precept so deeply, Marshall is able to create a coherent universe in her work. The characters in *Browngirl, Brownstones*—Selina, Silla, Deighton, Suggie—are psychologically related to Merle, Leesy, Vere, and Lyle. The Barbadian immigrants' obsession with brownstones, an obsession that is at the crux of her first novel, exists because places like Bournehills exist. The difference between the two novels is a difference of emphasis and scope rather than a shift in theme. The social analysis in *Browngirl, Brownstones* is done through the fulcrum of one West Indian immigrant family; the psychology of the major characters in *The Chosen Place, The Timeless People* is done through the presentation of the entire socioculture of Bournehills. In the first novel, the protagonist seeks an understanding of her world to find herself, as woman; in the second novel, we examine the many characters' psyches according to their sense of themselves as woman or man, black or white, oppressor or oppressed, to understand the particular world of Bournehills and how it came to be what it is. As Marshall herself matures, her emphasis moves from the way the world affects an individual psyche to how our many psyches create a world. Like Joyce in *Ulysses* and Baldwin in *Another Country,* Marshall moves toward a unity of, rather than a specialization of, experience.

That type of movement is one of the reasons why persistent creative artists are so important to a culture. In graphically depicting their own growth, in analyzing abstract concepts through the concrete experiences of particular human beings, they fuse the personal and the social areas that our fragmented world thrusts one against the other. Only when we see the oneness between politics and the individual psyche, oppression and the nature of human history, culture and the individual, their creative voices sing, will our species move beyond biting its tail to create its mouth. The wholeness of the creative process continually reminds us that we purposely sleep through much of our lives.

Paule Marshall's works, as psychopolitical images, elucidate the people who affect their culture and are affected in turn by their creation. Because of this thrust, her works remind us that all of us compose our own experiences in our minds and that our individual shapes are kinetically poised in a unified sculpture called the universe; that we all are continuity and process, shape and space, and that our sculpted creations are ourselves; that we change our world by changing our shapes, yet our world will change whether or not we want it to. Marshall's novels manifest history as a creative and moral process, for she graphically describes how we compose our own experiences in our minds as well as in the objective world; how we as individuals and whole cultures decide upon the moral nature of an act, a series of acts, a history. Above all, her work shows us that creative writing must be immersed in an act of honesty and love. The new child will come, when it has a mind to.

5

The Contemporary Fables
_____ of Toni Morrison _____

Toni Morrison's works are fantastic earthy realism. Deeply rooted in history and mythology, her work resonates with mixtures of pleasure and pain, wonder and horror. Primal in their essence, her characters come at you with the force and beauty of gushing water, seemingly fantastic but as basic as the earth they stand on. They erupt, out of the world, sometimes gently, often with force and terror. Her work is sensuality combined with an intrigue that only a piercing intellect could create.

Two of her three novels: *The Bluest Eye* (1970) and *Sula* (1974) reveal a consistency of vision, for they illustrate the growth of a theme as it goes through many transformations in much the same way as a good jazz musician finds the hidden melodies within a musical phrase. Both novels chronicle the search for beauty amidst the restrictions of life, both from within and without. In both novels, the black woman, as girl and grown woman, is the turning character, and the friendship between two women or girls serves as the yardstick by which the overwhelming contradictions of life are measured. Double-faced, her focal characters look outward and search inward, trying to find some continuity between the seasons, the earth, other people, the cycles of life, and their own particular lives. Often they find that there is conflict between their own nature and the society that man has made, to the extent that one seems to be an inversion of the other. Her novels are rich then, not only in human characterizations but also in the signs, symbols, omens, sent by nature. Wind and fire, robins as a plague in the spring, marigolds that won't sprout, are as much characterizations in her novels as the human beings who people them.

PART I

The Bluest Eye: **Truth in Timbre**

> It had occurred to Pecola sometime ago that if her eyes that held the
> pictures, and knew the sights—if those eyes of hers were different that
> is to say beautiful, she herself would be different. Her teeth were
> good, and at least her nose was not big and flat like some of those who
> were thought so cute. If she looked different and Mrs. Breedlove, too.
> Maybe—they'd say, "Why look at pretty-eyed Pecola. We mustn't do
> bad things in front of those pretty eyes."
>
> Pretty eyes, Pretty eyes, Pretty blue eyes, Big blue pretty eyes. Run,
> Jip, run. Jip runs. Alice runs. They run with their blue eyes. Four blue
> eyes. Four pretty blues eyes Blue-jay eyes, blue-like Mrs. Forrest's
> blue blouse eyes. Morning glory-blue eyes. Alice-and-Jerry-blue-
> story book-eyes.
>
> Each night, without fail, she prayed for blue eyes.[1]

Toni Morrison's *The Bluest Eye* presents a simple theme: the story of a
black girl who wants blue eyes as a symbol of beauty and therefore of
goodness and happiness. This statement of the theme, though, undercuts
the tragic complexity of such a desire, and complexity is precisely what
Morrison is somehow able to impress us with in her first novel. Yes, we
know that blue eyes, blond hair, fair skin, are the symbols of beauty valued
in the West, as proclaimed by romantic novels, movies, billboards, dolls, and
the reactions of people to golden objects. But do we really understand the
core of that myth and the value connotations it embodies? Perhaps one of
the most difficult artistic tasks to achieve is to take the known, what everyone thinks they understand, and really press its complexity and contours
against the psyche. This simple theme, the desire of a black girl for blue
eyes, is a real and symbolic statement about the conflict between the good
and the beautiful of two cultures and how it affects the psyche of the people
within those cultures. The theme is at the base of the conflict of artistic and
societal values between the Anglo-American and Afro-American cultures,
complicated by the psychopolitical dominance of one culture over another.
As such, this novel is a book about mythic, political, and cultural mutilation as much as it is a book about race and sex hatred.

How Pecola comes to want blue eyes demands more than just telling
Pecola's story. That is, Pecola's desire is more than the result of her own
personal story. It encompasses three hundred years of unsuccessful interface between black and white culture. Morrison's dilemma as a writer,
though, is that she cannot retell three hundred years; she must make Pecola's
story relevant to that history and yet be her own story. She must create both

a sense of intimacy with her characters, yet enough distance to give the theme its expansive substance, if she is to communicate the tragic complexity of such a "simple" theme. Perhaps even more than the usual novel, the way in which this theme is presented is crucial to the theme itself. Morrison's construction of the book is perhaps what gives the book its essential truth more than the particular events within it.

The Bluest Eye begins with prose familiar to a few generations of Americans, black and white:

> Here is the house. It is green and white. It has a red door. It is very pretty. Here is the family. Mother, Father, Dick and Jane live in the green and white house. They are very happy.[2]

Yes—the prose of our very first primer as we sat at our very first desk in our very first school and had our very first lesson in reading. There are pictures of Dick, Jane, Father, Mother, the cat, and the dog, accompanied by simple, punctuated sentences that are drilled into the mind as we first learn to read. Words have power. Pictures have power. Five-year-old children heard these words, saw these pictures across the landscape of America and even in the Virgin Islands where I was born, perhaps more than any other single word-picture image. Morrison plays the prose back at us again, somewhat accelerated, and then plays it again at high speed as if we were listening to a runaway tape recorder set up for programming. The speed, the frequency with which the words are said, run together, set the tonal modalities for the structure of this story about Pecola Breedlove and her mother and father; about Claudia and Frieda MacTeer and their mother and father; about Junior and his mother, Geraldine, and his father; about Maureen Peal and her mother and father; about Mr. Henry; about the whores; about Soaphead Church; and of course about the white family for whom Mrs. Breedlove works.

We are asked to meditate on these lines familiar to us from our childhoods, and to make sure that we do indeed continue to contemplate them, Morrison begins the objective part of each chapter of this book with a run-together fragment from the Dick and Jane primer, a fragment appropriate to the subject of that particular section. By removing the punctuation from these fragments, she heightens the lack of internal integrity essential to their simplistic order. For example "Autumn," the chapter about the house Pecola Breedlove lives in, begins with "HEREISTHEHOUSEITISGREEN ITHASAREDDOORITISVERYPRETTY". These undifferentiated words are juxtaposed to Morrison's integral description of Pecola's house.

> There is an abandoned store on the southeast corner of Broadway and 35th Street in Lorain, Ohio. It doesn't recede into its background of leaven sky, nor harmonize with the gray frame houses and black tele-

phone poles around it. Rather it foists itself on the eye of the passerby in a manner that is both irritating and melancholy. Visitors who drive to this tiny town wonder why it has not been torn down, while pedestrians, who are residents of the neighborhood, simply look away when they pass it.[3]

A voice intrudes, as the Dick and Jane prose recedes, a voice that will recur throughout the book. It is the voice of Claudia MacTeer as she speaks for herself and her sister when they were children. Her voice speaking to us gives the reader a personal feeling for this story, for Claudia takes us into her memories, personal experiences, girlish desires and fears, as she and her sister try to make sense of the often confusing world around them. In using the pronoun *we*, as she often does, she seems to be reliving our own sense of our parents, the fears about menstruation, the fascination with where babies come from—the intensely female and human mysteries into which all women, in some way, are initiated. In her introductory statement, and in the section that begins each chapter, she establishes the time, place, image, and structure of the novel as well as introduces the major characters of the book. She then becomes our central narrator.

Importantly, Claudia tells us in her introduction that this story takes place in the year 1940-41, from fall to fall, in the year when the baby Pecola had by her own father is born dead, in the year when the marigolds did not sprout. This nature image is the major structural element of the novel, for the book is divided into the seasons of the year, reflecting, sometimes ironically, on the tragedy of Pecola Breedlove. Appropriately, the year does not begin in January or in the spring, but in the fall when school starts according to the rhythm of a child's life. Autumn, too, begins the book because Pecola's story will not be the usual mythic one of birth, death, and rebirth, from planting to harvest to planting. Hers will proceed from pathos to tragedy and finally to madness, as the earth will not accept her seeds.

But isn't this story primarily Pecola's? Why is Claudia needed at all? The use of Claudia as the child narrator of Pecola's descent into madness seems to be one of Morrison's most brilliant strokes. Obviously Pecola does not have the necessary distance, space, or time to know what is happening to her. She cannot look at her own story in hindsight, for she goes mad. Claudia is telling Pecola's story after it has happened and after she has made some sense of it, a particular characteristic of hers throughout the book. But even more dramatically, this story is also Claudia's story. She does not experience the gravest effects of the myth of beauty as Pecola does. She is not seen as the ugliest of the ugly, but she does know that blue eyes and blond hair are admired by all and that she does not possess them. The dolls she receives at Christmas, the Shirley Temple mug, and so on are measures of her own lack of desirability. But Claudia fights back, resents the dolls, tries to make sense out of the contradictions she finds around her about love and beauty. She becomes the girl-woman in the book with whom we can identify, for most of us are not the extreme, as Pecola is, and do not overtly go mad. Claudia, then, becomes a way of giving voice to the graveness of Pecola's situation even as she herself is confronted with the same problems, although less intensely.

The main body of *The Bluest Eye* is divided into four chapters named for the seasons, a schema we are prepared for by Claudia's introductory statement in which she relates the failure of the marigolds to sprout with the death of Pecola's baby. "The seeds shriveled and died, her baby too." Nature images are constant throughout the book and help to organize its structure. At the center of this nature construct are the physical and psychological events that lead to the rape of Pecola and to her ill-fated pregnancy. The divisions into seasons beginning with autumn chart that development of events. These events, in fact, form the plot of this novel.

But the seasons are not only surface movement in the novel; they are ironic and brutal comments on Pecola's descent into madness. In spring, for example, lovers flow into each other and fertility rites are cyclically re-enacted, as nature comes back to life; yet it is in that season that Pecola is raped by her father, the only love she is to know. Her rape in the spring is preceded by a "false spring" in the winter, personified by Maureen Peal, the green-eyed, blond black who befriends her with her talk of babies and daddies and follows that wooing with the rejection, "I am cute! And you ugly! Black and ugly Black e mos." The images of the seasons erupt every way in this book as nature itself remains constant, seemingly aloof, although embodying the essence of memory:

> I have only to break into the tightness of a strawberry, and I see sum-mer—its dust and lowering skies. It remains for me a season of storms. The parched days and sticky nights are undistinguished in my mind, but the storms, the violent summer storms, both frightened and quenched. But my memory is uncertain; I recall a summer storm in the town where we lived and imagine a summer my mother knew in 1929. There was a tornado that year, she said, that blew away half of South Lorain. I mix up her summer with my own. Biting the straw-berry, thinking of storms, I see her. A slim young girl in a pink crepe dress. One hand is on the hip; the other lolls about her thigh waiting. The wind swoops her up, high above the houses but she is still stand-ing, hand on hip. Smiling. The anticipation and promise in her lolling hand are not altered by the holocaust. In the summer tornado of 1929, my mother's hand is unextinguished. She is strong, smiling and re-laxed while the world falls down about her. So much for memory. Public fact becomes private reality, and the seasons of a Midwestern town become the *Moirai* of our small lives.[4]

The seasons, the natural process of growth, will not wait for marigolds to be planted, will not alter their pattern because someone is crying, but will inflict cold, tornadoes, and beatings upon humanity. Morrison's view of nature is uncompromising. Nature is itself a whole system in which "natural" and "social" spheres do not compete. Since it is cyclical rather than linear, there is no point of completion. It is like life; it is life, mean though precious.

These three elements—the Dick and Jane primer backdrop, the modulated voice of Claudia, and the constant continuum between the mean, precious seasons and the growth of young black girls—are the fuse from which this story of a mutilated life bursts into sparks. The character of each of these elements tells us something specific about Morrison's intent in this book.

The Dick and Jane primer reminds us of the pervasiveness of the happy family, middle-American, romantic beauty myth so we are not tempted to see its effects on Pecola's life as unique or idiosyncratic. The primer confronts the grossness of standardized bland concepts projected as desirable, the norm. Where do Dick and Jane exist? Probably only on the pages of that primer. But young children are led to believe that others are happy because they are white and perhaps because they are pretty, are not too noisy, or are living an orderly life, whatever line of demarcation or difference they can perceive as marking their own existence. The more confusing, different, poverty-ridden or depressed that a child's life is, the more she will yearn for the norm the dominant society says provides beauty and happiness. Reality is compared to the visual-word picture. Morrison contrasts her own values with examples of houses varying according to the societal norm of order and beauty. So she shows us how Geraldine's house with its prissy orderliness reflects her lack of vitality, her frigidity. However, when Pecola sees it, she thinks it is a beautiful house. We can feel her belief that this house must be full of happiness and love—hence the impact of rejection, exclusion from these desires, when Geraldine so harshly throws her out, or when we view that spacious kitchen belonging to the rich white family that Mrs. Breedlove works for: "her skin glows like taffeta in the reflection of white porcelain, white woodwork, polished cabinets and brilliant copperware." Pecola is destined to mar that kitchen and be harshly expelled by her own mother. These dwellings are contrasted to the ugly storefront that Pecola lives in, where the only living things are the coal stove, and where everyone feels ugly and fights with each other.

While the ever-present mimicking Dick and Jane words are used to give the book expansiveness, Claudia's voice brings us close to the characters as she and Frieda tell us Pecola's story, their own siftings against the backdrop of grownups who touch golden dolls with awe. So her voice guides us through the real happenings of life for her—the moment when Pecola begins to "ministrate," and their wondering if she is going to die—or her sensing the beauty and sorrow of her mother's voice as she sings the blues. The solidity of the MacTeer family is the image, the real image, of a struggling family from a young girl's point of view in contrast to the empty Dick and Jane ideal. The intimacy of growing up with a love that surrounds her, a love that is so firm in its manifestations that it might not be fully appreciated until she is much older, explodes the myth of the Dick and Jane family-beauty type.

Dick and Jane has its societal implications in our particular cultural context and Claudia's voice individualizes that context. The seasons reinforce the mythic quality of life embodied in every live particle, as they ebb and flow, are beautiful in their terribleness or gentleness. At the core of this mystery are sensuality and sexuality, exciting and problematic, but constant and real as instinctively perceived by young girls struggling from childhood into womanhood. Their experiences at this turning point quiver with possibilities: rape perhaps; the yearnings of old men like Soaphead and Mr. Henry who tenderly try to recapture their own youth or purpose in life by touching them; the girls' own excitement over the mysteries of their bodies; and of course their wonderings about love and beauty. Love, as sensual and spiritual, is what these young girls want; love, they intuit, is possible for anyone. In contrast, the societal concept of beauty sets up a hierarchy of desirability that proclaims that love is deserved only by a few. Perhaps, because grownups are distorted by the pain of their lives, they deny their own capacity for love by tearing that capacity in others apart. Pummeled by the complexity of a mean precious nature, they fear the funk of love that is necessary for the spirit to grow. In their intense yearning for, yet deep fear of, love, they distort it by giving it unattainable romantic characteristics. Beauty precedes love the grownups seem to say, and only a few possess beauty. But the seasons go on—beyond beauty—in their many transformations. So there are marigolds and dandelions, winters that are a hateful knot, springs that are warmer but whose twigs deliver stings that last long after the whipping is over, and summers that are like tight strawberries.

As structural motifs, these three elements form the building blocks of the book. Externally the first section in each chapter begins with Claudia's voice as she reminisces about that particular season, its meaning in her life and in Pecola's. Then this section is followed by seemingly objective sections headed by Dick and Jane fragments and told by an omniscient narrator who can go backward and forward in time and space, can escape the limitations of a specific human consciousness. In these sections we learn the backgrounds of our major characters: Mr. and Mrs. Breedlove, Geraldine, Soaphead Church, all of the characters who in the immediate present help to cause Pecola's downfall. We see them as they are seen and as they see themselves, so we can understand how they got to be as they are.

Intrinsically, each chapter is unified by a particular idea that permeates the atmosphere in which Pecola is drifting, an idea that is also related to that season of the year. The chapter "Spring" illustrates how the fabric of interrelatedness between structure and theme is central to this book's character.

"Spring" begins with:

> The first twigs are thin, green and supple. They bend into a complete circle but will not break. Their delicate showy hopefulness shooting from forsythia and lilac bushes meant only a change in whipping style.[5]

It is Claudia speaking, and she goes on to tell us that Mr. Henry touched Frieda on her breasts and her Daddy beat him up and cast him outside. Frieda is afraid that she is ruined and will get fat. She and her sister decide that the whores are ruined but don't get fat because they drink whiskey. Marvelous logic! So they go searching for Pecola since her father drinks whiskey. Directed by the whores (Pecola's only grownup friends), they find her, we are told, at Mrs. Breedlove's employers' home, but only after we hear about the change in landscape from the ugliness of their part of town to the city park "laid out with rosebuds, fountains, bowling greens, picnic tables, sweetly expectant of clean white well-behaved children and parents." Pecola is waiting outside to take the wash to her house. As Mrs. Breedlove goes to get it, the three black girls, nervous in this beautiful, white kitchen, see a little girl who looks like the dolls they get at Christmas. She is looking for Polly, obviously Mrs. Breedlove. When Pecola touches the berry cobbler her mother has made for this girl-doll, she drops it, burning herself and marring the floor, the perfect kitchen, with blueberry juice. Mrs. Breedlove slaps Pecola and comforts the little girl-doll while she banishes the three black girls from Paradise.

Claudia's section, along with two other events, Cholly Breedlove's rape of his daughter and Soaphead Church's gift of blue eyes to Pecola Breedlove, are the only events that take place in the spring of 1941. These events are the plot of the chapter. But Morrison is not so much interested in communicating what happened as how it happened. The first twigs of spring bend into a complete circle but will not break. So this chapter, "Spring," is circular rather than linear. Accustomed as we are to the order of linear structures, the reverberations of "Spring" must, at first, have a dizzying effect on the reader—as dizzying as the effects of spring 1941 on the characters in this book. Morrison is not interested in the march of words epitomized by the Dick and Jane prose; that formation does not communicate the essence of her characters' spring or their thought processes as they try to graft one set of cultural values unto another. The organization of this chapter is that of the sounding of motifs and the exploration of their reverberations. The chapter is a jazz composition rather than a sonata. Chords

are sounded and then transformed and resounded as they are affected by
other chords. Morrison's composition would lose its essence, its force, if
reduced to linear structures. Cyclical as nature, circular as spring's first
twigs, this chapter defies linear analysis.

Claudia's section sounds the thematic chords of this chapter: the inverted
figure of Daddy, the older man who molests girl-woman, and the inverted
figure of Mother, the woman who denies her children for other children.
Mr. Henry's misdemeanor, which reminds us that old men yearn for love,
for touching, is but a subtle preparation for Cholly's rape of his daughter
and for Soaphead Church's attraction to young girls in their respective sections of this chapter. Mrs. Breedlove's rejection of Pecola for the daughter
of her employer is as much an act of love-hate as Cholly's tragic action is.
By exploring the sound reverberations in the lives of Pauline Breedlove,
Cholly Breedlove, and Soaphead Church, each in a distinct section of this
chapter, Morrison creates an atonal composition.

The cadence of Pauline Breedlove's section begins with an ironic note:
"SEEMOTHERMOTHERISVERYNICEMOTHERWILLYOUPLAY
WITHJANEMOTHERLAUGHSLAUGHMOTHERLAUGH."
Two voices, as in a duet, tell her story: the voice of the all knowing narrator and the distinctive voice of Pauline Breedlove herself. It is important
that we hear her story in her own sound patterns and images, for her manner of perceiving the world, primarily in rural tones and images of color, is
a key to her wasted life. But her sense of herself is too limited, so we also
need the more expansive sounds of the narrator to explore fully the disso-
nance in Mrs. Breedlove's life.

Possessing a slight limp from her second year, Pauline Breedlove learned
early to be separate and unworthy. "Restricted as a child, to the cocoon of
her family's spinning she cultivated quiet and private pleasure, she liked,
most of all to arrange things. . . . To line things up in rows. . . . She missed
without knowing what she missed—paints and crayons." Her own narration
emphasizes this quality. She speaks always in terms of colors. For example,
when she first meets Cholly she describes it this way:

> "When I first seed Cholly, I want you to know it was like all the bits of
> color from that time down home when all us children went berry
> picking after a funeral and I put some in the pocket of my Sunday
> dress, and they mashed up and stained my hips. My whole dress was
> messed with purple, and it never did wash out. Not the dress nor me.
> I could feel that purple deep inside me. And that lemonade Mama
> used to make when Pap came in out the fields. It be cool and yellow-
> ish, with seeds floating near the bottom. And that streak of green
> them june bugs made on the trees the night we left from down home.
> All of them colors was in me. Just sitting there. So when Cholly came
> up and tickled my foot, it was like them berries, that lemonade, them

streaks of green the june bugs made all come together. Cholly was thin then, with real light eyes. He used to whistle and when I heard him, shivers come on my skin."[6]

Pauline Breedlove has the eye of an artist, a fascination with color and arrangement. Her life, though, with its move to the city where she is seen as "country," her growing dependence on Cholly, her need for quiet and private pleasures contrasted with her husband's extroverted nature, result more and more in privation, disappointment, and sorrow. She gets pregnant and, oppressed by the loneliness in her two-room apartment, begins going to the movies.

> There in the dark her memory was refreshed, and she succumbed to her earlier dreams. Along with the idea of romantic love, she was introduced to another—physical beauty. Probably the most destructive ideas in the history of human thought. Both originated in envy, thrived in insecurity, and ended in disillusion. In equating physical beauty with virtue, she stripped her mind, bound it and collected self-contempt by the heap.

> . . . She was never able after her education in the movies, to look at a face and not assign it some category in the scale of absolute beauty, and the scale was one she absorbed in full from the silver screen.[7]

When she has Pecola, her comment is, "Eyes all soft and wet. A cross between a puppy and a dying man. But I knowed she was ugly. Head full of pretty hair, but Lord she was ugly." The die is cast. Pecola, her own child, is assigned a bottom category in the scale of absolute beauty and the possession of beauty is equated with self-worth. Pecola, too, will learn to be separate and unworthy.

Having had children, Mrs. Breedlove takes on the role of the bread-winner and returns to the church. These two dominant chords in her life interact. The church allows her to bear the ugly Cholly like "a crown of thorns" and her ugly children "like a cross." Her job at the home of a well-to-do family allows her her fill of color and line and satisfies her need to arrange things. Here she finds "beauty, order, cleanliness and praise," a private world that she never introduces to her own family. What holds her to Cholly, then? It is the funk of love (a theme throughout the book), the bits of color floating up in her when he makes love to her. "When he does I feel a power. I be strong. I be pretty, I be young."

The dissonances in Pauline Breedlove's section lead us irrevocably to the third part of this composition, to an exploration of her husband's life. Beginning with "SEEFATHERHEISBIGANDSTRONGFATHERWILL YOUPLAYWITHJANEFATHERISSMILINGSMILEFATHERSMILE

SMILE," Morrison immediately introduces the dominant chord progression in her exploration of Cholly Breedlove's essence. The reverberations of the mystery of birth and rebirth through sex and parenting give unity to his section. This father has no mother or father, his mother having abandoned him when he was four days old and his father having disappeared almost immediately after his birth. Cholly's only knowledge of his father is his name, Samson Fuller, Morrison's ironic comment on the stereotype. Cholly is, in fact, raised by his old Aunt Jimmy and more distantly by a nice old man, Blue Jack, who used to tell him stories about his adventures with women. When Aunt Jimmy dies one chilly spring, in typical Morrison style, of peach cobbler, the chord patterns of Cholly's life are transformed. Morrison uses Aunt Jimmy's illness and funeral as both a ritualistic enactment of a vividly female culture that strengthens the sinews of black Rural America and as Cholly's initiation into manhood.

As the old woman dies, her friends come to wait with her, hugging their memories of illness to their bosoms. In a hauntingly lyrical crush of words, Morrison tells us the story of those old black women reared in the South and in so doing relates their lives to that of Pauline Breedlove:

> Then they had grown. Edging into life from the back door. Becoming. Everybody in the world was in a position to give them orders. White women said, "Do this." White children said, "Give me that." White men said, "Come here." Black men said, "Ly down." The only people they need not take orders from were black children and each other. But they took all of that and recreated it in their own image. They ran the houses of white people, and knew it. When white men beat their men, they cleaned up the blood and went home to receive abuse from the victim. They beat their children with one hand and stole for them with the other. The hands that felled trees also cut umbilical cords; the hands that wrung the necks of chickens and butchered hogs also nudged African violets into bloom; the arms that loaded sheaves, bales and sacks rocked babies into sleep. They patted biscuits into flaky ovals of innocence—and shrouded the dead. They plowed all day and came home to nestle like plums under the limbs of their men. The legs that straddled a mule's back were the same ones that straddled their men's hips. And the difference was all the difference there was.[8]

As Cholly listens to them talking and dreams that his penis is changed into a long hickory stick caressed by one of the old women, we are subtly prepared for his initiation into manhood, for his first sexual encounter with a woman—a woman who will probably follow the pattern of her granny. At the funeral, a celebration of life and death, Cholly and a young girl, Darlene, go to pick berries just as Pauline does in her own youth, so far away and yet so near. In this orgiastic atmosphere led on by the instinctive cues of the female, his maleness asserts itself. But this mythic scene, complete with grape-stained lips and feasting, complete with the compelling images of the transformation of death into life, is distorted by the intrusion of two white men who turn Cholly's first sexual experience into a public pleasure show. "Get on wid it nigger," they squeak, "make it good." Cholly can do no more than make believe and, in a most logical movement of the human mind, hates not the white men who humiliated him but the black woman who "had created the situation, the one who bore witness to his failure, his impotence." He is at once initiated into the rituals of potency and impotency, and the woman is testament to both.

Wildly thinking that Darlene might be pregnant, he runs away, retracing his father's footsteps even as he goes looking for him in Macon. His personal cycle is completed as he finds his father there and is rejected by him. Cholly then becomes free. "Abandoned by his mother in a junkheap, rejected for a crap game by his father, there was nothing to lose. He was alone with his own perceptions and appetites and they alone interested him. It was in this godlike state that he met Pauline Williams." What we grasp about Cholly's life is that once having tasted the freedom of narcissism permitted only to the gods, he could not abide the dullness of married life.

Having explored the dominant chords of Pauline and Cholly Breedlove's lives, Morrison executes a marvelous leap of time from past years into the spring of 1941. For in the patterns that continue, as if they were circles, to dominate these parents' lives, lies the logic inherent in the rape of Pecola. All of the chord progressions are sounded simultaneously as, drunk one day, Cholly Breedlove watches his daughter washing dishes and senses her love for him. Confronted by his own unworthiness, his own lack of godliness, he hates her until she shifts her weight and repeats the same pitiful gesture that drew him to her mother. The circle of love-hatred seems to be completed in this chapter as he tries to fuck her tenderly, to somehow reconcile the love-hate within, toward Pecola, his wife, and himself.

But spring does not end there; the perversity of natural sensuality Cholly experienced in that spring of Aunt Jimmy's death, the sheer weight of the sameness of married life, his own sense of his own unworthiness, is not yet resolved even by the love-hate Cholly gives his daughter, for Pecola is left in the spring with the burden of it, with the experience of love-hate at the essence of the act itself. She must now find her way through this vortex of opposite strivings and it is to a spiritual source, to Soaphead Church, that she goes for reconciliation, for salvation, for rebirth.

Soaphead's section completes this circle of the chapter. As a fuller exploration of the chord sounded by Mr. Henry, Soaphead loves little girls whose bodies seem to him the least offensive of all human beings. Like Mr. Henry, he is a clean old man. But unlike Mr. Henry, this philosopher's attraction for little girls is rooted in his intense dislike for human beings in general, who in their physical and cultural forms are imperfect, in a continual state of decay. In short, he is a misanthrope. Morrison appropriately begins his section with "SEETHEDOGBOWWOWGOESTHEDOGDOYOUWANT TOPLAYWITHJANESEETHEDOG" for Soaphead clearly identifies with an old mangy dog who sleeps in front of his entrance and whose decrepitness creates great revulsion in him.

Soaphead's articulation of a philosophy of misanthropy is a culmination of the many chord progressions sounded by the main characters in this chapter. His distorted view of life flows from the same causes that transform Mrs. Breedlove into a cruel martyr of a mother, the same causes that impress upon Cholly Breedlove his own unworthiness, his own ugliness, the same causes that will inspire Pecola Breedlove to ask this clean old man to give her blue eyes. But he goes beyond their seemingly impetuous actions by intellectualizing and conceptualizing their common condition. Through the character of Soaphead, Morrison expands the theme of spring from that of thwarted rebirth in the lives of individuals to a statement about the tragedy of cultural mutilation.

As his former self, Elihue Micah Whitcomb, Soaphead had come from a mulatto West Indian family dedicated to preserving and heightening its British blood, not only in terms of color and shade but in the culture it represents. His family was:

> . . . industrious, orderly and energetic, hoping to prove beyond a doubt De Govineau's hypothesis that "all civilizations derive from the white race, that none can exist without its help, and that a society is great and brilliant only so far as it preserves the blood of the noble group that created it."[9]

More directly, Elihue's schoolmaster father developed his own legacy of Anglophilia into a narrow intellectual statement of the unworthiness of man, undoubtedly only slightly concealing his own distaste for himself and his son. Elihue inherits this view of man, for as he grows up he sees the sterile ugliness of the need to be British, this need to erase color, all vitality, all funk, out of life. Elihue is the tragic mulatto who is both bred to, yet aware of, the waste in the urge to acculturize. He knows the nonlife at the center of his father's narrow view of life. Morrison describes this disease so well in her description of Elihue's marriage with Velma, a lovely, laughing, big-legged girl.

> She was to have been the answer to his unstated, unacknowledged question—where was the life to counter the encroaching non-life? Velma was to rescue him from the non-life he had learned on the flat side of his father's belt. But he resisted her with such skill that she was finally driven out to escape the inevitable boredom produced by such a dainty life.[10]

Leaving the island, he tries the usual professions open to one of his class and finally sinks into "a rapidly fraying gentility." When he comes to Ohio, the folk with their usual sagacity zero in on his essence. They find his English awe-inspiring, his lack of funkiness amazing, and declare him supernatural, a perception that results in his decision to become a Reader, Advisor and Interpreter of Dreams. When Pecola comes to him with her fantastic but logical request for blue eyes, he immediately understands her need: "Here was an ugly little black girl asking for beauty." Her request makes total sense to him, for he, more than any other character in the book, intellectualizes the pain, the self-mutilation, inherent in that request, so much so that he writes an arrogant and ironic letter to God, "TO HE WHO GREATLY ENNOBLED HUMAN NATURE BY CREATING IT." God had obviously done a poor job of creation, which Soaphead, by granting Pecola's request, is trying to correct. But not before he uses Pecola to get rid of the mangy dog he hates so much; not before he pays tribute to his own belief in her ugliness as he "gives" her in a godlike manner blue eyes.

"Spring" ends with Soaphead slipping into an "ivory sleep" as the old dog Bob is found dead. In contemplating its circular structure, its ironically rhythmical patterns, its theme of inversion in which old men are inverted Daddies struggling for a meaning in life by touching the first twigs of spring, in hearing its melody of thwarted sexuality (atonal though sweet) in which the intrusion of another culture into the characters' lives waylays their instinctive desire for life, we are stunned by the terrors of nature to which human beings are prone. In arranging such a pattern of sound, Morrison has wrested out of the March winds, out of the reawakening of nature, her characters' desire to be reborn, even if tragic forms are their only fruit. "Spring" is a fertility rite inverted.

Each chapter, like "Spring," has a unifying sound idea, recurrent images, translucent connectives, as each section explores in depth a variation of the theme played throughout. But not only is the structure of the book circular, it is also elliptical, for not only is each chapter of the book itself coherent, it is also linked to every other. Morrison's transitions are in the form of her characters. The focal character may be Pecola, but all of the other characters in varying degrees suffer from the insanity that will manifest itself in her madness. The story moves, connects piece by piece, through the presentation of one character after another who shows us some aspect of that insanity. In "Winter," Maureen Peal, the "high yellow dream child with long brown hair braided in two lynch ropes," has got what Geraldine (who also appears in this chapter) will struggle all of her life to get next to. Geraldine, not as singular as Maureen Peal, in this pyramid of beauty and funklessness and shade, belongs to a distinctive group of women who:

> . . . go to land-grant colleges, normal schools, and learn how to do the
> white man's work with refinement: home economics to prepare his

food; teacher education to instruct black children in obedience; music to soothe the weary master and entertain his blunted soul. Here they learn the rest of the lessons begun in those soft houses with porch swings and pots of bleeding heart: how to behave. The careful development of thrift, patience, high morals, and good manners. In short, how to get rid of the funkiness. The dreadful funkiness of passion, the funkiness of nature, the funkiness of the wide range of human emotions.[11]

Geraldine will brush her son's hair forever in abortive attempts to wipe out the subtle and telltale signs of niggerism. She, in her prissy asexual cleanliness, is identified with cats, as Soaphead Church in his mangy cleanliness is identified with an old dog. She breeds Soapheads, the only end to which her generation could come, for as her son Junior already grasps, there is a dainty, cold self-hatred at her core. So Maureen Peal is connected to Geraldine who is connected to Soaphead who in turn is connected to Mr. Henry and so on. All of them are connected to Pecola who dramatically manifests their insanity by revealing the disease for what it is.

Pecola is the passive center of the novel, the one to whom things happen and whose only action, her prayer for and receipt of blue eyes, renders her tragic. Her tragic flaw is her particular vulnerability and her generic ill-luck to be born black and female, to be born into the chasm between two cultures. She falls into that chasm's bottomlessness while others hang on by their toenails or seem to straddle it with one foot on either side, sometimes with an amazing lack of balance. The section in the book that belongs to her, the section in which the part of her with blue eyes converges with the part of her without them is not only a terror-filled dialogue but is conclusive in its judgment of where all of the other characters really reside. Harrowed by an unfulfilled need for love, she finds a friend in the other part of herself, the part that can admire her newly acquired eyes. Morrison heads this section "LOOKLOOKHERECOMESAFRIENDTHEFRIENDWILLPLAY WITHJANETHEYWILLPLAYAGOODGAMEPLAYJANEPLAY" The friend will play with her only if she has the bluest eyes of all. Who is the fairest of us all?

In a sense, everyone in the town understands what has happened to Pecola, that the natural order has been inverted by the unnaturalness of human actions. They cannot look at her, because, as Claudia says, "All of us—all who knew her—felt so wholesome after we cleaned ourselves on her." They had all raped her. Claudia knows this, that Pecola's madness was not only caused by the fatal love of her father, but was the "fault of the earth, the land of their town." We come to know this not only through the terrifyingly connected structure of this novel but also through Morrison's style, which moves both toward and beyond her characters at the same time.

Because Morrison is always both telling Pecola's story and relating it to a wider circumference, her intense use of piled-up similes and metaphors is especially effective. You can hardly read a paragraph without being whirled into a circulating throb of asymmetrical likenesses. Listen to her description of Frieda and Claudia's response to the conversation of the grownup women. The comparisons move toward the characters while they take on an eternal vibration:

> Their conversation is like a gently wicked dance: sound meets sound, curtsies, shimmies and retires. Another sound enters but is upstaged by still another: the two circle each other and stop. Sometimes their words move in lofty spirals; other times they take strident leaps, and all of it is punctuated with warm-pulsed laughter—like the throb of a heart made of jelly. The edge, the curl of the thrust of their emotions is always clear to Frieda and me. We do not, cannot, know the meanings of all their words, for we are nine and ten years old. So we watch their faces, their hands, their feet, and listen for truth in timbre.[12]

The novel is sound, truth in timbre, as Claudia, Frieda, Pecola, all of us, learn our truths not in what is said but from the pitch, the timbre, of our society's sound. Language as tonality and as dance, African linguistic characteristics, are at the center of this book's truth as Morrison refuses to compose her characters' world in linear order, for that is not the pattern of its sound. Rather it is her metaphors in motion, her continual and overlapping improvisations on the theme, her delving into the infinite possibilities of the insides of language chords, rather than the mere sounding of the chord that moves us into the lives of her characters and beyond them into the life of life itself, into the sound of the sound itself.

> The pieces of Cholly's life could become coherent only in the head of a musician. Only those who talk their talk through the gold of curved metal, or in the touch of black and white rectangles and taut skins and strings echoing from wooden corridors, could give true form to his life. Only they would know how to connect the heart of a red watermelon to the asfetida bag to the muscadine to the flashlight on his behind to the fists of money to the lemonade in a Mason jar to a man called Blue and come up with what all of that meant in joy, in pain, in anger, in love, and give it its final and pervading ache of freedom.[13]

As if she were a musician, Morrison connects Pecola Breedlove's desire for the bluest eyes to Mrs. Breedlove's restricted spirit and Cholly Breedlove's sense of unworthiness, to Geraldine's fear of funk and Soaphead Church's sterility, to Maureen's fate as an eternal dream child and Claudia's ache to be whole. By exploring the devastating effects that the

Western ideas of beauty and romantic love have on a vulnerable black girl, this novelist also demonstrates how these ideas can invert the natural order of an entire culture. The vortex, at which two conflicting orders meet, Pecola becomes the scapegoat for that part in all of us that needs to see our own fears of unworthiness embodied in some form. As black and female, Morrison concludes, the Pecolas of America are an accessible dumping ground.

PART II

Sula: **The Pattern of a Fable**

> Sula was a heavy brown with large quiet eyes, one of which featured a birthmark that spread from the middle of the lid toward the eyebrow, shaped something like a stemmed rose. It gave her otherwise plain face a broken excitement and blue-blade threat like the keloid scar of the razored man who sometimes played checkers with her grandmother. The birthmark was to grow darker, as the years passed, but now it was the same shade as her gold-flecked eyes, which to the end were as steady and clean as rain.[14]

Toni Morrison's first novel, *The Bluest Eye*, reveals the inversions of an order that result in a black girl's belief that she possesses the greatest treasure, the bluest eyes imaginable. As such, it is a patterned fabric in which the warp is the myth of beauty and desirability in our society itself, while the weft, the part that shows, is the personal history of Pecola Breedlove. In *Sula*, her second novel, Morrison again takes on an apparently simple theme, the friendship of two black girls. One, Nel Wright, follows the pattern of life society has laid out for her, and the other, Sula Peace, tries to create her own pattern, to achieve her own self. Again, as in *The Bluest Eye*, the theme is but a sign of all that the novel explores, for the search for self is continually thwarted by the society from which Sula Peace comes. So the novel is not only about Nel Wright and Sula Peace, it is most emphatically about the culture that spawns them. In *The Bluest Eye*, Pecola's destiny is ultimately determined by the myth of beauty and goodness one culture has foisted on another. In *Sula*, the patterns of both cultures are distinct, yet share common factors. Sula's destiny is charted by the mythology of Evil and Nature her hometown ascribes to and by the view the Bottom as well as the larger society hold of woman, her span and space. In exploring this community's system of beliefs, Morrison weaves a fable about the relationship between conformity and experiment, survival and creativity. This mythological system is continually discerned in the novel's fabric through death, so ordinary in its eternal presence that it might otherwise be missed, through the drama of time as a significant event, and through the pervasive use of nature as both a creative and destructive force. As in *The Bluest Eye*, the novel's patterns help to transform a seemingly obvious theme.

Overtly, the novel is divided into an introduction, two parts—one devoted to years in the twenties, to Sula and Nel's growing up, and the other to years in the late thirties and early forties, to these women, now grown—and finally, as if an epilogue, there is 1965, a year of remembrance and understanding for Nel Greene. But Morrison immediately signals her reader that this tale about the friendship between Nel Wright and Sula Peace is integrally related to the survival of their community. The novel begins not with the presentation of these characters but with the death of their hometown. In *Sula*, as in *The Bluest Eye*, Morrison uses the motif of inversion, of derangement, as the natural order is turned upside down as a result of human society.

The introduction announces the pervasive presence of Death, as the Bottom is being torn down to make room for a golf course. We begin with the end, the death of a community of black folk, which is being deleted by the onward march of "progress," a community in which pain was so much a part of the pleasure of living that the Bottom's mores might be misleading. Then we leap from end to beginning, a beginning that was a joke, a nigger joke, because the laughter is so much a way of dealing with the pain. The Bottom, the Negro neighborhood of the town Medallion, was a white man's gift of land to a slave who had performed some heavy duties for him. Although the Bottom was really hill land where planting was backbreaking and the weather harsh, the master had persuaded the slave that this land was more desirable than valley land, that it was called the Bottom because it was the bottom of Heaven—"best land there is." Inverted, the truth is inverted, and so the Bottom on the top came to be.

This little nigger joke of how the Bottom came to be is juxtaposed in the novel to the origins of National Suicide Day, the Bottom's unique holiday. The beginning is the end, so to speak. National Suicide Day had been initiated by Shadrack, a shell-shocked soldier "who was not so much afraid of death or dying as the unexpectedness of both. It was a way of controlling the fear of death." In the essence of ritual, he initiated a day devoted to that fear, "so that everyone could get it out of the way."

What does National Suicide Day have to do with what follows—the story of Nel and her family, the story of Sula and her family, the story of their friendship? Their story, the story of the Bottom, is punctuated by death. Death occurs in each chapter and is the beginning of, or climax of, the experience in that particular section of the novel. Death becomes a way of focusing experience. As each year gives way to another, so each death gives way to a new view of life, a new discovery, a new feeling for truth.

Death is the haunt, personified by Shadrack, that moves the story; the tale of the Wright and Peace families and particularly of Nel and Sula, is the matter with which we are preoccupied. So the chapters proceed as if we are being shown the history of these families and finally the intertwining of two lives, Sula and Nel's, as they affect the Bottom, that nigger joke. The distinctive characteristics of these families from the Bottom, then, alert us to the specific belief system of their community, and the introduction of the novel, the juxtaposition of its end and its beginning, and the origins of National Suicide Day are indications that this story is a lesson in the nature of survival and continuity.

As the beginning is in the end, the end is in the beginning. Time becomes important only as it marks an event, for the people of the Bottom do not see its reckoning as an autonomous terminology. So each chapter in *Sula* is headed by a year, a time that allows us to focus on the climax of that section. The delineation of a particular year is a focus, not a limitation, as Morrison uses with great craftsmanship, this cultural characteristic of the Bottom. In adapting this quality to the novel, she heightens the magic of the written word—the flexibility to move from time to time, from one setting to another, without the need for changing props or signaling a new drift of images. So each chapter is not about the particular year for which it is named—rather some crucial event happens in that year which demands background, its whys and hows, the reasons for the event's significance. As the author, she is beyond time, collapsing the past, present, and future into the now so we might understand and feel the significance. The structure, then, so apparently neatly defined by the march of time, by a chronological pattern, is always transforming itself, for in fact we do not move forward in a straight line. Rather a particular point in time is but the focus of intertwining circles of other times and events. It is as if we were hearing an old African folktale—mythological in tone—in which content revitalizes an empty terminological system. The then is in the now; the now in the then; and the teller spins ever-intricate webs of connectiveness, until the web is completed or broken.

The mythological tone of this tale is heightened further by Morrison's pervasive use of nature images. Throughout *Sula*, images of fire, water, wind and earth are closely linked to the eternal presence of death and the Bottom's concept of time. As a result, the novel projects an integral world view, for the qualities of creativity and destructiveness are continually transforming the images of nature.

Morrison's use of nature images is not arbitrary. As in *The Bluest Eye*, the way in which the characters perceive nature is crucial to an understanding of their universe:

In spite of their fear, they reacted to an oppressive oddity, or what they called evil days, with an acceptance that bordered on welcome. Such evil must be avoided, they felt, and precautions must naturally be taken to protect themselves from it. But they let it run its course, fulfill itself, and never invented ways either to alter it, to annihilate it or to prevent its happening again. So also were they with people.

What was taken by outsiders to be slackness, slovenliness or even generosity was in fact a full recognition of the legitimacy of forces other than good ones. They did not believe death was accidental— life might be, but death was deliberate. They did not believe that Nature was ever askew—only inconvenient. Plague and drought were as "natural" as springtime. If milk could curdle, God knows robins could fall. The purpose of evil was to survive it and they determined (without ever knowing they had made up their minds to do it) to survive floods, white people, tuberculosis, famine and ignorance. They knew anger well but not despair, and they didn't stone sinners for the same reason that they didn't commit suicide—it was beneath them.[15]

Because the author probes the philosophical system compressed in these few paragraphs, this novel becomes not only an intense tale of two women's friendship but also a forceful drama of contending mythic beliefs. Her characters' philosophy of life contains no idyllic view of nature, no sympathy with the natural as an ideal, except to survive it. Theirs is a philosophy grounded in a history of struggling continually to survive, a philosophy that exhibits a cynicism about the limits of living. Nature's signs, although they are seldom controlled by the actions of men, must, in this view, relate to the course of human events. Rain falls alike on good men and bad; all are subject to the plague of robins. But the plague must mean something. As Eva greets Sula when she unexpectedly shows up in the Bottom after ten years' absence: "I might have knowed them birds meant something." Nature *is* a sign that can be read, and usually its message relates to the lives of the folk.

While the structural elements of Death, Time, and Nature unify the novel, the story of the Wright women and the Peace women specify the community's perception of itself, for its view of women is inexorably connected to its concept of survival. Part I of this patterned tale emphasizes the myriad forms of woman's behavior that the community incorporates, even as it dramatizes the beginnings of Nel and Sula's friendship. In using these two very different families, the author dramatizes not only the levels of this community's tolerance in relation to women but also its spiritual richness and poverty.

Nel's mother had been born in the Sundown House in New Orleans. The rest of her life was about getting as far away from the wild blood that brothel represents as she could. A high-toned lady, she fashioned her own daughter to be obedient, to be bland: "she drove her daughter's imagination underground," for fear that it might revert. Our introduction to Helene Wright and to Nel in the chapter "1920" comes, as it often does in this novel, through death. Helene's grandmother, who had taken her away from the Sundown House and raised her under "the dolesome eyes of a multicolored Virgin Mary," has died. Her funeral means that Helene has to do what she most fears—come close, too close, to the Sundown House. She will have to acknowledge her own mother, the whore who smells like gardenias and darkens her eyebrows with burnt matches. The trip South is significant, hence the marking of the year, for it is the first and last time Nel will leave Medallion. It is an opportunity for her to see her own mother, so adored by her father and so held in awe by the Bottom, reduced to "custard" by a white conductor. It is during this trip that she learns she is herself: "I'm me," Nel whispers. Each time she said the word "me, there was a gathering in her like power, like joy, like fear." It was her new sense of me-ness that allowed her to cultivate a friend, Sula Peace, of whom her mother initially disapproves.

Sula's ancestry is counterpoint to Nel's. The tone of their respective houses emphasizes the contrast:

> Nel, who regarded the oppressive neatness of her home with dread, felt comfortable in it with Sula, who loved it and would sit on the red velvet sofa for 10 to 20 minutes at a time—still as dawn. As for Nel, she preferred Sula's woolly house where a pot of something was always cooking on the stove; where the mother, Hannah, never scolded or gave directions; where all sorts of people dropped in; where newspapers were stacked in the hallway, and dirty dishes left for hours at a time in the sink, and where a one-legged grandmother named Eva handed you goobers from deep inside her pockets or read you a dream.[16]

As Helene Wright, the light-skinned lady, has a most dubious background, so the Peace women are convoluted, marvelous folk. As portrayals of black women, they are as complex and nonstereotypical as any you will find in literature. Only such ancestral vitality and complexity could have produced Sula, as undefinable as she is black, as unique as she is a woman. When we are first introduced to Eva, her grandmother, and Hannah, her mother, we might at first mistake them for the banal stereotypes of black women in literature and film. Eva, as the mammy, is willing to save her children at all costs, even to the point of sticking her leg under a train to sell it. Hannah, as the loose, comely black woman, will "fuck practically anything." But even as we meet them, any comparisons with the "mammy" or the "loose woman" image is immediately put to rest.

Far from being the big-breasted, kind, religious, forever coping, asexual, loving-white-folks mammy, Eva is arrogant, independent, decidedly a man lover who loves and hates intensely. She is strong by virtue of her will, wit, and idiosyncrasies rather than because of her physique. That strength is nurtured and sustained by her hatred for Big Boy, the unfaithful father of her three children, a hatred that she says keeps her alive and happy. Her utterances throughout the book fall on the mean side of sharpness, refined by a rich imagination and a colorful folk wit. She answers what she considers to be foolish questions with nippy answers. So when her daughter Hannah asks her mother if she ever coddled her children, Eva's answer is richly to the point:

> "Play? Wasn't nobody playing in 1895. . . . What would I look like leapin' round that room playin' with youngins with three beets to my name? . . . No time, there wasn't no time. Not none. Soon as I get one day done here comes a night. With you coughin' and me watchin' so TB wouldn't take you off and if you was sleepin' quiet I thought, O lord they dead and put my hand over your mouth to feel if the breath was comin'. What you talkin' 'bout did I love you girl. I stayed alive for you can't you get that through your thick head or what is that between your ears, heifer?"[17]

She loved her children enough to stay alive and keep them alive; she needn't be physically endearing to them. Thus she retreats to her upstairs bedroom where she spends most of her time, but from which she directs the lives of her children, friends, strays, and a constant stream of boarders.

If Eva has got any of the traditional mammy qualities, it is that she is domineering, without any reason to feel that she should be otherwise. She does as she pleases. As a mother she had given life, and so when her son Plum returns from the war and attempts to "crawl back into her womb," she acts in her usual decisive manner; she burns him to death. Her explanation to Hannah for her actions reverberate with the hidden power inherent in the act of creativity, the power to destroy:

> "After all that carryin' on, just gettin' him out and keepin' him alive, he wanted to crawl back in my womb and well. . . . I ain't got the room no more even if he could do it. . . . He was a man, girl, a big old growed-up man. I didn't have that much room. I kept on dreaming it. Dreaming it and I knowed it was true. One night it wouldn't be no dream. It'd be true and I would have done it, would have let him if I'd've had the room but a big man can't be a baby all wrapped up inside his mammy no more; he suffocate. I done everything I could to make him

leave me and go on and live and be a man but he wouldn't and I had to keep him out so I just thought of a way he could die like a man not all scrunched up inside my womb, but like a man."[18]

Like the primeval Earth Mother Goddess, feared and worshipped by man, like the goddesses of antiquity, older even than the biblical Eve, Eva both gives life and takes it away. She performs a ritual killing inspired by love— a ritual of sacrifice by fire.

In conjuring up this ritual, Morrison dramatically fuses her major structural elements, for she uses Time as the significant event and fire as a destructive element in describing an act that is the most unnatural death of all, a mother's killing of her own son. Eva's burning of Plum takes place in the year 1921 and is the climactic event ending that chapter. The motif of death is resounded here as it was in the chapter "1920," but this time it is not death as a result of old age, but a killing. Although Plum's death ends "1921," Eva's explanation of her actions does not occur until two years later, in 1923, the year she will witness Hannah's accidental death by fire. Between these two chapters, "1921" and "1923," the chapter "1922" focuses on an accidental death by water. Like water, fire has always been a sign of creativity and destructiveness in the human imagination. Morrison uses this forceful symbol in her brilliant treatment of a taboo subject, a mother's murder of her son. But she does not stop there. In weaving her fable, the author connects Eva's destruction of her creation, Plum, to Nature's accidental burning of the beautiful Hannah.

Hannah, Eva's second daughter, is a lovely character. Widowed young and left with her daughter Sula, she returns to her mother's house, evidently intent on never marrying again, perhaps because she has inherited from her mother the love of maleness for its own sake. "What she wanted, after Rekus [her husband] died and what she succeeded in having more often than not, was some touching everyday." But far from being the seductress traditionally dressed in red, who manipulates men to her own ends, Hannah is funky elegance, making no special effort to be alluring other than her natural sensuality, setting no demands on the men she knows. She remains independent in her self, for although she would make love to practically any man, she is extremely careful about whom she sleeps with, for "sleeping with someone implied for her a measure of trust and a definite commitment." So she becomes, as Morrison puts it, "a daylight lover," sex being a part of the ordinary and pleasant things she does every day, rather than a hidden activity at night. Hannah's personality, though, is not wound around sex; she emerges as the practical actor in the bustling house she lives in—the manager, so to speak. Now and then we get glimpses of her questionings, her wonderings, as in her fatal question to Eva about Plum's death. She is honest, as Eva is, but not in her mother's flamboyant fashion. Her succinct appraisal of her feelings for Sula, whom she says she loves but doesn't like, is spoken in anything but dramatic tones.

Just as Plum's murder is enmeshed in the recurring dream of incest that Eva cannot dispel, Hannah's terrible death is foreshadowed by dreams, strange human actions, and omens from nature. In her manner of writing around the point of focus, of playing variations on top of variations, Morrison tells us the second strange thing that happens first. Hannah asks her mother a pointed question, "Mamma, did you ever love us?" in her effort to understand why her mother killed her only son. In true Hannah fashion, it had taken her two years to broach the question, a question that must be answered before she dies, even if it means tangling with her ornery mother. The urgency with which Hannah approaches her mother is, of course, in the realm of human choice; the first strange omen, though, was beyond human control. There had been an unusual wind the night before Hannah's questionings, wind without rain that brought more heat rather than a cooling rain to the Bottom. Then there had been Sula's unusual craziness the day before as if she didn't know what hit her, coupled with Hannah's dream of a wedding in the red dress. Those familiar with dream books, as Eva was, know that a wedding signifies death. But the signs were flying so hot and heavy, Eva scarcely had time to notice any of them. Thoroughly thrown off by the weirdness of the day, Eva cannot find her comb, her favorite object, in her room where no one ever moved anything. As she is looking for it, she sees Hannah burning.

What Morrison does in creating this tragedy of Hannah's burning, reminiscent of the burning of witches, is to pile up sign upon sign, some caused by human beings themselves, others beyond their control, that in hindsight can be read as indications of an imminent tragedy. What a concentration of images, as the earthly and the supernatural, the seemingly trivial and the substantial mesh, it would seem, in a "perfection of judgment" upon Eva, who burns her only son only to see her daughter steamed to death because of a shift in the wind. The author has, in the classic sense, distilled the folk's sense of time by compressing the unseen with the known, the seemingly indifferent and idiosyncratic forces of nature with the order of events willed by human beings. Whatever goes around comes around. As if continuing that never-ending spiral, Eva insists that she was sure she saw Sula watch her mother burning, not with terror but interest. Eva's presumptuous act of burning her own son has triggered a series of effects that will haunt her many years hence when Sula will do battle with her. Her entire family is scorched by her act. In breaking a taboo, Eva provokes not only human repercussions but nature's wrath as well.

By dramatizing significant events in the lives of diverse characters such as Helene Wright and Eva and Hannah Peace, the novel outlines the precise perimeters of the Bottom's tolerance in relation to a woman's behavior.

This community absorbs many styles—Helene's ladylike and hypocritical demeanor, Hannah's elegant sensuality, even Eva's arrogant murder of her son—as long as they remain within its definition of woman as wife, mother, or man lover. The Bottom's apparent toleration of these many styles is as restrictive as it is generous. Morrison focuses on this cultural characteristic in her presentation of the development of Nel and Sula's friendship. In addition, by placing the beginnings of their friendship between chapter "1921," when Eva burns Plum to death, and chapter "1923," the time of the accidental burning of Hannah, Morrison reminds us of the impact their female relatives are having on these impressionable twelve-year-old girls.

Out of their awareness that their lives, as black females, are restricted by their community and by the outer society, Nel and Sula are drawn to each other. As only-girl children, each takes the other as sister, sharing each other's dreams of freedom and excitement:

> So when they met, first in those chocolate halls and next through the ropes of the swing, they felt the ease and comfort of old friends. Because each had discovered years before that they were neither white nor male, and that all freedom and triumph was forbidden to them, they had set about creating something else to be. Their meeting was fortunate, for it let them use each other to grow on. Daughters of distant mothers and incomprehensible fathers (Sula's because he was dead; Nel's because he wasn't), they found in each other's eyes the intimacy they were looking for.[19]

Nel and Sula's friendship is sustained not only by their recognition of each other's restrictions but also by their anticipation of sexuality and by an ultimate bond, the responsibility for unintentionally causing the death of another. However, although the two girls share these strong bonds, they are different, for Sula, who is the adventurer, often allows "her emotions to dictate her behavior," and Nel is more cautious, more consistent. As a result, in this chapter, Sula appears to be the more focal actor of the two.

The chapter "1922" is deceptive in its flow, for it is so innocent in its springtime visions, so bittersweet in its images of budding twelve-year-old girls, that the drama of Chicken Little's drowning catches us off guard. But a note of pain, ever so slightly touched on, begins a shift in tone when Sula overhears her mother's comment that she may love her, but she does not like her. The pain of her mother's assertion is mingled with the beginning of sexual stirrings that she and Nel feel as they play by the river. Overflowing with the energy of repressed pain and pleasure, the emotional Sula swings the little boy, Chicken Little, until he falls into the river, never to be seen again.

Because of the feelings that led to it, this accidental death by water is

Sula's baptism into her search for some continuity between the natural world and the social world, between the precariousness of life and the inevitability of death. The author emphasizes the impact this death has on Sula by having Shadrack, as well as Nel, witness it. A veteran of the witnessing of horrific death, Shadrack attempts to give Sula some sense of its meaning. As the originator of National Suicide Day, he assures her of her own permanency, that she need not have fear of death. Because of his own singular concern with this fear, his one utterance in the book, the word *always*, takes on mythic proportions. Although Shadrack does not intend the meaning Sula attributes to this word, he is in a sense right, for Chicken Little's death and the emotions that surround it will always be with her, not the drowning itself so much as the feeling that she cannot rely either on herself or on others. Perhaps the old women at Chicken Little's funeral are right when

> they danced and screamed, not to protest God's will but to acknowledge it and confirm once more their conviction that the only way to avoid the Hand of God is to get in it.[20]

Morrison concludes Part I by reiterating her major structural elements, for Part I ends not with the death of someone but with a wedding, the wedding of Nel and Jude in the year 1927. Their marriage becomes *the* event in the Bottom, bringing together the community in a moment of feasting, revelry, and renewal. But as Eva has already told us, and as Hannah's death clearly illustrates, the dream of a wedding means death. This wedding seems to mean death, not only for Nel and Sula's girl friendship but for Jude and Nel's previous sense of themselves.

The delineation of Nel and Sula's personalities and the particular roads they take are finely drawn in this chapter, particularly in relation to the mores of the Bottom. Just as Sula was more focal in the chapter about these young girls' personal explorations of life and death, so Nel is the major actor in this chapter about the community's initiation of young adults into its fold. Jude chooses Nel because she has no desire to make herself and delights in caring about someone else. Like so many young men in his community, he begins thinking of marriage because he needs desperately to accomplish something of significance, this something being a job at helping to build the new River Road:

> It was while he was full of such dreams his body already feeling the rough work clothes, his hands already curved to the pick handle, that he spoke to Nel about getting married. She seemed receptive but hardly anxious. It was after he stood in lines for six days running and saw the gang boss pick out thin-armed white boys from the Virginia hills and

the bull-necked Greeks and Italians and heard over and over, "Nothing else today. Come back tomorrow," that he got the message. So it was rage and the determination to take on a man's role anyhow that made him press Nel about settling down. He needed some of his appetites filled, some posture of adulthood recognized, but mostly he wanted someone to care about his hurt, to care very deeply.[21]

Jude's reasons for pressing Nel into marriage reinforce our sense of the Bottom's definition of woman. As his helpmate, Nel is a buffer between his desire for his own autonomy and the restrictions the outside world places on him. Her marriage to him will replace the need he so intensely feels to have some impact on the world and thus enable him to accept his state.

As the Bottom dances and eats, as Nel responds to Jude's kiss, Sula takes another road distinct and apart from the community. We are left to contemplate Nel and Sula's childhood as reflected in the structural lines of Morrison's tale. Nel Wright's sense of her own identity had begun with her trip to her great-grandmother's funeral and the beginning of her friendship with Sula Peace. Our first insight into Sula's ancestry begins with our hesitant comprehension of Eva's fire murder of her only son to save his manhood. Sula's personality is gravely affected by the events that surround the watery death of Chicken Little. Her mother, Hannah, as if a witch, is seared to death in so tragic and senseless a way that supernatural omens are needed to justify it. As their childhood ends, all of these events reach their logical conclusion. Nel, the daughter of the proper Helene Wright, marries Jude, losing the sense of her own identity she had gotten a glimpse of in her friendship with Sula, and Sula, daughter of the distinctive Peace women, leaves the Bottom. The patterned story of Nel and Sula's friendship, woven as it is with threads of their community's culture and their families' histories, is rhythmically embroidered with knots of death and stunningly colored by the elemental forces of Nature.

Part I explores the many styles of women's behavior that the Bottom is willing to absorb, while it traces the friendship of Nel and Sula as young girls. In contrast, Part II emphasizes the forms that this community will not tolerate, while it examines the friendship and estrangement of Nel and Sula as adult women. Foremost to Part II is the Bottom's concept of evil, for that is the way in which they characterize intolerable behavior. Although there is a progression in theme, however, the structural elements of this fable remain the same. The author immediately reiterates her framework by beginning Part II with an uncommon freak of nature, a plague of robins. Like the marigolds that would not sprout in *The Bluest Eye*, this oddity of nature holds sway in the imagination, conjuring images of dread or at least of the unknown.

In Part II, as in Part I, Nature's signs are intertwined with the persistent recurrence of death, and the time when a particular death is focused upon is the core around which each chapter is built. However, although the deaths in Part I are primarily physical, the deaths in Part II are emotional and spiritual as well. In the chapter "1937," Nel and Sula's friendship is presumably killed because Sula sleeps with Jude, Nel's husband. In the chapter "1939," Sula and Ajax's relationship is killed by Sula's attempt to possess Ajax. In 1940 Sula dies physically, but we feel to some extent that her death is due to spiritual malnutrition as much as any physical cause. In 1941 a significant number of folk in the Bottom are killed in their attempt to destroy the tunnel that they were not allowed to build. In effect they bring about their own deaths because they have been spiritually as well as physically drained by poverty, harsh weather, and starvation—a power-lessness. Death is not just a physical occurrence. Its presence is related to the folk's spiritual needs left unfulfilled by Nature and society.

Related to death, in Part II, is the figure of Sula and the images of nature that accompany her. Interestingly, the elements of air and earth are as pervasive as the elements of fire and water in the previous section. So in the chapter "1937," Sula's return is heralded by a plague of robins and by "the peculiar quality of that May," a quality that Nel alone notices. More than anything, Sula's lover, Ajax wants to fly a plane. Sula thinks of Ajax's body in images of gold, alabaster, and loam, which she waters, and of sex with him as "the high silence of orgasm." As Sula dies in chapter "1940," she remembers the word *always* that Shadrack had uttered on the day of Chicken Little's drowning and feels her death to be "a sleep of water always." In keeping with that image of water, her funeral is concluded by a shower of rain. The collapse of the tunnel in chapter "1941" is preceded not only by Sula's death but by the sudden change from extreme cold to intense heat, which causes the earth to shift and the river to overflow. On that climactic January, Shadrack watches his ritual, National Suicide Day, come to life before his very eyes as water, earth, wind, and fire combine to create a holocaust. Part II then begins with an oddity of nature and ends with a natural disaster, one seeming to announce the return of Sula to the Bottom, the other seeming to underscore her death.

In addition to the elements of Death and Nature, Time, in Part II, con-tinues to be crucial to Morrison's patterning of her fable. The way in which the events are arranged is not so much chronology as it is the juxtaposition of two views about the nature of living. By using Nel and Sula, two parts of an intense friendship, as the embodiment of these views, Morrison per-sonalizes the philosophical content of her tale. But these points of view would not assume mythic proportions as they do in this novel if they were merely idiosyncratic, if they were not set within the context of a culture. This novel is a fable because it presents a culture's philosophy about life and death, good and evil.

The community sees Sula as the embodiment of evil. All of their ills and sufferings take visual form in her being. From the year 1937, when Sula returns to the Bottom, to the year 1940, when she dies, a presence charges the Bottom with an energy, the fuse of which is to defeat her by surviving her. What is it about Sula Peace that turns this community into a buttressed fort against her? The reasons are not so much explanation as intersecting circles of fear, the greatest one being the fear of difference.

Ironically, Sula is both the sum of her ancestors and greater than each part. Like Eva, she is tough, ornery, and nippy. Her first action upon her return to the Bottom, in fact, is to do battle with her grandmother and to banish her to an old folks home, contrary to the mores of the Bottom. But Sula's expulsion of Eva is not her mortal sin. She and her grandmother clash on the issue that will emphasize her difference in a community that believes it needs consistency to survive: Sula wants to make herself rather than others. In a scorching dialogue between Sula and her grandmother, the perfection of judgment upon Eva comes full circle. Eva assaults Sula with the question:

". . . When you gone to get married? You need to have some babies. It'll settle you."

"I don't want to make somebody else. I want to make myself."

"Selfish. Ain't no woman got no business floatin' around without no man."

"You did."

"Not by choice."

"Mama did."

"Not by choice, I said it ain't right for you to want to stay off by your-self. You need . . . I'm a tell you what you need."

Sula sat up. "I need you to shut your mouth."

When Eva replies that God will strike her down, Sula retorts:

"Which God? The one who watched you burn Plum? . . . Maybe one night when you dozing in that wagon flicking flies and swallowing spit, maybe I'll just tip on up here with some kerosene and—who knows—you may make the brightest flame of them all.[22]

As if she had carefully studied her grandmother, Sula introduces the one threat that would drive fear into Eva's heart. In so doing she dethrones the haughty mistress of the house. What is most interesting, though, is Eva's resistance to Sula's need to make herself, a concept totally alien to one who loves maleness for its own sake. Yet Sula has inherited this need for independence, this arrogance, this orneriness, at least partially from the Eva who had the gall to destroy her only son to save his maleness.

Like Hannah, Sula sleeps with the husbands of her neighbors indiscriminately. But although Hannah made the men feel complete and seemed to compliment the women by wanting their husbands, Sula sleeps with them once and discards them. Unlike her mother, Sula does not experience sex as a pleasant pastime. Orgasm becomes the moment for her when she feels her full strength and power at the same time that she experiences complete aloneness. Orgasm, for Sula, "was not eternity but the death of time and a loneliness so profound the word itself had no meaning." In sex she knows not her partner but herself.

Because of her drive for self-knowledge, and because of the imagination she brings to the memories of her ancestors and to her own experiences, Sula emerges as a unique woman. In two beautifully terse analyses, Morrison illumines her character:

> Sula was distinctly different. Eva's arrogance and Hannah's self indulgence merged in her and, with a twist that was all her own imagination, she lived out her days exploring her own thoughts and emotions giving them full reign, feeling no obligation to please anybody unless their pleasure pleased her. As willing to feel pain as to give pain, to feel pleasure as to give pleasure, hers was an experimental life—ever since her mother's remarks sent her flying up those stairs, ever since her one major feeling of responsibility had been exorcised on the bank of a river with a closed place in the middle. The first experience taught her that there was no other that you could count on; the second that there was no self to count on either. She had no center, no speck around which to grow.[23]

> She had been looking along for a friend, and it took her a while to discover that a lover was not a comrade and could never be—for a woman. And that no one would ever be that version of herself which she sought to reach out to and touch with an ungloved hand. There was only her own mood and whim, and if that was all there was, she decided to turn the naked hand toward it, discover it and let others become as intimate with their own selves as she was.

> In a way, her strangeness, her naivete, her craving for the other half of her equation was the consequence of an idle imagination. Had she paints, or clay, or knew the discipline of the dance, or strings; had she

anything to engage her tremendous curiosity and her gift for metaphor, she might have exchanged the restlessness and preoccupation with whim for an activity that provided her with all she yearned for. And like any artist with no art form, she became dangerous.[24]

Sula has the distinction of being herself in a community that believes that self-hood can only be selfishness. Her view of life is different from others, as if the birthmark above one of her eyes has either distorted or enlarged her vision. It is with maddening recognition that we grasp Sula's tragedy—she is too full, and yet too static, to grow. She has stared into that abyss where nothing in life can be relied on—where nothing really matters. Like Cholly Breedlove in *The Bluest Eye*, she has developed the freedom of narcissism allowed only to the gods. Such freedom is not allowed to mere mortals as the oldest stories of all cultures testify. Sula is unique, though, even in the company of mortals who try to live life as if they are divine, for she is a woman. Her life, according to the customs of all traditions, is not hers to experiment with, to create or destroy. Her life is meant to result in other lives. So like Pauline Breedlove in *The Bluest Eye*, she is an artist without an art form. When Sula stares into the abyss that sex so clearly evokes for her, she is not looking for another entity but for another version of herself, for a total union possible only when each perceives the other as possibly being his or her self. Since woman is not usually perceived by man in that total sense, Sula abandons any attempt at union and seeks only herself. Since she cannot have everything, she will at least, or at most, have herself. Marked at birth, she will pursue her own uniqueness.

But such total absorption leads to destructiveness, for the world, used to compromise, will not accept, cannot understand, such concentration—perhaps it must not, to maintain even a slim semblance of order. Using the inexplicable fact that Shadrack is civil to Sula while he shuns everyone else, convinced that she is committing the unforgettable sin—sleeping with white men—and buttressed by her disregard for their God-ordained ways, the town turns Sula into a witch, conjuring spells against her power and acting righteously to prove themselves better than the ignoble she-devil. This lone woman's effect on her community recalls the always perplexing mystery of humanity's need for an evil one, for a devil:

> Their conviction of Sula's evil changed them in accountable yet mysterious ways. Once the source of their personal misfortune was identified, they had leave to protect and love one another. They began to cherish their husbands and wives, protect their children, repair their homes and in general band together against the devil in their midst.[25]

All things have their use and even Sula's evil nature is used by her community to validate and enrich its own existence. As pariah, she gives them a focus through which they achieve some unity, at least temporarily, just as Pecola's madness in *The Bluest Eye* is used by the townsfolk as evidence of their own sanity, their own strength, their own beauty. The need human beings continually exhibit for a scapegoat, so they can justify themselves, is one of the mysteries of human existence that Morrison consistently probes in her works. Why is it that human beings need an enemy, or a martyr, to come together, to feel their own worth, or merely to survive? Why is it that human beings are fascinated with "evil," creating images in its likeness, as children create monsters? It is significant, too, the emphasis the author places on women as accessible scapegoat figures for communities, for any obviously conscious disregard of cultural mores on their part seems to represent not only a threat to the community but to the whole species as well— hence the preponderance of witches, pariahs, and insane women in the history of humanity.

Most importantly, through Morrison's characterization of Eva, Hannah, and Sula, we see that it is not merely social deviance that makes one a pariah. That cursed label is given only to one whose behavior seems so different from, so *at odds with*, the prevailing norm that it cannot be absorbed into the unconscious of the community. In this case, from her birth, the community's unconscious had already been prepared to accept Sula as distinct. It is significant that Sula's birthmark is perceived in different ways, depending on the perspective of the beholder. When Morrison first describes it, "it is something like a stemmed rose" that adds excitement to an otherwise plain face. To Shadrack, who reveres fish, it is the mark of a tadpole, identifying Sula as a friend. To Jude, the mark resembles a rattlesnake, the sting of which is taken away by Sula's smile. To the folk, the mark is Evil, the mark of Hannah's ashes, identifying Sula from her very beginning as a devil. So Sula, not Eva or Hannah, is a pariah because she is distinctly different, because she is consciously seeking to make herself rather than others, and she is totally unconcerned about what others think; in other words, she does not care.

Although Sula does not care about what the community thinks, she does care about Nel, the friend to whom she returns in the Bottom, and she comes to care about Ajax, her lover, for a time. Morrison weaves in a specific pattern the strands of the community's belief system together with the estrangement of Nel and Sula and the love affair of Ajax and Sula so we might better understand the complexity of both points of view. First, the author tells us about the community's view of Nature and Evil, after which we experience the estrangement of Nel and Sula and the community's designation of Sula as a witch. Finally, the story of Sula's and Ajax's relationship is followed by Sula's death and the death of the folk in that tunnel. In carefully charting her pattern, Morrison asks us to contemplate the meaning of her design.

The story of the apparent dissolution of the strong friendship between Nel and Sula occurs within the context of the Bottom's need to band against

Sula and as such is the embodied formulation of the gap between Sula and the community from which she comes. Unlike the other folk in the Bottom, Nel is elated when Sula returns. Her joy is expressed, as their fear is, in terms of nature. She

> . . . noticed the peculiar quality of the May that followed the leaving of the birds. It had a sheen, a glimmering as of green, rain-soaked Saturday nights (lit by the excitement of newly installed street lights; of lemon yellow afternoons bright with iced drinks and splashes of daffodils).[26]

For Nel, the world again becomes magical and interesting because of Sula's presence. She emphasizes their unity, how talking to Sula was like talking to herself. Yet Sula's gift of magic becomes a spiritual death for Nel because these two women are no longer one. They have taken different roads in life and have formed the meaning-ness of their lives into different patterns. Nel's life, in essence, revolves around Jude, her husband, and their three children, while Sula's life revolves around her own exploratory imagination. When Sula sleeps with Jude, obviously not so much as an act of passion, but more as an exploratory act, or even, we suspect, as a means to more intimacy with Nel, she breaks the one taboo that could shatter their girlhood friendship. Their respective reactions to this act counterpoint one another, revealing their different value systems.

In her soliloquy, Nel stares into that abyss that Sula experienced so sharply when she overheard Hannah admit that she did not like her. That is, Nel learns that one can never wholly rely on anyone. She remembers Sula's words, "The real hell of Hell is that it is forever," and counters "Sula was wrong. Hell ain't things lasting forever, Hell is change." Unable to get away from her self, which is pain, and the pain, which is her self, she learns, too, as Sula had, that there is no self to rely on. Her pain and her fear of it become in her mind a dirty ball of fur and string signifying nothing. What Sula does for Nel, as she has always done in their friendship, is to share her experimental knowledge with her. By so doing Sula underscores the illusion on which Nel's life is based. From a practical point of view, Nel has been prepared solely for the role of being a handmaiden to Jude or to someone like him. By sleeping with Jude, Sula strips Nel of her illusion, leaving her with nothing she can rely on. In contrast to Sula, who turns this jarring knowledge into a reason for exploration, Nel *knows* that "her thighs are forever empty," that her life is finished, and that she nonetheless longs for those who had crushed her:

> That was too much. To lose Jude and not have Sula to talk to about it because it was Sula that he had left her for.[27]

In one stroke, Nel loses the bases of her emotional life, her husband, Jude, and her only friend, Sula. What else is there for her to do but die— slowly.

Between Nel's soliloquy about her pain and Sula's reactions to their broken friendship, Morrison inserts the community's judgment of Sula as a witch and Sula's acceptance of that judgment. The folk's judgment of Sula is partly based on Sula's infidelity to her friend Nel; in part, Sula's acceptance of their judgment is her realization that her only true friend has become one of *them*. Sula had thought of Nel as being one with her and finds out, at least from her point of view, that Nel is just like all the women she has known who hold onto their men "because they were only afraid of losing their jobs." Nel becomes like the others, the people she visualizes as spiders, afraid of experiment, afraid of living. So their friendship freezes to death, Sula surmises, because Nel becomes dead like the rest of the town.

These are Nel and Sula's perceptions about what has happened, perceptions on opposite sides of the spectrum. But Morrison's unrelenting probing assails us with a complicated truth that lies somewhere between the pain and emptiness of Nel, husbandless with three children, left to live without any hope of really living, and Sula's pure view of people who are afraid to live because they are possessive, because they do not want to experience pain and therefore never experience pleasure. As Sula explores her feelings about her estrangement from Nel, she characterizes the women of the Bottom in this way:

> The narrower their lives, the wider their hips. Those with husbands had folded themselves into starched coffins, their sides bursting with other people's skinned dreams and bony regrets. Those without men were like sour-tipped needles featuring one constant empty eye. Those with men had had the sweetness sucked from their breath by ovens and steam kettles. Their children were like distant but exposed wounds whose aches were not less intimate because separate from their flesh. They had looked at the world and back at their children, back at the world and back again at their children, and Sula knew that one clear young eye was all that kept the knife away from the throat's curve.[28]

But Sula, too, is not immune from the need for permanence and consistency. Morrison juxtaposes Sula's caustic analysis of the women in the Bottom with her relationship with Ajax, a relationship in which Sula discovers the desire to be possessive.

Sula and Ajax's love relationship emerges as the fullest communication between a man and woman in Morrison's works. As persons, they are well suited to each other. Ajax, beautifully male and heroic (as his name implies), had been the object of Nel and Sula's adolescent dreams of anticipated sexuality. His two loves, his conjure woman mother and airplanes,

tell us that he expects women to be mentally as well as physically interesting, and that he wants more than anything to fly, far above the limits set for
him. Like Sula, he resists limitations and ties. But unlike her, he has found
an object other than himself on which to focus his imagination, although it
is interesting that he, too, will never be able to fulfill his dream, will never
be able to fly a plane. They love each other; in that they find another version of themselves in each other, at least for a while. He is attracted to Sula,
suspecting that "this was perhaps the only other woman other than his
mother he knew whose life was her own, who could deal with life efficiently
and who was not interested in nailing him." Their relationship solidifies
because they have genuine conversations, the real pleasure that Sula is
seeking. But having discovered this pleasure, Sula wants to keep it, possess
it, always have it when she wants it. So in the manner of age-old seduction,
she adorns herself, cleans the house, and whispers to him, "Lean on me,"
words that epitomize the relationship between Nel and Jude, words that
thrust the concept of dependence and therefore of possessiveness into their
relationship. Knowing the signs, Ajax rushes off to watch the planes that he
will never be allowed to fly.

Now, Sula experiences the pain of absence she had unwittingly inflicted
on her friend Nel. Perhaps women feel wronged when men leave them, not
only, or sometimes not at all, because they will lose their jobs, but because
of the pain of absence. Sula experiences:

> An absence so decorative, so ornate, it was difficult for her to under-
> stand how she had ever endured, without falling dead or being con-
> sumed, his magnificent presence.[29]

Yet she knows that the relationship would have ended eventually, for had
he not left, her insatiable curiosity would have compelled her to dig deeper
and deeper into his psyche until she hurt him. Realizing the essential loneliness of her stance in life, she sings, "There aren't any more new songs,
and I have sung all the ones there are." What else is there left for her to do
but die?

Although Nel and Sula have taken opposite paths, they are both dying.
But Nel is dying, as Sula says, "like a stump," while Sula feels that she is
"going down like one of those redwoods." Death brings them together
again when Nel comes to see Sula on her deathbed. Both thirty, the evil
Sula is dying physically, the Bottom feels, as retribution for her sins, while
the virtuous Nel's "hot brown eyes had turned to agate, and her skin had
taken on the sheen of maple struck down, split and sanded at the height of
its green." Sula had lived gloriously before she was struck down; Nel, on
the other hand, endures physically, but only at the price of never having
fulfilled herself. Their conversation, an echo of Eva's conversation with
Sula, concerns how much one is allowed to live:

"You can't have it all, Sula."

"Why? I can do it all, why can't I have it all?"

"You *can't* do it all. You a woman and a colored woman at that. You can't act like a man. You can't be walking around all independent-like, doing whatever you like, taking what you want, leaving what you don't."[30]

Their exchange illuminates the difference between their philosophies. Sula exclaims:

"You think I don't know what your life is like just because I ain't living it? I know what every colored woman in this country is doing."

"What's that?"

"Dying. Just like me. But the difference is they dying like a stump. Me, I going down like one of those redwoods. I sure did live in this world."

"Really? What have you got to show for it?"

"Show? To who? Girl, I got my mind. And what goes on in it. Which is to say, I got me."

"Lonely, ain't it?"

"Yes. But my lonely is *mine*. Now your lonely is somebody else's. Made by somebody else and handed to you. Ain't that something? A second-hand lonely."[31]

As Nel leaves her, Sula crystallizes the difference.

"How you know?" Sula asked.

"Know what?" Nel wouldn't look at her.

"About who was *good*. How you know it was you?"

"What you mean?"

"I mean maybe it wasn't you. Maybe it was me."[32]

In her final speech in this novel, Sula questions the community's insistence on its own goodness and its designation of anything that falls outside its ken as evil. She does this most specifically in relation to their view of woman, which she proclaims is entirely to the community's use without any concern for the women who must live it. In spite of the community's judgments, however, and despite their estrangement, Nel and Sula still relate to each other as they had in childhood. Although the Bottom has labeled the behavior of one of them as evil and the other as good, they continue to complement one another. As the exploratory half in their relationship, Sula had always been the one to share with Nel what it was to experience this or that. So Sula had been Nel's source of liberation from stern parents or from a rigid community that sought to destroy any imagination she had. Nel had been Sula's source of stability when crises occurred, as in the death of Chicken Little. When Nel experiences the pain of Jude's absence, it is to Sula that she wants to talk, an impossibility since Sula is the reason for his leaving. When Sula is dying, her last thought is to share with Nel this most personal of experiences. "Well, I'll be damned," she thought, "it didn't even hurt. Wait'll I tell Nel." We later learn that when Sula is dead, Nel is the one in the Bottom who makes the arrangements for her funeral and is the only one who formally attends it. The practical element in their relationship, Nel always performs well in a crisis.

In the pursuit of complex truth, Morrison has juxtaposed the world of Nel next to the world of Sula, the world in which practicality and survival are foremost to the world in which exploration and imagination make life worth living. Which world view holds the answer to life? Does either? Nel does as she is told; any sparkle she has is rubbed down to a dull glow so she can become a sensible, comforting wife, so she can do those things, however tedious, necessary for survival. But her world is dependent on another, the world of her husband or her children. Since these worlds collapse, she is left without a context. Sula pursues herself, exploring her emotions and imagination. Her world is hers, but left without a focus for her imagination, she becomes destructive, and because her stance seems contrary to the survival of her community, she is left alone, estranged from others. Finally, she turns in on herself, but the self, as her experience with Chicken Little or as her relationship with Ajax proves, cannot be totally relied on either.

Although Sula dies, Morrison does not want us to conclude that the philosophy of the Bottom is superior. The folk's major premise is that the way to conquer evil is to survive it, to outlast it. So when Sula dies, the folk feel they have won, that a brighter day is dawning, that there will be work for black men in building the tunnel, which has been planned, abandoned, and replanned. The chapter "1941" makes it plain that the evil they need to conquer cannot merely be outlasted, and that Sula's presence in the Bottom has little to do with brighter days. If anything, her absence makes things worse, for without a pariah, the folk revert to not caring about each other. What becomes clear is that Nature will always inflict disasters on them, that the evil of racism will result in jobless men and women, and that death will be always with them. With or without a pariah, evil days continue, and although the philosophy of survival may be useful in combatting them, it is a limited method. As if reminding the Bottom that it is still vulnerable to catastrophe, regardless of Sula's death, the natural fall of the year is replaced by an early frost, destroying the crops, resulting in sickness of the body and in a spiritless, stingy Thanksgiving. Then the frost is followed by the false hope of a summery January, a heat that will cause the earth to shift in the tunnel they all yearn to build. In fact, if anything, Sula's death, coupled with the natural and social ills that affect them, bring mass death to the Bottom.

Consistent in the novel, Shadrack appears as the figure who stands for the fear of death. Ironically, this shell-shocked soldier realizes through the death of Sula that his National Suicide Day ritual does not ward off death. He had reassured Sula, his only visitor in all those years, that she would *always* be. Yet she, too, had died and would never come again. On January third, on National Suicide Day, he pays no attention to the details of his ritual for he no longer believes in its efficacy, and, ironically, on this particular day, national suicide happens not in ritual but in fact. Looking at death in the sunshine and being unafraid, laughing folk follow Shadrack:

> As the initial group of about twenty people passed more houses, they called to the people standing in doors and leaning out of windows to join them; to help them open further this slit in the veil, this respite from an anxiety from dignity, from gravity, from the weight of that very adult pain that had undergirded them all those years before. Called to them to come out and play in the sunshine—as though the sunshine would last, as though there really was hope. The same hope that kept them picking beans for other farmers, kept them from finally leaving as they talked of doing; kept them knee-deep in other people's dirt; kept them excited about other people's wars; kept them solicitous of white people's children; kept them convinced that some magic "government" was going to lift them up, out and away from the dirt, those beans, those wars.[33]

Revitalized by false hope, they dance to the site of promise—the tunnel—and in an act of defiance try to kill the tunnel they were forbidden to build. The heat, the false hope, causes the earth to shift and the water to break. Many are suffocated, drowned, or crushed to death as Shadrack rings his bell, proclaiming the unexpectedness of death. Too long insistent on outlasting evil, worn down by natural and social forces, the folk's one defiant gesture is built on a false hope that keeps them in shackles.

Morrison's fable emphasizes the paradox inherent in the philosophy of survival. True, when one is not able to destroy evil, one must try to outlast it. But human beings have to demand more from life than mere survival, or they may not survive at all. To really live life, there must be some imagination, some exploration, so there can be some creative action.

The last chapter of the novel, "1965," hammers this point home, for although some of the folk have survived and there has been some progress, the Bottom and its distinctiveness have disappeared. Ironically, black folk had moved from the Bottom only to realize too late that hill land had become valuable. In terms of monetary value, it had become, in fact, what the white farmer had told his slave a hundred years before, "the bottom of Heaven."

Structurally, this chapter acts as the Bottom's eulogy, weaving all the novel's threads together into a completed fabric. Nel is, as she must be, our point of view character, for through Sula, she has participated in another world view, distinct from her own. She alone can recognize the pattern that was being woven all those years. In talking with Eva, the mother who has outlasted her progeny, Nel is confronted with the waste and arrogance inherent in living solely to make others. Confronted by Eva's meanness, Nel recognizes the Bottom's narrowness, finally its undoing, even as she can still appreciate its marvelous distinctiveness. Nel's conversation with Eva also reminds us of the futile deaths that pervade this book: the death of Plum, Chicken Little, Hannah, and finally Sula. In confusing Nel with Sula, Eva reminds Nel of the unity of feeling she once had with this cursed woman. As if to heighten our awareness of the death of the Bottom, Nel goes to the cemetery, the only remaining monument of this community. On her way she passes Shadrack, the symbol of the fear of death throughout this novel. It is fitting that these two should be our final witnesses to this fable for they represent throughout the novel the personal embodiment of the community's concept of survival that is rooted not in the wish to live but in the fear of dying.

As a result of her confrontation with the pattern of her life, Nel realizes the emptiness she had felt all of these years was not the pain of Jude's absence but that of Sula's. It is with Sula that she had experienced the excitement of being human and had had the opportunity to go beyond the Bottom's narrow principle of survival. Through Sula, she could have transformed her own life just as the Bottom might have. If she and it had sought to understand what Sula meant, if she and it had explored the possibilities of life, perhaps Sula might have survived, Nel might have lived, and the Bottom might still be. As it is, the tale of Sula, the marked woman, and her community, the Bottom, remains the stuff out of which legends are made.

PART III

The Vision and Craft of Toni Morrison

Toni Morrison's first two novels reveal a consistency in vision and craft. In creating fables, she weaves together the quest of young black girls for womanhood with the cultural values of their communities. She structures her tales by showing how the mythological system of their communities, specifically their concepts of time, nature, and death, relate to their definition of woman. By so doing, she dramatizes the effects this definition has on her girl-women.

Although Morrison's major characters all struggle toward womanhood, their sense of what it means is drastically different. For Pecola, womanhood means being loved; for Nel, it is a straight narrow line; and for Sula, to be a woman means self-fulfillment. Morrison's first novel, *The Bluest Eye*, explores the reasons why it is so difficult for black women to achieve the definition of womanhood ascribed to by American society and still remain true to their racial identity. The second novel, *Sula*, penetrates further beyond the norms of any community, black or white, although through them, to a deeper analysis of selfhood as woman. Realizing that the dominant norms are both impossible or undesirable, Sula pushes beyond them. So there is a development in the concept of womanhood and selfhood from one book to the next.

The pursuit of womanhood, as it affects their wholeness, begins in earnest at that vulnerable age when Pecola and Sula are caught between the physical stages of girlhood and womanhood. It is at this quivering point that Pecola is raped and begins her search for blue eyes, and that Sula discovers the hard emotional fact that no one, not even her mother, or even herself, can be totally relied on. The approach of adolescence marks the growth of their body sexuality and the emergence of their mind consciousness. Along with sexuality comes the desire for knowledge, the knowledge of self. In both Pecola and Sula's quest for wholeness and self-knowledge, sexuality becomes the vehicle. Pecola's rape by her father is the culmination of the lie her community and family have been trapped by. "It was the only love she was to know," in her search for love, for womanness. The act itself embodies the love-hate lacerating not only her father's life but the life of her community. At age twelve, Pecola experiences sex as an act of love-terror, so she goes mad. Sula's sexuality is not fully explored in the novel until she is twenty-seven years old, but again her knowledge of herself as woman is determined largely by her attitude toward sex. She uses the act itself as a means to self-knowledge rather than intimacy with another, for she doubts the possibility of true communication with men, who would be her lovers but not her friends. Sex verifies for her the awesome powerfulness and loneliness of her self.

The community's final rejection of both Sula and Pecola relates to these women's experience of sex. The rape of Pecola and her subsequent madness completely alienates her from her community; the folk's insistence that Sula sleeps with white men becomes the damning reason for labeling her a devil. Because a particular society's definition of womanhood and therefore of the female self often incorporates that group's view of sexuality and of nature, both novels are explorations of cultural and mythic beliefs. In both novels, these beliefs are the bases for the behavior of the families and the communities from which Pecola and Sula evolve.

In *The Bluest Eye*, the emphasis is placed on the inversion of truth caused by one culture's attempt to impose its value system inappropriately on another culture. So the effect, even if it seems successful as in Geraldine's case, is grotesque. Pecola cannot and should not want to be a blue-eyed, straight-haired lady. But since that image is imposed on her as the means to wealth, love, and happiness, she is defeated by her own culture's inability to separate image from substance. Since she is *the* vulnerable character in the book, she is awake to the contradictions in the very air she breathes. Pecola's family has already been defeated by society's racism and callousness; the community of women around her, as well as her mother, Pauline, have fastened onto the prevailing concept of beauty as the reason why they cannot become all that they want to be. How, then, can Pecola become a woman, how then can she be loved, since she does not have the physical characteristics necessary for happiness? Since Pecola, sensitive and poor, is frightened by life, she does not question the norm, does not fight the images that attack her essence. But then neither do any of the other black women in the book. They are all attempting to straddle the gulf between image and substance, at the price of self-hatred. Only Claudia and Frieda, girl-children as they are, rebel against the norm, but they have yet to be assailed by the beautiful terror of adolescent fantasizing. This test, the need to be seen as all things beautiful and good in the eyes of another, still lies ahead of them. Pecola's end is tragic because she, unlike her elders, cannot lie to herself; in totally believing the efficacy of the image, she reveals its absurdity. Her doom underscores the hidden tragedy, the waste in the lives of all of the black women in the novel.

Sula, in contrast, rejects her own culture's definition of woman, as a being meant to make someone else, whether that someone be man or child. She seeks herself. But the community's norms, nonetheless, are crucial to her survival and development. Because she rejects them, she becomes isolated even unto death. Her presence challenges the value system at the core of the community's existence so they reject her desire to recreate the definition of a woman to suit her own sensibility. Both Pecola and Sula's communities, then, are hindrances to them in their quest for womanhood, although Pecola differs from Sula in that she accepts the norm; it is just that she cannot achieve it.

The conflict between Pecola and Sula's vision and the visions of their communities is heightened by the ever-present image of *eyes*. Pecola wants the impossible blue eyes, a desire transmitted to her by her community and a desire that distorts her and their abilities to perceive reality. One of Sula's eyes is indelibly marked at birth, proclaiming her distinctive vision. She is as she is. Although Pecola seeks to elevate herself to the level of a desirable human being by possessing those blue eyes, Sula pursues her own divinity, refusing to restrict her essence to the limits set by the human beings around her. Thus her attempt to be more than human flies not only in the face of the prevailing definition of woman, but even the concept of what man should try to do. But the community reacts to these two women in much the same way, turning Pecola into a dumping ground for their own feelings of help-lessness, inverting Sula's godlike narcissism into witchcraft. Pecola's mad-ness makes everyone feel sane; Sula's evilness heightens everyone's goodness, thus uniting their communities. Both characters, although one seeks to con-firm and the other to reject the communities' norms, are rendered tragic, as the community uses them to aggrandize itself.

Illuminating the theme of distinctive vision, Morrison weaves the threads of the outlandish, the extraordinary, into the normal fabric of her characters' worlds. Both books begin with an inversion of the truth: in *The Bluest Eye*, the inversion about the beautiful and the true is introduced as the failure of the marigolds to sprout. In *Sula*, the origins of the Bottom is itself an in-version. Even dramatic acts at the center of these complex tales are con-sequences of the waste and horror of inversion. Pecola is raped in spring, the season of love, as the lie at the center of her father's vision of himself overwhelms him, and Eva, preferring infanticide to potential spiritual incest, burns her junkie soldier son to death in an attempt to save his maleness. Her fiery act haunts her generations as she witnesses her daughter's fiery acci-dental death and is herself threatened with a fire death by her granddaughter Sula. The family is torn asunder, its members' roles inverted, as father rapes daughter, mother kills son, and granddaughter threatens grandmother.

Such disorder can only end in death of the body or spirit. Death, a most natural occurrence in life, is too often summoned before its time as the only resolution to disharmony in these inverted worlds. Counterpointing the natu-ral flow of birth, death, and rebirth, the seasons shift abnormally or have abnormal effects. In *The Bluest Eye*, the natural surge of blood lust in the spring results in rape; in *Sula*, the unnaturally cold fall followed by a warm winter causes the earth to shift, killing many folk of the Bottom. As if re-sponding to the disharmony caused by humankind, Nature goes awry.

The theme of inversion, as well as the structuring of the novel, in fact, is most often reiterated by the seasons, Nature's timing. In *The Bluest Eye*, the novel's structure is defined in terms of the seasons, a natural phenome-non that will not yield to the sentimentality of humankind. Morrison's winters are harsh compositions, her springs inverted melodies of love. In *Sula*, the years as enumerated by man—1921, 1922, and so on—are signifi-cant as they signal an event of consequence and as they juxtapose the view of Sula and the view of her community. Here, too, Nature presents signs, omens that can be read or distorted by the folk, as when the plague of robins in the spring seems to announce Sula's return to the Bottom. Thus each year defines a section of the novel, but only as poised entry or climactic ending to the illumination of the characters' collective actions.

Because Morrison's probings are so relentless, her sounds so authentic, and her appreciation of complexity so profound, we are able to recognize, as do Claudia and Nel, the patterning of beauty and waste in the history of Pecola and Sula and their communities. As a result, *The Bluest Eye* and *Sula* teach us a lesson about the integral relationship between the destructive limits imposed on the black woman and the inversions of truth in this society.

6
Novels for Everyday Use:
_____The Novels of Alice Walker_____

Alice Walker's works are quilts—bits and pieces of used material rescued from oblivion for everyday use. She takes seemingly ragged edges and arranges them into works of functional though terrifying beauty. She has published books of poetry, _Once_ (1968), _Revolutionary Petunias_ (1973); _Good Night Willie Lee, I'll See You in the Morning_ (1979); a book of short stories, _In Love and Trouble, Stories for Black Women_ (1973); a children's book about Langston Hughes; ed. anthology on Zora Neale Hurston (1979); and two novels, _The Third Life of Grange Copeland_ (1970) and _Meridian_ (1976).

The bits and pieces are not random fabric. Like their quilter, they originate in the South. The daughter of a Georgian sharecropper, Walker is the significant black woman novelist of our generation to concentrate on the sensibility of the South as a way of perceiving the perennial conflict between the human spirit and societal patterns. She has long insisted that until the solids and prints of the South are sorted out and stitched into clarity, the relationship in this country between men and women, blacks and whites, will continue in disarray.

As a craftsman, Walker sorts out the throwaways, the seemingly insignificant and hidden pieces of the lives of Southerners, particularly black families, and stitches them into a tapestry of society. Who is to blame for the waste in our lives, she asks? Ourselves? The society that seems at every turn opposed to blossoming? The wrath of God? The question of responsibility for personal action and societal change is one recurrent motif in the complex quilts that Walker makes out of thrifty sentences, knotted questions, tight metaphors, terse sections. Her novels continually stitch a fabric of the everyday violence that is committed against her characters and that they commit upon one another in their search for regeneration, and regeneration is what they as black people desire.

The exploration, then, of the process of personal and social growth out of horror and waste is a motif that characterizes Walker's works. For her, the creativity of the black woman is essential to this process. In her classic essay, "In Our Mothers' Gardens" (1974), Walker asks, "How was the creativity of the black woman kept alive, "when the freedom to read and write . . . sculpt, paint or expand the mind with action, did not not exist." In searching for the means to her own artistic and political freedom, Walker investigates the legacy of the past. To deepen our understanding of the plight of her maternal ancestors, she not only calls upon her own personal history but upon Jean Toomer, who perhaps more than any other writer of the past had focused on the repressed creativity of black women:

> When the poet Jean Toomer walked through the South in the early twenties he discovered a curious thing: Black women whose spirituality was so intense, so deep, so *unconscious* that they were themselves unaware of the richness they held. They stumbled blindly through their lives: creatures so abused and mutilated in body, so dimmed and confused by pain, that they considered themselves unworthy even of hope. In the selfless abstractions their bodies became to the men who used them, they became more than "sexual objects," more even than mere women: they became Saints. Instead of being perceived as whole persons, their bodies became shrines: what was thought to be their minds became temples suitable for worship. These crazy "Saints" stared out at the world wildly like lunatics—or quietly, like suicides and the "God" that was in their gaze was as mute as a great stone.
>
> Who were these "Saints"? These crazy loony women? Some of them without a doubt were our mothers and grandmothers [author's emphasis].[1]

What Walker discovers is that some of these women were not "Saints," but "Artists," "who were driven to a numb and bleeding madness for which there was no release." In contrast to these mute women who were physically and psychologically abused, a few, like Phyllis Wheatley and Nella Larson were preened by black and white society to escape the horror. They, too, suffered, for they struggled in the mire of confused identity and were torn by what Walker calls "contrary instincts." As creative women, however, they struggled to sing even as they were denied the freedom to express their own voice and thus "kept alive, in so many of their ancestors, the *notion of song.*" Still others held onto the creative spark by using daily parts of their lives such as storytelling, singing in church, root working, quilt making, and, as Walker's mother did, their gardens as mediums for their creative expression. The artist Walker describes the impact that one of these everyday art forms had on her:

> For example: in the Smithsonian Institution in Washington, D.C. there hangs a quilt unlike any other in the world. In fanciful, inspired and yet simple and identifiable figures, it portrays the story of the Crucifixion. It is considered rare, beyond price. Though it follows no known pattern of quiltmaking and though it is made of bits and pieces of worthless rags, it is obviously the work of a person of powerful imagination and deep spiritual feeling. Below this quilt I saw a note that says it was made by "An anonymous Black woman in Alabama, a hundred years ago."
>
> If we could locate this "anonymous Black woman from Alabama", she would turn out to be one of our grandmothers, an artist who left her mark in the only materials she could afford, and in the only medium her position in society allowed her to use.[2]

In her search for our mothers' gardens, Walker describes a legacy from which the creativity of the contemporary black woman can flower. To develop further, the black women of her generation must garner wholeness from the bits and pieces of the past and recreate them in their own image. Walker then uses the often unheralded heritage of black women, the creative sparks as well as the history of restrictions, as the foundation of her artistic vision. A feminist, she explores the relationship between this tradition and societal change as crucial to the search for freedom—not only for woman, but for man, the child, the society, the culture, the land.

This theme, though, is never ostentatiously stated in Walker's works. Rather it is revealed through her skillful, often subtle narrative. She is at her best a storyteller. We can feel her delight, sheer delight, in telling stories, in mingling bits and pieces of hard reality and lyrical fantasy. Like a quilter, she is economical; her stories are thrifty; there are no bulges or long stretches of the same material, no waste. Her tales are marvelous themselves, intriguing the imagination with wondrous touches juxtaposed to the mundane; velvet pieces lie comfortably next to the most used flannel. Her craft of words, in fact, becomes a potential model for regeneration. Search for the bits of plain and fancy, the memories of pain and pleasure, and lay them out, examine them, rearrange them, and remake them. The pattern at first may be beautiful only in its terror, but until that terror is faced and explored, precarious contentment may be possible, but not rebirth.

PART I

The Third Life of Grange Copeland:
A Saga of Degeneration and Regeneration

The plot of Alice Walker's first novel, *The Third Life of Grange Copeland*, exposes the pattern of terror over a span of sixty years in the lives of one black family of sharecroppers. Grange Copeland abuses his wife, Margaret, and neglects his son, Brownfield, because he feels himself less than a man in a land where his entire life is indebted to the white boss. As he grows older, he feels trapped by his family, for they hold him to this life. Increasingly he feels guilt because he can neither protect his wife from the white hairy arms of Shipley nor make possible a better life for his son. As he drinks solace from the overflowing breasts and bar of Josie, the local whore, Margaret takes on lovers, reacting to Grange's abuse by abusing herself. When her husband leaves his life of indebtedness for the North, Margaret poisons herself and her young, illegitimate baby.

Deserted by his parents, Brownfield, a young man of sixteen, follows his father's path only to end up working for and sleeping with Josie. While he is employed at the Dew Drop Inn, Brownfield meets and falls in love with Mem, Josie's schoolteacher niece. In love and passion they marry—only to repeat the pattern of depression and abuse Grange and Margaret had already drawn. In spite of Mem's efforts to better her life and the lives of her daughters Daphne, Ornette, and Ruth, Brownfield drags her down. Feeling less than a man, he, too, buries himself in Josie only to lose even her to the father that deserted him.

The pieces, slightly rearranged, remain essentially the same. Walker graphically tells the story of Brownfield and Mem's deterioration. In revenge for his father's rejection, Brownfield kills his newborn albino son, a white baby that looks like his father. In a moment of terrible strength, Mem threatens her husband with a gun and tears his defenses apart. In a clear drunken stupor, after years of mangling guilt and self-hatred, Brownfield murders Mem, leaving his own children, as his father had done before him, to fend for themselves.

Grange, who has returned from the North, takes on the responsibility of raising Ruth, his youngest grandchild, with the same vigor that he had shunned the responsibility of raising his own son. Ruth in her innocence gives Grange a new life. Jealous and angry, the imprisoned Brownfield plots with Josie, Grange's now neglected wife, to wrest the girl from her grandfather. After he leaves jail, Brownfield manages to have a white judge give the custody of the sixteen-year-old Ruth to him, her father but also the man who has killed her mother. Calmly, deliberately, Grange kills his son Brownfield in the court of justice to make life possible for Ruth. Grange, in turn, is shot at his home by the sheriff's men.

That is the plot. The story is marked throughout by the motif of physical and spiritual murder, by suicide and infanticide, by wife beating and killing, set against a background of the horror of racism in the South. The pervasive pattern of this quilt is kin killing.

Why is this novel saturated with murder and violence of all kinds? Isn't Walker substantiating the pervasive myth that black people, particularly black men, are by their very nature violent and that they inflict the full range of their violence on their own blood? Doesn't Grange's neglect of Margaret and Brownfield's abuse of Mem give fuel to the idea that black men hate their women, and doesn't Mem's attack on Brownfield reinforce the covert fear of many black men that black women are always trembling with the desire to castrate them? In fact, doesn't *The Third Life of Grange Copeland* effectively prove the racist myths about Afro-Americans?

It is as if Walker consciously selects all the nasty bits and pieces about black people that they as well as white people believe. Then she examines each bit, lucidly arranges the pieces so we might see the savage nibblings of everyday oppression at the souls of black Southerners.

Of all the savage nibblings of racism, the most poisonous bite is the abnegation of responsibility for one's own soul. The novel, through its juxtaposition of parts, relates the monstrous ramifications that result from blacks believing what society, at every turn, teaches them—that they are not capable of being responsible for their own actions, that white folks are to blame for everything. This abnegation of responsibility is what it means to be a "nigger." All of the bits and pieces of violence in the book are arranged to reiterate this motif—a motif that Grange Copeland in his one true communication with his son Brownfield explores:

> By George, I *know* the danger of putting all the blame on somebody else for the mess you make out of your life. I fell into the trap myself! And I'm bound to believe that that's the way the white folks can corrupt you even when you done held up before. 'Cause when they got you thinking they're to blame for everything they have you thinking they're some kind of gods! You can't do nothing wrong without them being behind it. You gits just as weak as water, no feeling of doing *nothing* yourself. Then you begins to think up evil and begins to destroy everybody around you, and you blames it on the crackers. *Shit*! Nobody's as powerful as we make them out to be. We got our own *souls*, don't we?[3]

Yet the dilemma for poor black Southerners is not as simple as all that. In every corner of this novel, the reader feels the tight control the white bosses have over the black sharecroppers and how this control, although seemingly focused on a work relationship, fends its way into the relationships between black men, black women, and black children.

Through her graphic description of the Copelands' everyday lives, Walker illuminates a basic strategy of racism. Because it is so obvious, we often forget that the most effective way to control anyone is by confusing his or her sex definition according to the norms of society. The masculine thrust in this society manifests itself in forms of power and acquisition, phantom qualities to which neither Grange nor Brownfield Copeland have access. The female, according to southern norms, should present herself in images of passivity, chastity, and demure beauty and should receive from men the rewards of security, comfort, and respect, rewards that neither Margaret nor Mem Copeland can exhibit. Although physically grown, the black adults in this novel are never treated by the majority culture as men or women or even as boys or girls. They are seen as sexual beings without the human qualities necessary for sex definition, except in purely physical terms.

Because Walker covers three generations of the Copeland family, she is able to show us how consistent and deep-rooted this strategy of racism is. By having one figure, the figure of Grange Copeland, persist throughout this generational span, Walker dramatizes the possibilities of change. Throughout the eleven economical sections of this novel, however, the author refuses to let her readers forget society's insistent, often stolid, attempt to control the psychological as well as the material conditions under which black people struggle. She graphically lays out her patterns by tracing in the first half of the novel the degenerate effects of racism on the Copeland men, women, and children and by demonstrating the process of regeneration in the second half. Two elements, then—the need to accept responsibility for one's life, for self-definition, and the obvious fact that much of it, at least in this time and place, is beyond one's control—form the axis of the novel's cyclical patterns. This novel poses the question: In the grip of physical and psychological oppression, how do you "find a place in you where they can't come?" How do you hold onto self-love?

The obvious answer is to go somewhere else, to go North. That is why, I believe, Walker begins the novel with Brownfield's northern cousins' visit at his backwoods home. That is why we are first shown an escape route based on history. But the North, the promised land, has got its own share-cropping system as the death of Brownfield's northern uncle reveals. Still, the land up North is a dream of hope for the Copeland men, who at least are mobile if nothing else. Grange deserts Margaret to go north where he believes he will escape white people's control. The young Brownfield wants to go north with his cousins.

He wants to go, for the cycle of his father's days are fixed in hopelessness. Walker carefully stitches a square that will be repeated in this quilt, when she describes Grange Copeland's week, every week:

On Monday, suffering from a hangover and the aftereffects of a violent quarrel with his wife the night before, Grange was morose, sullen, reserved, deeply in pain under the hot early morning sun. Margaret was tense and hard, exceedingly nervous. Brownfield moved about the house like a mouse. On Tuesday, Grange was merely quiet. His wife and son began to relax. On Wednesday, as the day stretched out and the cotton rows stretched out even longer, Grange muttered and sighed. He sat outside in the night air longer before going to bed; he would speak of moving away, of going North. He might even try to figure out how much he owed the man who owned the fields. The man who drove the truck and who owned the shack they occupied. But these activities depressed him, and he said things on Wednesday nights that made his wife cry. By Thursday Grange's gloominess reached its peak and he grimaced respectfully, with veiled eyes, at the jokes told by the man who drove the truck. On Thursday nights he stalked the house from room to room and pulled himself up and swung from the rafters of the porch. Brownfield could hear his joints creaking against the sounds of the porch, for the whole porch shook when his father swung. By Friday Grange was so stupefied with the work and the sun he wanted nothing but rest the next two days before it started all over again.

On Saturday afternoon Grange shaved, bathed, put clean overalls and a shirt and took the wagon into town to buy groceries. While he was away his wife washed and straightened her hair. She dressed up and sat, all shining and pretty, in the open door, hoping anxiously for visitors, who never came.

. . . Late Saturday night Grange would come home lurching drunk, threatening to kill his wife and Brownfield, stumbling and shooting off his shotgun. He threatened Margaret and she ran and hid in the woods with Brownfield huddled at her feet. Then Grange would roll out the door and into the yard, crying like a child in big wrenching sobs and rubbing his whole head in the dirt. He would lie there until Sunday morning, when the chickens pecked around him, and the dog sniffed at him and neither his wife nor Brownfield went near him. Brownfield played instead on the other side of the house. Steady on his feet but still ashen by noon, Grange would make his way across the pasture and through the woods, headlong, like a blind man to the Baptist church, where his voice above all the others was raised in song and prayer. Margaret would be there too, Brownfield asleep on the bench beside her. Back home again after church, Grange and Margaret would begin a supper quarrel which launched them into another week just about like the one before.[4]

Although Brownfield had dreamed, had believed, that his life would be different from his father's, twenty years later he finds himself caught in the same square.

> It was a year when endless sunup to sundown work on fifty rich bottom acres of cotton land and a good crop brought them two diseased shoats for winter meat, some dried potatoes and apples from the boss's cellar, and some cast-off clothes for his children from his boss's family. It was the summer that he watched, that he had to teach, his frail five-year old daughter the tricky, dangerous and disgusting business of handmopping the cotton bushes with arsenic to keep off boll weevils. His heart had actually started to hurt him, like an ache in the bones, when he watched her swinging the mop, stumbling over the clumps of hard clay, the hot tin bucket full of arsenic making a bloodied scrape against her small short leg. She stumbled and almost fell with her bucket, so much too large for her, and each time he saw it his stomach flinched. She was drenched with sweat, her tattered dress wringing wet with perspiration and arsenic; her large eyes reddened by the poison. She breathed with difficulty through the deadly smell. At the end of the day she trembled and vomited and looked beaten down like a tiny, asthmatic old lady; but she did not complain to her father, as afraid of him as she was of the white boss who occasionally deigned to drive by with friends to watch the lone little pickaninny, so tired she barely saw them, poisoning his cotton.
>
> That pickaninny was Brownfield's oldest child, Daphne, and that year of awakening roused him not from sleep but from hope that someday she would be a fine lady and carry parasols and wear light silks. That was the year he first saw how his own life was becoming a repetition of his father's. He could not save his children from slavery; they did not even belong to him.
>
> His indebtedness depressed him. Year after year the amount he owed continued to climb. He thought of suicide and never forgot it, even in Mem's arms. He prayed for help, for a caring President, for a listening Jesus. He prayed for a decent job in Mem's arms. But like all prayers sent up from there, it turned into another mouth to feed, another body to enslave to pay his debts. He felt himself destined to become no more than overseer, on the white man's plantation, of his own children.
>
> That was the year he accused Mem of being unfaithful to him, of being used by white men, his oppressors; a charge she tearfully and truthfully denied.[5]

Like his father before him, Brownfield at first dreams of going North, but even these dreams finally die. Imprisoned in his own life, he, like Grange, begins to see his wife as a trap and gives her the blame for this failure. Both Grange and Brownfield know inside themselves that Margaret and Mem are not to blame for the waste in all of their lives. But since they cannot get near the true cause of their poverty, their wives are accessible targets upon whom they can vent their frustration.

The true cause of their misery is the racist sharecropping system. Thus, another figure that appears throughout this novel is the figure of the powerful white boss. Brownfield as a boy is puzzled at how the white man who drove the truck could turn his father into stone, and his young soul is filled with terror of this man who could by his presence alone transform his father into something "that might as well have been a pebble or a post or a piece of dirt, except for the sharp bitter odor of something whose source was forcibly contained in flesh." As if harnassed by that childhood memory, the man Brownfield does not even maintain his father's stony silence (in its way a form of protest) before the boss; for "he had no faith that any other place would be better," or that he could do anything about the restrictions on his life.

Again the bits and pieces are slightly different, but the pattern remains the same. It would be madness, Grange and Brownfield know, to bite the hands that feed them. It would be madness to believe that they could defeat the sharecropping system. Knowing what their society denies, that they are men, the Copeland males try to free themselves first by working hard. When this fails, they hate themselves for their impotence, their inability to fulfill the masculine urge to power. Finally, they use whatever power they feel they have, primarily their power over their women, in a destructive way. Their masculine urge is blocked and therefore turns in on itself. So Grange abandons his family and goes North where he learns the harshness of invisibility and Brownfield attacks the only vulnerable person available to him, his lovely wife.

The lives of their wives, too, follow a similar pattern. Both Grange and Brownfield marry sweet, virginal women who had had a girlhood brimming with hope. Margaret and Mem at first believe, as do their husbands, that through love, kindness, fortitude, orderliness, they can create and maintain a good home. The wives are programmed to be demure and pretty, to plant flowers, be chaste. If they do these things well, they believe they will receive their just rewards. Because they believe in the definition of woman dictated by society, neither Margaret nor Mem are emotionally prepared to understand, far less cope with, their reality. So when the rewards do not materialize, when in fact they are abused and blamed by their men for their failure, the wives believe they have not done their part well.

Depressed by their condition, Margaret and Grange fight as if to preserve some part of the feeling of being alive. Crushed by the deadly labor of her days, and the neglect of her husband, the kind, submissive Margaret becomes "a wild woman looking for frivolous things, her heart's good times in the transient embrace of strangers." But in spite of, even because of, her amorous adventures, she believes that she is at fault; she blames herself, without knowing what she can do, for everything, especially for not being able to deliver her husband from his lot in life. So when Grange leaves her, Margaret accepts the responsibility for his failure and the pain of her loss. "She was curled up in a lonely sort of way, away from her child, as if she had spent the last moments on her knees."

Brownfield chooses a wife, much like his memories of his mother before she became a wild woman. When he first meets her, Mem is a schoolteacher, plump and quiet, with demure slant eyes. In the beginning of their relationship she tries to teach Brownfield how to read; he feels she can help him to rise above his ignorance. At first she is for him a lady, "the pinnacle of his achievement in extricating himself from evil and the devil and aligning himself with love." In the fashion of hopeful young men, Brownfield tells Mem on their wedding day: "We ain't always going to be stuck down here, honey, don't you worry." She believes him. Walker tells us about their initial happiness, so we can see that they were originally passionate and hopeful. But unceasing labor with no chance of reward is a cesspool they cannot get out of:

> Over the years they reached, what they would have called when they were married, an impossible and *unbelievable* decline. Brownfield beat his once lovely wife now, regularly, because it made him feel, briefly, good. Every Saturday night he beat her, trying to pin the blame for his failure on her by imprinting it on her face; and she, inevitably, repaid him by becoming a haggard automatous witch, beside whom even Josie looked well-preserved.[6]

Mem's response to her husband's abuse is not quite the same as Margaret's. She begins to deteriorate; she loses the school speech and the plump beauty that Brownfield had coveted. "Her mildness became stupor; then her stupor became horror, desolation and at last hatred." Framed by the children she bears, those who live and the many who die, she wants to find a door but cannot. For most of the novel, we feel that she cannot act because she does not believe or understand what is happening to her. Eventually, she becomes so desperate that she must believe in, fight for, something. The goal she puts all her energy into, as do many women, is a house, a house that can become a home, because it is stable and comfortable and commands respect.

The woman's desire to have a house becomes the major conflict in the

battle between the Copelands, as it had been between the Boyces in Paule
Marshall's *Browngirl, Brownstones*. It is not the acquisition of a house that
causes the conflict so much as the fact that the women in question find the
inner as well as the financial resources to accomplish their goal while the
men cannot. For their part, both Mem and Silla become so desperate in their
struggle for survival and stability, in their engulfing desire to have a home
for their children, that they are willing to confront their men and if necessary move them out of the way. In one bold stroke, they are forced to redefine their definition of themselves as women, thus inevitably assaulting
the men's definition of themselves as men.

Mem's determination to have a house and Brownfield's fear of her growing strength is the dominant motif in Part Five. The way in which Walker
puts this section of her quilt together is a good illustration of her particular
style. Part Five is divided into six short sections of tiny bits and slightly
larger pieces, as the quilter sorts out the appropriate fabric for her pattern.
Two pieces of fabric recur in this section: Brownfield's fear that Mem will
find a house for *his* family when he could not and his equally powerful fear
of his white boss, Captain Davis.

A lover of succinct units, Walker customarily begins each of her sections
with a tight topical sentence. In this case, the first sentence of Part Five is:
"Brownfield did not believe Mem would be able to find a house." The *be
able* is crucial here, for Brownfield tells us that he *could not* find a decent
house "the first and only time he had looked for one." One page long,
chapter 19 shows the relationship between Brownfield's sense of his own
inadequacy and the abuse Mem receives from him for her initiative.

Chapter 20, about one and one-half pages long, presents the other recurring piece of fabric in this square. Brownfield receives an "offer" from his
white boss, Captain Davis, to go to work for his son, Mr. J. L., who of
course would provide the sharecroppers with a shack. Brownfield does not
want to work for Mr. J. L. but he cannot refuse Captain Davis: "Yassur,"
he said finally, hypnotized by the old man standing in the sun. One is reminded of Brownfield's first childhood experience of the white boss as the
man who turned his father into stone.

Brownfield must of course tell his family that he has committed them to
work for Mr. J. L. In the slightly longer chapter 21, he forces his weakness
on them. This scene has as its focus the image of Brownfield as an animal.
In being unable to refuse Captain Davis's offer, his wife and her children
perceive him as less than human. In fact, Brownfield himself acts as if he,
too, has come to believe this:

> When her father was eating Ornette could not think of him as anything
> but a hog.[7]

A shiver of revulsion ran through his wife. "He's just like a old dog. . . ."[8]

"I ain't never going to marry nobody like him," Daphne swore to herself, watching the big ugly hands that smell always of cows and sour milk."[9]

"I already told you," she (Mem) said, "you ain't dragging me and these children through no more pigpens."[10]

"If I was a man," she (Mem) thought, frowning later, scrubbing the dishes, "if I was a man I'd give every man in sight and that I ever met up with a beating, maybe even chop up a few with my knife, they so pig-headed and mean."[11]

The following chapter (chapter 22) is built on the tension caused by Mem's ability to find a house and Brownfield's refusal to accept that fact. Even after years of abuse, Mem apologizes to Brownfield for her accomplishment. In spite of what it has cost her, she stills holds onto society's definition of Brownfield's and her respective roles:

"I'm real sorry about it, Brownfield," said Mem, whose decision to let him be man of the house for nine years had cost her and him nine years of unrelenting misery. He had never admitted to her that he couldn't read well enough to sign a lease and she had been content to let him keep that small grain of pride. But now he was old and sick beyond his years and she had grown old and evil, wishing every day he'd just fall down and die. *Her generosity had shackled them both* [author's emphasis].[12]

Although apologetic, Mem is determined to make the move, not so much for herself but for her children who, she believes, must now be her primary concern. Brownfield may also want to believe this, but he is caught between his wife's determination and the wishes of his white boss. Walker emphasizes this internal conflict of his by placing two very short chapters next to each other. In chapter 23, Captain Davis informs Brownfield that the deal has been made. As usual, the white man treats Brownfield like chattel; as usual, Brownfield, although angry, responds obsequiously. In chapter 24, Mem informs Brownfield that not only has she got a house in town, but she has got a job there, too. In the space of one day, Brownfield's manhood has been insulted by his white boss and threatened, he feels, by his wife.

Brownfield is too afraid of his boss to challenge him in any way. So it is not surprising that in chapter 25, the climactic chapter of Part Five, he takes out his feelings of anger on Mem. In contrast to the rest of this section, this chapter is long, divided into two smaller parts: Brownfield's customary assault on Mem and her reaction. Strengthened by her recent victories, as well as by her determination to save her children, Mem's response is not her usual one:

> "You going to move where I says move, you hear me?" Brownfield yelled at her giving her a kick in the side with his foot. "We going to move to Mr. J. L.'s place or we ain't going nowhere at all!"[13]

> "Open your eyes!" Mem's voice was as even as a dammed-up river. Slowly he stopped turning and opened his eyes, squinting them stickily to keep out the light. Mem was propped up against the wall on her side of the bed, holding a shotgun. At first he saw only the handle, smooth and black and big, close to his head like that. One of Mem's long wrinkled fingers pressed against the trigger. He made a jump, half toward her, half away from her. He felt a sharp jab on his body down below the covers, the shooting pain caused him to wince and thrash on the bed.[14]

The struggle between the determined Mem and the frustrated Brownfield that is dramatized in this section is a compression of the dominant motifs of Part Five. In the bed that has caused her such agony, Mem recites the long year of hardship and abuse that she has endured because of their insistence on holding onto the South's definition of woman and of man. But Brownfield does not hear her words; he only sees himself as trapped between his crazy wife and his all powerful boss. In an attempt to get Mem to put down the gun, to get her to accept her state, he threatens her with his ultimate authority, the big white boss, Captain Davis. Mem's insistence that Captain Davis does not see Brownfield or any other black man as a man, and her refusal to accept Brownfield's abnegation of his responsibility for his acts, assaults Brownfield's definition of himself.

Walker risks hell and brimstone when she stitches together the remnant of a black man's lost pride with the new cloth of a black woman's mounting strength. Although Brownfield has consistently brutalized Mem, to maintain his sense of his own manhood, her attack on him might be seen by many as a betrayal, as unwomanly. At the core of this scene is Mem's acknowledgment that Brownfield responds only to acts of a brutal castrating nature, that this is the way he relates to her and her children, and that this mode of action is the only one that commands his respect. And why shouldn't it be? All of his life he has had to respect the white boss's power and the castrating mode is the form that this power usually takes. Mem finally resorts to his mode of behavior in order to get her husband to act for his own benefit. In the process she challenges the double standard by which society judges her and her husband's actions. In order to help him regain his manhood, in order to force him to break away from the belief that says he is not responsible for his actions, she forcefully shows him his lack of manliness. Most importantly, she insists on being treated as a human being rather than an object. Mem has no choice. If she does not challenge Brownfield's definition of masculinity, she and her children will not survive. She must use her own skills, even if Brownfield feels diminished by them, or her entire family will be destroyed.

Part Five ends with Brownfield's "Yes ma'am." For the moment, Mem has begun to gather strength. But Part Six reminds us that she must maintain and develop her strength even further by redefining herself as a woman, for it begins, "Brownfield lay in wait for Mem's weakness." Brownfield's reaction to Mem's attempt to make him take responsibility for his actions reveals the source of his definition of himself as a man. Although his life is more human in their new house, he is willing to destroy it all, since he has not made it possible in the same way that white men are able to:

> "I done waited a long time for you to come down, Missy," he said when he came home, reeking of alcohol for the first time in almost three years. "This is what I can afford and this is what you going to have to make do with. . . .
> "You was going to have your house, straight and narrow and painted and scrubbed, like white folks. You was going to do this, you was going to do that. Shit," he said, "you thought I fucked you 'cause I wanted it? Josie better than you ever been. Your trouble is you just never learned how not to git pregnant. How long did you think you could keep going with your belly full of childrens?"[15]

Brownfield has been lying in wait for the weakness of the womb. Ironically, Mem's strength, her having children, is also her weakness. Just as the male's inescapable need to take on the forms of masculinity in his society turns him against himself, so the female's distinctive quality, her womb, turns in on her. Even the indomitable strength that flows from motherhood undermines the definition of what her society tells her a woman should be. To save her children Mem must become aggressive rather than passive; she must be willing to create security and comfort for herself rather than have it delivered to her, and she must be willing to do it alone, without a man.

Having taken responsibility for her own actions, Mem's definition of herself as a woman changes. Although she is temporarily defeated by Brownfield, she intends to get well, leave her husband, and hold on to the life she had a glimpse of in her moment of strength. No longer does she plant flowers; no longer will she be the demure wife. But since Brownfield's definition of himself as a man does not change, is in fact assaulted by Mem's redefinition of herself, he must destroy her. No wonder that he kills her with the very gun with which she first proclaimed her recent independence. Tormented by his inability to change, he cannot allow her to. Mem dies violently as did Margaret, a generation before. Like Margaret, "her bloody repose had struck them instantly as a grotesque attitude of profound inevitable rest."

So much for the stereotypical strong black woman who conquers all. Walker calls up the other side of that strong black woman image, as well as the reason why it is emphasized so much in American mythology. That image is necessary because so many black women, like Margaret and Mem, have been crushed and utterly destroyed precisely because they are black and because they are women. Their blood flushes the Copeland quilt with the colors of violent death and with the threads of degeneration. Now the children are left to fend for themselves in a world that will naturally abuse them. Margaret and Mem are examples of Walker's first group of black women, the most abused of the abused. It is important to note that these women are destroyed when they begin to gather strength or to rebel.

Just as their husbands are defeated by an internal as well as an external disorder, both Margaret and Mem are destroyed not only by their husbands and their society but by their "stupid belief that kindness can convert the enemy." They have tried to be women in the traditional southern Christian sense. Margaret tries to rouse Grange to concern by abusing herself, and Mem believes that she can give her own strength and its rewards to Brownfield. Even as they rebel, these women lived and died with their husbands, rather than themselves, foremost on their minds. Brownfield, musing in his jail cell, fixes Mem's essence for us:

> If she had been able to maintain her dominance over him perhaps she would not stand now so finished, a miniature statue, in his mind, but her inherent weakness, covered over momentarily by the wretched muscular hag, had made her ashamed of her own seeming strength.[16]

Fat Josie is the one black woman in the book who is neither virginal nor wifely, and who does not depend on a man for her financial needs. In fact, her profession feeds on the despair of the men around her. But although she is economically independent, Josie's life is another example of the way in which the society's definition of woman and man conflict with one another.

At age sixteen, Josie becomes a whore because her father rejects her when she becomes pregnant. In an attempt to win back his love, she uses her body, her only asset, to earn money to buy him gifts. Walker's presentation of young Josie's fall as a woman is marked by her analysis of the difference between society's view of her lovers, who are encouraged to express their manhood through their sexuality, and its punishment of the woman who succumbs to them. Although the young Josie is expected to attract men through her body, she is also expected to be a virgin. This irresoluble conflict is powerfully dramatized when the very pregnant Josie literally falls at the birthday party she gives for her father:

> Her mother stood outside the ringed pack of men, how many of them knowledgeable of her daughter's swollen body she did not know, crying. The tears and the moans of the continually repentant were hers, as if she had caused the first love-making between her daughter and her daughter's teen-age beau, and the scarcely disguised rape of her child that followed from everyone else. Such were her cries that the men, as if caught standing naked, were embarrassed and they stooped, still in the ring of the pack, to lift up the frightened girl, whose whiskied mind had cleared and who now lay like an exhausted, overturned pregnant turtle underneath her father's foot. He pressed his foot into her shoulder and dared them to touch her. It seemed to them that Josie's stomach moved and they were afraid of their guilt suddenly falling on the floor before them wailing out their names . . . "let'er be," growled her father. "I hear she can do tricks on her back like that."[17]

Forevermore, in her dreams that foot continues to ride Josie. Her father, whom she calls a witch, continues to haunt her. The relish with which Josie does her job, then, is partly based on the anger towards her father, laced with an insatiable desire for the love she never had. Throughout the novel she is presented as a devouring cat, voracious and sly.

Ironically, Josie the whore is also the continuing thread between the various generations of Copelands. As a whore, she is indispensable to the system of sexual and racial conflict within which the frustrated husbands and the anguished wives suffer. She is both Grange and Brownfield's whore, later Grange's wife, and finally Brownfield's co-conspirator. She feels Margaret has taken Grange away from her and hates her. Since Mem is her niece, it is through her that Brownfield meets the budding schoolgirl. But Josie is also angry at Mem for taking Brownfield away from her and feels obligated to wreck his marriage. Years later, Josie the fat whore is replaced by Ruth Copeland, her innocent step-granddaughter, in Grange's affections. If there is any character in this novel who finds her way into the innards of all the principals, it is Josie. She is the destructive link between father and son. But in using men, Josie is used by them for purposes beyond her single-minded desires. Continually living her father's judgment of her, Josie "felt somehow she was the biggest curse in her life and that it was her fate to be an everlasting blunderer into misery."

So much for the stereotypical loose black woman who gets what she wants through sex. Unlike the stereotype, Josie not only fucks but feels. Although men are encouraged by the society to release their frustrated manhood through her and others like her, she is seen by them as an object to be used rather than a person. In the final analysis she gets nothing but sleepless nights and perhaps a long, wasted life. She sleeps with Grange and then Brownfield, conspires against their wives and children, and finally helps to cause the death of Grange, the man she wants. She ends up as Brownfield had begun, "mumbling what had become for her the answer to everything: 'the white folks is the cause of everything.' "

The children of this book, though, do not conceive of white folks as the source of *their* problems. Trapped by their youth, they are the ones most affected by their parents' patterns of self-hatred. In their prepubescent period they catch this disease by abhorring their parents, and then as their sexuality begins to manifest itself and they become parents, that hatred turns in on them. The children of Brownfield—Daphne, Ornette, and Ruth—delineate the complexity of cause and effect. Who is responsible for their condition— their parents, who are themselves victims, or are their parents victims only because they allow themselves to be? At what point does their responsibility end and the inevitability of fate begin. Is their condition fixed, no matter what they do? Is it too much to ask of a human being that he or she keep the spirit intact in spite of a barrage of attacks?

Throughout the novel, children give us their feeling, their sense of confusion about their parents and the life imposed on them. In fact, one way in which the novel could be described is as a two-child narrative. The first narrative flows through the consciousness of the child Brownfield who never really grows up, who never believes he is a man. The second is concerned with the child Ruth as she struggles into adulthood. At the center of each of these narratives is the figure of Grange, first as the daddy that Brownfield never had and then as the transformed Grange who is Ruth's father in place of her real daddy, Brownfield. Certainly the child point of view is recurrent in Walker's quilting, particularly the point of view of the child who feels rejected or abandoned by the father.

In this novel, as in her short stories, Walker puts much emphasis on the relationship between the fathers and their children. Since the society in which the children develop their sense of values is patriarchal, their belief in their own worth is very much related to the ways their fathers judge them.

Thus the novel begins with a child, Brownfield, as he tries to understand his father. At ten he loves his mother; already his father seems unreachable. Grange hardly ever talks to his son, hardly ever admits his existence. Practically the only words we hear him speak directly to Brownfield when he is a child are, "I ought to throw you down the goddam well," words Brownfield tells us that are not spoken in anger but with pity and regret. Of course, Brownfield is too young to understand that Grange sees in his son the continuation of a life of slavery. Unable to free his son from bondage, he regrets that Brownfield exists at all.

At ten, Brownfield gets a headache, like any child would, trying to comprehend his parents' actions. By fifteen, he has given up trying. By now even his mother eludes him, for her attentions are riveted on securing some small, if fleeting, happiness for herself. Enveloped by the depression of their lives, his parents no longer see him. Even when Grange leaves her home forever, he cannot bear to touch Brownfield or acknowledge any feelings of tenderness for him:

> Brownfield pretended to be asleep, though his heart was pounding so loudly he was sure his father would hear it. He saw Grange bend over him to inspect his head and face. He saw him reach down to touch him. He saw his hand stop, just before it reached his cheek. Brownfield was crying silently and wanted his father to touch the tears. He moved toward his father's hand, as if moving unconsciously in his sleep. He saw his father's hand draw back, without touching him. He saw him turn sharply and leave the room. He heard him leave the house. And he knew, even before he realized his father would never be back, that he hated him for everything and always would. And he most hated him because even in private and in the dark and with Brownfield presumably asleep, Grange could not bear to touch his son with his hand.[18]

Forevermore, Brownfield will repeat to himself and to everyone else that Grange was never a daddy to him, as indeed he was not. When Margaret kills herself, the son realizes that even she would prefer to die for the father rather than live for the son.

In tune with his father's despair, Brownfield begins his abuse of his own children when he realizes that he is caught in the same square of life that his father before him had been caught in. So Daphne, his first child, receives love and tenderness from him until he realizes that he cannot free her from a life of slavery. Also, Brownfield himself never grows up, so it is difficult for him to give the love that he never received. He is forever seeking his father's love even as he hates him. The only way that he can resolve that emotional contradiction is in some way to destroy his father.

Many of the characters in this novel waver between an intense love for the father and an equally intense self-hatred engendered by the rejection of the father. The father's rejection of his child is very much related to his view of that child's future as man or woman. So Grange rejects Brownfield because he believes he cannot give his son the qualities of power that will fit the society's definition of a man. Brownfield becomes an abusive father when he realizes he cannot give his daughters the gifts that will allow them to be ladies. Josie's father rejects her because she loses her virginity before marriage and therefore can never, in his eyes, be a lady. The society's definition of a person's worth as man or woman distorts the love between father and child.

In the course of the novel, Walker stitches together squares that grotesquely reveal how dependent the children are on the humaneness or inhumaneness of their father. One of these squares, perhaps more than any other in the book, lays out the damage done to Brownfield by his father, and by his own inability to accept responsibility for his soul. Brownfield tells Josie that his last child, a boy, was white, not real white but an albino baby who looked just like Grange. In his insanity, the figures that have controlled his life—the daddy who rejected him and the white man—seem to mesh in this baby. Brownfield deliberately kills his only son:

> "An' one night when that baby was 'bout three months old, and it was in January and there was ice on the ground, I takes 'im by the arm when he was sleeping, and like putting out the cat I jest set 'im outdoors on the do' steps. Then I turned in and went to sleep. . . . I never slept so soundly before in my life—and when I woke up it was because of her (Mem) moaning and carrying on in front of the fire. She was jest rubbing that baby what wasn't no more then than a block of ice. Dark as he'd *ever* been though, sorta *blue* looking."[19] . .

Brownfield explains his action. He killed his son, his future, because he doesn't believe there is any future. The instinct in all living things to see their offspring as the future is reversed in Brownfield's mind. For him his son is despair not hope: "I jest didn't *feel* like going on over my own baby who didn't have a chance in the world whether I went on over him or no." In Brownfield's twisted mind, his despair, his futility, meshes with his hatred of his father and his hatred of himself, for his father's blood flows through him to his son: "I got sick of keeping up the strain." His act is the essence of self-hatred.

The bereft children of the book—Brownfield, Daphne, Ornette, and Ruth —invent ways of ameliorating their pain. Left with no vessel for their trust and faith or the experience to understand what is happening to them, fantasy, particularly about fatherhood, becomes their outlet. The child Brownfield's persistent daydream, a fantasy that he first has after his northern cousins' visit, lasts for five years. Dreaming this dream becomes his favorite occupation:

> He saw himself grown-up, twenty-one or so, arriving home at sunset in the snow. In this daydream there was always snow. . . . In his day-

dream he pulled up to his house, a stately mansion with cherry-red brick chimneys and matching brick porch and steps, in a long chauffeur-driven car. The chauffeur glided out of the car first and opened the back door, where Brownfield sat puffing on a cigar. Then the chauffeur vanished around the back of the house, where his wife waited for him on the kitchen steps. She was the beloved and very respected cook and had been with the house and the chauffeur and Brownfield's family for many years. Brownfield's wife and children— two children, a girl and a boy—waited anxiously for him just inside the door in the foyer. They jumped all over him, showering him with kisses. While he told his wife of the big deals he'd pushed through that day she fixed him a mint julep. After a splendid dinner, presided over by the cook, dressed in black uniform and white starched cap, he and his wife, their arms around each other, tucked the children in bed and spent the rest of the evening discussing her day (which she had spent walking in her garden), and making love.

There was one thing that was odd about the daydream. The face of Brownfield's wife and that of the cook constantly interchanged. So that his wife was first black and glistening from cooking and then white and powdery to his touch; his dreaming self could not make up its mind. His children's faces were never in focus. He recognized them by their angelic presence alone, two bright spots of warmth; they hovered about calling him "Daddy" endearingly, while he stroked the empty air, assuming it to be their heads.[20]

At age ten, Brownfield's first daughter Daphne calls herself the Copeland Family Secret Keeper and makes her childhood days bearable by telling her younger sisters stories about the good old days when Brownfield had been a good daddy. In the only way she knows how, the older daughter tries to sow in the younger ones the seeds for regeneration. But the memories are not enough; in fact, they help to make Daphne a nervous child:

She tried so hard to retain some love for him, perhaps because of her memories of an earlier time, that she became very nervous.[21]

In spite of her efforts to remain whole, Brownfield's attitudes condition Daphne and her sisters' development. His nickname for the nervous Daphne is "Daffy"; as an adult she would become a mental patient. Ornette, Brownfield's second daughter, who has no memory of her father's tenderness, is jolly and tough by the age of eight. By the age of four, Ruth, the third daughter, tells her father: "You nothing but a sonnabit."

Ruth, who is the focus of the second half of the book, is born at the same time in the midst of degeneration and regeneration. From her birth, Brownfield does not relate to her as a father. Her mother delivers her herself because her father is too drunk to get the midwife; and on the morning that she is born, Grange, her grandfather rather than Brownfield, builds a fire, cooks stew for the weak Mem, and takes care of the older children. He, rather than Brownfield, takes on the responsibility of the father mainly because he feels guilt about his neglect of his own son. Ruth's benevolent father image is, from her very beginnings, the figure of Grange. When Mem is killed, "Ruth alone could not be pried loose from her grandfather's arms." Rather than going North with her mother's father, she insists on that gloomy Christmas Day that she remain with her father's father, an insistence that results in a bond that will transform the oldest and the youngest of the Copelands.

Part One to Part Seven of this quilt continually reiterates the cyclical motifs of spiritual and physical degeneration within the Copeland family, the most bloody motif being Brownfield's murder of his wife in the presence of their children. Given that climactic act, one would expect the hopeless Copeland pattern to continue. But ironically, Brownfield's murder of Mem breaks the pattern, at least for Ruth. Hope creeps into her life when her grandfather, Grange, resolves to be a father to her, as he never was to Brownfield.

From Part Seven through Part Eleven, about one-half of the book, the grandfather and the granddaughter give each other new life. A new pattern evolves as Grange, the impotent, rejecting father, becomes an involved, caring human being, and as the young child Ruth both seeks her identity through her elder and yet helps him to understand his own life.

Certainly a change in texture is one of the vivid differences between the first and the second half of the book. The first half is gray in its desperation, sharp in its bleakness, tense in its rhythm; the second half, although not without intense tensions or murders, has splashes of golden days, some laughter, and much tenderness. At Grange's farm, ambrosia-making days are mellow marathons, spiced with color and tales, as this section of the book reminds us that there is another side to black life in the South. In helping her to grow, Grange gives Ruth a feeling for her peoples' lore, history, and culture. And he teaches her to dance, for in the dance is the essence of black folk:

> They danced best when they danced alone. And dancing taught Ruth she had a body. And she could see that her grandfather had one too and she could respect what he was able to do with it. Grange taught her untaught history through his dance; she glimpsed a homeland she had never known and felt the pattering of the drum. Dancing was a warm electricity that stretched, connecting them with other dancers moving across the seas. Through her grandfather's old and beautifully

supple limbs she learned how marvelous was the grace with which she moved.[22]

Almost always, though, even in the good times, there is an undercurrent of questioning in Walker's stories. In this novel, this undercurrent is the difficult questions that children ask themselves about their ancestors and the world, the answers to which are often complicated and terrifying. Just as the ten-year-old Brownfield wondered about his parents' actions, his father's silence, and his mother's submission, Ruth wonders about her father and mother, about her grandfather's relationship with her father, and about her grandfather's life before she came to live with him. Brownfield could not penetrate his father's stony silence, and Grange gives Ruth not so much answers but the knowledge he has learned in his three, maybe four, lives.

In the talks Grange and Ruth have about themselves and the world, teacher becomes student and student, teacher. At first, precisely because he loves her, Grange wants Ruth to understand the nature of her world, how white folk have caused the misery of black folk and how she must learn to hate them, better still, to avoid them:

> "They are evil."
> "They are blue-eyed devils."
> "They are your natural enemy."
> "Stay away from them hypocrites or they will destroy you."
> "They killed your father and your mother."[23]

But Ruth will not believe that white folks killed her mother, for she had seen her father do it. More than anything, she wants to understand how her father got the way he did: "Ruth turned her father's image over and over in her mind as if he was a great conundrum." In her innocence she knows what she had seen but cannot comprehend its complexity. Can she forgive her father for killing her mother even if she understands that he is a victim? Grange wants his granddaughter to understand the world's cruelty so she might survive and she, at her young age, wants to know love so she can be whole.

Even as Grange instructs his granddaughter in the ways of the cruel world and in understanding how racism affects her life, Ruth's love and her questions lead him into self-examination and reflection. Through the clarity of the third life she gives him, his first and second lives begin to make some sense:

> "The white folks hated me and I hated myself until I started hating them in return and loving myself. Then I tried just loving me, and then you, and ignoring them much as I could. You're special to me be-

cause you're a part of me; a part of me I didn't even used to want. I want you to go on a long time, have a heap of children. Let them know what you made me see, that it ain't no use in seeing at all, if you don't see *straight*!"[24]

Old patterns may be torn apart, but they leave old scraps, untied ends. The structure of the first half of the novel is continuous with the second, for although the pattern of Ruth and Grange's life together is new, Brownfield's pattern remains the same. The chapters in which Grange and Ruth are transforming their souls set next to sections in which Brownfield, along with Josie, Grange's now-neglected wife, conspire against his family. Like a ragged but necessary piece of cloth, Brownfield's schemes to hurt Grange interrupt the new pattern. Although Grange feels that "his one duty in the world was (is) to prepare Ruth for some great and herculean task, some magnificent and deadly struggle, some harsh and foreboding reality, . . . It maddened Brownfield that his father should presume to try to raise his child."

What Brownfield feels most in prison is aloneness, the same intense aloneness he had experienced when his parents deserted him. The repetition of this traumatic feeling verifies for him the reasons behind his tragic life:

> "Yeah," said Brownfield, "you'd think more peoples would think about how they ain't got no more say about what goes on with 'em than a pair of shoes or a little black piece of writing in a newspaper that con't move no matter what it stands for. How come we the only ones that knowed we was men?"[25]

The *was* is important, for certainly Brownfield no longer looks at himself as a man but as a force, a force to bring down his father, for Grange's neglect of him represents to Brownfield his father's inability to preserve his own humanity and defend it from the all powerful white man. Brownfield so intensely hates himself that he must hate the one who gave him, if nothing else, existence.

When he leaves prison, nine years of aloneness later, he is clear about what he wants to accomplish in his worthless life. He intends to take Ruth away from his father. He intends to continue the pattern of kin killing. His strategy in pursuing his goal reveals his essence; at his center is the need to be destructive because he feels sorry that he exists at all. More complex than mere self-hatred, his self-pity verifies his own total involvement with himself while denying him any capacity for regeneration.

In the last section of the novel, it is almost as if we are at its beginning. In pursuing his goal, Brownfield confronts his father, only to find that Grange is finally capable of relating to him as a father. In giving his son the sum of the wisdom he had acquired in his three lives, Grange tries to transform the old pattern. In admitting to his son grave errors, the old man insists that Brownfield be a man, that he take some responsibility for his life:

> "I'm talking to you, Brownfield," said Grange, "and most of what I'm saying is *you got to hold tight a place in you where they con't come.* You can't take this young girl here and make her wish she was dead just to git back at some white folks that you don't even *know.* We keep killing ourselves for peoples that don't even mean nothing *to* us!"[26]

But Brownfield is no longer a receptive ten-year-old; his soul has hardened into a changeless stump, for he so hates and pities himself that he cannot reach out to others. In his one meeting with his daughter Ruth, he reveals his inability to change. Although he feels some grief and guilt about the pain he has inflicted on his family, he is unwilling to allow his daughter her life. When Ruth says, "If you love me leave me alone!" he exclaims: "No, I can't do that. I'm a *man*. And a *man's* got to have *some* thing of his own." Brownfield's concept of love is based on his definition of manhood that he has learned from the white folks, the acquisition and the possession of things.

Ruth's innocence, though, does have some impact on Brownfield. It causes him to think about what love might be. He is surprised that "Ruth still ran toward something. This annoyed Brownfield. What did she see in the world that made her even want to grow up?" For a brief moment he sees himself as a human being capable of loving and being loved. But he cannot sustain that moment, for his soul has accepted the fixed nature of reality as he has known it—"The changelessness was now all he had—. . . . He must continue hard as he had begun." Brownfield continues hard, lives the old pattern out until the quilt of kin killing is completed. When he succeeds in having a white judge give Ruth to him, he feels he has triumphed over his father. He has kept the saga of degeneration intact. In effect, he becomes like the white man whom he hates.

But new patterns exist as well. In the one grand, ironic twist of the novel, the new mode of existence takes on the tactics of the old to survive. Grange kills Brownfield, his only son, in the presence of the white judge, to save Ruth, his granddaughter. All of the elements of the novel coexist in this act. Grange kills his son—the old pattern of kin killing; but he spills the blood of his son to save his granddaughter, the new pattern. He does this not only to thwart the power of the white folks that Brownfield has enlisted but also in the very presence of the white judge, the symbol of racist disorder in the South. Grange knows, of course, that in sacrificing his unregenerative son to his granddaughter in the presence of white law, he has also killed himself. The sheriff's men follow him to the home he had vowed to hold inviolate against the white man and there they kill him, gun in hand. He dies as if he were a motherless child, "rocking himself in his own arms to a final sleep."

We know that Grange in killing his son reverted to the old pattern so Ruth, the new pattern, might not just survive but live. His act is based on his vision of what life could be for her:

> And still, in all her living there must be joy, laughter, contentment in being a woman; someday there must be happiness in enjoying a man, and children. Each day must be spent, in a sense, apart from any other; on each day there would be sun and cheerfulness or rain and sorrow or quiet contemplation of life. Each day must be past, present and future, with dancing and wine-making and drinking and as few regrets as possible. Her future must be the day she lived in. . . . Survival was not everything. *He* had survived. But to survive *whole* was what he wanted for Ruth.[27]

We know, too, that Grange's bloody act is necessary if Ruth is to survive whole. It is as if he uses up all of the cloth intended for the old quilt so a new one might be started. Yet in killing Brownfield and himself, Grange has left Ruth alone. Can she avoid the unworkable definition of woman by which her mother and her grandmother were trapped? Must she confront and be defeated by the self-hatred of a man like her father, a self-hatred that is a result of the racist fabric of the South? Can she, as a woman survive whole?

Because Alice Walker's quilt is so compactly made, we cannot help but ask questions that go beyond the Copelands's specific history. To what extent can individuals within a deranged society overcome the destructive male and female definitions that are thrust upon them? What is the relationship between responsibility for one's actions and the hardships that society imposes on us? Does the knowledge of the attacks on the spirit suffice in our struggle to hold onto our souls? The paradox of death-giving-life remains. We wonder if it must be so.

PART II

Meridian: The Quest of Wholeness

Alice Walker's second novel, *Meridian*, proceeds naturally from *The Life of Grange Copeland*, as the younger generation from the older. Again, her illumination of the potent process of personal change unifies the bits and pieces of southern life as was true in *The Third Life of Grange Copeland*. Again, the image of the child as a continuing possibility is one of the dominant motifs of the novel. Again, the black woman's struggle is focal to the novel's theme. Whereas Walker's first novel is deep in its penetrating concentration on the Copeland family, her second novel expands the theme of a procession of generations to the history of black people in the South up to a peak period in the 1960s. Like Paule Marshall's second novel, *The Chosen Place, The Timeless People*, Walker's *Meridian* is more inclusive in its scope without losing the depth that comes from concentration on one family at a particular time.

In this story so like a quilt of complex and multiple pieces, Walker gives a vibrant and connected personal and collective history rather than a generalized and sterilized account of the sixties. Meridian, the major character in this book, is a black woman who allows "an idea—no matter where it came from—to penetrate her life." The question that permeates this book and her life is the nature of social change and its relationship to the past and the future, a question that is at the crux of the Civil Rights Movement. In other words, what does one take from the past, which is still often present, to create a new future? What does one throw away? This question is specific in the novel to black people in America as they acknowledge a past born in suffering, fed by violence, conditioned by powerlessness—as they try to create a future, a glowing child out of the past. Again, the intersection of degeneration and regeneration coexist in this novel as they did in *The Third Life of Grange Copeland*. How do you change the pattern of life without destroying what is essential and good in it? Grange Copeland's last bloody act, killing his son to save his granddaughter, haunts *Meridian*. At the vortex of the book's many strivings is the relationship of violence to change. Is it necessary, is it right, or when is it right to kill to create? Meridian wonders if she could kill for the revolution? And if she could, would she be destroying what she is trying to recreate—the respect and love for life in a society that does not value the lives of every one of its children.

Although both Walker novels examine the impact that social conditions have on personal growth, the difference between the two is as instructive as the similarities. The emphasis in *The Third Life of Grange Copeland* is on the necessity to accept responsibility for one's life, despite overwhelming social restrictions. *Meridian*, however, specifically explores the relationship between a movement for social change and the personal growth of its participants. *Meridian* is a novel of ideas, for Walker attempts to let its constructive elements develop out of her analysis of the history and philosophy of southern blacks, who were the foundation of that movement.

The difference in emphasis between the first novel and the second is crystallized in the difference between their major female characters. Certainly Mem is one of those pitiful "Saints" that Walker described in her essay, *In Our Mothers' Gardens*, for the author's presentation of this character emphasizes the oppression that eventually destroys her rather than the creative sparks that would enable her to hold on. The major character of the novel *Meridian*, on the other hand, is a combination of the three types of black women that Walker described in her essay. Like some of her ancestors, Meridian is a "looney" woman who is physically and psychologically abused. Like Phyllis Wheatley and Nella Larsen, she is given the opportunity to become an exception, torn by "contrary instincts." And like the contemporary black woman that Walker envisions, Meridian becomes an artist by "expanding her mind with action." In *Meridian*, Walker encompassed the past, the present, and the future as her major character uses her heritage to change her society, even as she seeks her own expression. Meridian then is not only a character, she is the embodiment of the novel's major concept, the relationship between personal and social change.

However, since a novel by definition contains its elements through a causal flow of events, one major problem that a writer who is primarily interested in analyzing an idea must solve is the way in which this flow will take place. That is, the structure of the novel must be organic to the ideas, lest the peculiar ability of the novel, its ability to put flesh on ideas, give way to abstract analysis. This problem is heightened when the major idea to be embodied is how the characteristics of an individual human personality relate to the political, racial, and sexual composition of a peculiar society. As a novelist, Walker cannot give us the entire history of this country, in relation to the issues of sexism and racism. As a writer who clearly prefers succinct units, she would not want to. She attempted to solve this problem by using each of the major elements—its plot movement, its motifs, and its characters—as an economic way of adding specific dimensions to the novel.

Walker's presentation of the plot is integrally connected to *Meridian's* central idea. The novel tells us the story of a black woman, Meridian Hill, who grows up in a small southern town. After an early marriage and divorce, she gives up her child to accept a scholarship to go to college. While in college she is an active participant in the Civil Rights Movement. She falls in love with Truman Held, a black political activist from the North with whom she becomes pregnant. But when he becomes involved with Lynne Rabinowitz, a Jewish civil rights volunteer, Meridian aborts her baby and has her tubes tied. Truman later marries Lynne, and the relationship between these three characters continue even when the Civil Rights Movement gives way to the idea of violent revolution. Meridian, who is not sure that she can kill, even for the revolution, continues to practice nonviolent resistance in a world that no longer respects it. In her quest for an answer to her questions about the relationship between violence and change, she undergoes a personal transformation and is able to absolve her feelings of guilt about her inability to be a mother. At the end of her quest, she passes on her struggle for wholeness to Truman Held.

This may be an outline of the major events that take place in *Meridian*.

But it certainly is not the movement of the plot. The sequence of events is itself a visual representation of the term *revolution*, the moving backward to move forward beyond the point at which you began. Walker indicated her order of presentation to the reader by calling the book and her major character *Meridian* (an echo of Jean Toomer's prophetic poem about America, *The Blue Meridian*) and by listing at the beginning of the novel its many definitions, the essence of which is an ascending series of intersecting circles toward the highest point.

The first chapter, which follows this list, acts as an additional clue to the reader, for it is an outline of the sequence of events as they will be presented in the rest of the novel. Even its name, "The Last Return," suggests the movement backward to move forward. In spite of the fact that the book will largely be occupied with the period of the sixties, it begins with a point of time in the seventies when the strategy of nonviolent resistance is no longer widespread, at a time when the dramatic demonstrations of the Civil Rights Movement have ended, and when most observers would say that the Movement was over. Thus we are invited to see the sixties as history. But the character Meridian continues to practice nonviolent resistance as if it were the present rather than the past. Because of her intransigence, this initial scene invites us to question her sanity or at least the inappropriateness of her actions in time and space.

Because of its tone of slapstick absurdity and its lightning quick movement, this chapter may be a shock to some readers as Walker presents to us the major ideas of her novel in the form of American rituals elongated to such an extent that the absurdity of their essence leaves us unsettled.

It begins with Truman's return to the South. He is seeking Meridian and finds her in Chicokema, a small southern town whose Indian heritage lingers only in its name. Dominated now by white interests, the town is distinguished by its possession of an old army tank bought during the sixties to defend its white inhabitants against outside agitators. In more recent times, its folksy nature has been enhanced by "Marilene O'Shay, One of the Twelve Human Wonders of the World: Dead for Twenty-five Years Preserved in Lifelike Condition." This dead white woman is presented as the epitome of Southern Womanhood—"A Goddess," "Obedient," "Pure," "Beautiful." In fact, her husband had killed her when she betrayed him with another man. According to the mores of the South, he had been forgiven by family, as well as the civil authorities, because his victim was female and had committed adultery. Piling necromancy upon murder, he has put together this replica of his wife to make money. In keeping with the reality of southern life, "Blacks cannot look at this human wonder, except on their day, Thursday."

With biting surreal stitches, Walker satirizes the lavish trademarks of the South—the white woman protected, indeed mummified, by the sanctimonious rhetoric of her society, but losing even these questionable privileges when she exercises any sexual freedom; the white man using even his kin to make money; the sanctification of violence in the pursuit of protection; the exclusion of black folk even from participating in the lunatic activities of their white counterparts; the preservation of Indian culture in the town's name even after the conquering race has extinguished the original natives. The absurdity of this scene is heightened even more when we watch Meridian employ the weapon of nonviolent resistance against the fortress of values that protects Marilene O'Shay's preserved dead body.

When Truman finally talks to Meridian, our curiosity is further piqued by his assertion that Meridian, who after all lives in America, owns nothing, that she becomes paralyzed from time to time but lives a life of wandering, and that she has "volunteered to suffer." As if daring us to pass judgment on the outmoded and crazy actions of her major character, Walker sardonically smiles at the absurdity of Truman Held, a decidedly nonrevolutionary painter, dressed as he is in a Che Gueverra hairdo and Mao jacket, but whose objections to Meridian's life-style sound practical and sane. The contrast between Truman's pragmatic point of view and Meridian's insistent struggle is crucial to this book's inquiries.

> Truman watched her struggle to regain the use of her body.
> "I grieve in a different way," he said.
> "I know," Meridian panted.
> "What do you know?"
> "I know you grieve by running away. By pretending you were never there."
> "When things are finished it is best to leave."
> "And pretend they were never started?"
> "Yes."
> "But that's not possible."[28]

Both Truman and Meridian grieve for the Movement, for the idea that nonviolent action could change the "absurdity" of the Chicokemas all over the South. They grieve in their own way for the collective action that thrived for a few years in the blood-soiled soil of the South, only to be replaced by an equally blood-soaked idea. The new idea was to change their personal lives, as well as the history of the South. Walker juxtaposes the intransigence of Chicokema to the intransigence of Meridian, while juxtaposing that critical moment in the North when the action of nonviolent protest is replaced by the idea of violent revolution.

Mentally we find ourselves no longer listening to Truman and Meridian talk in a small southern town in the seventies. Now we are sitting with Meridian, her best friend Anne-Marion, and other black students in a New York apartment ten years before Truman will make his last return to the

South. Meridian is confronted with the question, "Will you kill for the Revolution?" A positive answer to this query meant entry into or exclusion from many circles. We know that this scene occurred among black students and intellectuals after the major protest demonstrations had caused so many of them to wonder if allowing oneself to be hit on the head accomplished very much, if volunteering to suffer was not a weak posture. We have lived this history. Meridian's essential characteristic, her resistance to accepting the easy solution, her refusal to speak the word without living its meaning, reminds us of the many who succumbed to group pressure whether or not they believed what they were saying, and the many who simply would not, could not, say yes without fussing, fighting, questioning.

In creating this historic scene, Walker announces her major motifs. What Meridian is held by is her past: the children of the South; the face of her mother in church as she insists that Meridian say the word and be saved; her father's perennial conversation about the plight of the Indian; the collective soul of her people that she hears in the music. Held by these memories, she cannot say yes. Instead, she goes back to the South to remain close to the people until she can make such a decision and mean it. She resolves to stay within the action of the sixties until she can formulate effective action for the seventies.

The New York scene together with our experience in Chicokema formulate the basic idea of the book: the way in which political movements affect personal lives and how personal lives are the marrow of political movements. So it follows logically that we find ourselves back in Chicokema as Truman and Meridian speak of their personal past; of Lynne, Truman's wife; of his dead child Camara; of Anne-Marion, Meridian's former best friend who still writes her letters of anger and fury. In fusing dream, action, counterpuntal times and places, and motifs and characters, Walker shows us the way to her pattern, a pattern that will be arranged and rearranged as we question Meridian's way of life, her persistent identification of her body with her soul, her past with her present. This insistence is both her strength and her weakness:

> *Truman:* I've never understood your illness, the paralysis, the breaking down . . . the way you can face a tank with absoluted calm one minute and the next be unable to move. I always think of you as so strong, but look at you.[29]

As an embryo, the first chapter presents us with the whole, the rest of the novel will give flesh to Meridian's essence. The book is an unraveling of the reasons for her continued nonviolent protest, as conditioned by her own past and the history of the South, a history that has led her to ask impossible questions and pursue seemingly absurd paths. But Walker's sensitive analysis of Meridian's essence will not move forward in a straight line. As in "The Last Return," Part I, called "Meridian," will travel from a time in the seventies backward beyond Meridian's specific existence to the lives of her mother, grandmother, and great grandmother and then forward to the seventies. Like Part I, the section called "Truman Held," will also proceed from a time outside the drama of the sixties and will go backward only to move forward to the time of the book's beginning. Only the last section, "Ending," will move forward beyond Chicokema to that moment when Meridian resolves her quest. But even then Truman replaces her in the search for wholeness, a search with which the novel begins.

By using time as a circular movement rather than a chronological pattern, the author is able to connect the parts of Meridian's life that are related to her cultural milieu, as well as to the nature of the Civil Rights Movement of which she is a part. Thus the particular events that Walker chooses in her dramatization of the reasons for Meridian's recalcitrance are not random. They are selected with great care so we might understand the influences on Meridian as she develops from a sensitive black girl-child who feels her mother's undercurrents of frustration and resentment to a pensive woman who continues despite the apparent ineffectiveness of the act to use her body to manifest her spirit. In describing Meridian's development, Walker is always taking great pains to heighten those threads that run throughout the life of any young girl in Meridian's particular cultural milieu: the discovery of sex as sordid, the importance of a man in one's life, the possibility of vision, the emptiness of a premature marriage, the hassles of "happy motherhood." Because of the author's resistance to the easy road of generalization, Meridian's development is most specific, but because her pattern exists within the history and culture of her milieu, it intersects with the rhythmic patterns of many others. So when Walker describes Meridian's relationship with Eddie, her boyfriend who would later become her husband, she is not only analyzing Meridian's personal history but prevailing cultural patterns as well:

> Being with him did a number of things for her. Mainly, it saved her from the strain of responding to other boys or even noting the whole category of Men. This was worth a great deal, because she was afraid of men . . . and was always afraid until she was taken under the wing of whoever wandered across her defenses to become—in a remarkably quick time—her lover. This, then was probably what sex meant to her; not pleasure but a sanctuary in which her mind was freed of any consideration for all the other males in the universe who might want anything of her. It was resting from pursuit.
>
> Once in her "sanctuary," she could, as it were look out at the male world with something approaching equanimity, even charity; even friendship. For she could make male friends only when she was sexu-

ally involved with a lover who was always near—if only in the way the new male friends thought of her as "So-an-So's girl."[30]

What we begin to see as we examine Walker's quilting is that personal history is an index to cultural history. Her analysis of Meridian's lapse into an early marriage is as much history as the Saxon students' reaction to President Kennedy's funeral on television, an event that involved millions of viewers. Throughout the novel, our quilter composes patterns of events that show how personal and public history mesh to make up the collective process of the sixties. At every turn, every personal experience is selected for emphasis as an indication of the personal history of many, and every public experience is given personal dimensions.

Just as the movement of the plot embodies the concept of revolution in relation to Meridian's personal and social milieu, so recurrent motifs add a philosophical dimension to the novel. As if they were the common threads of a fabric, Walker uses the images of black children and black mothers, of nature and music, and of the relationship between the body and the spirit in every chapter. She is able to use them as compressed images precisely because she concentrates on one of them in each chapter as indicated by its title.

At the crux of all of these images is the concept of animism, which Walker insists is one thing that Afro-Americans have retained of their African heritage. She defines *animism* as "a belief that makes it possible to view all creation as living, as inhabited by spirit"[31] and in so doing stresses the oneness of the natural and the human world. In *Meridian*, Walker attributes this view of the world not only to Afro-Americans but to the original inhabitants of America, the Native Americans. They are, throughout the novel, the motif that stands for the union of the land and its people. So the book begins with a quotation from Black Elk, which fuses the dominant motifs of the novel, even as it presents the dream of Nature's wholeness destroyed:

> I did not know then how much was ended. When I look back now I can still see the butchered women and children lying and scattered all along the crooked gulch as plain as when I saw them with eyes still young. And I can see that something else died there in the bloody mud, and was buried in the blizzard. A People's dream died there. It was a beautiful dream . . . the nation's hope is broken and scattered. There is no center any longer, and the sacred tree is dead.[32]

As this quotation suggests, Walker uses motifs that illuminate the concepts of wholeness and fragmentation, both of which are related not only to Meridian's past and present but also to the Civil Rights Movement. By describing her quest as a search for health, Meridian insists that to be whole, there must be a unity of body and mind. So, too, the central action of the Civil Rights Movement, body resistance to manifest the protest of the mind, attempted to demonstrate this oneness. The process of putting one's body on the line, of resisting oppression without inflicting violence, is crucial to the Movement's spirit—the desire to change without destroying, to maintain the integration of body and spirit, to resist separation and alienation.

The image in the novel that most fully expresses the concept of animism is *music*, which for Walker is itself "the unselfconscious sense of collective oneness."[33] The texture of *Meridian* is punctuated with the expression of the people's collective soul, music—not only music as an individual or extraordinary accomplishment, but as a part of the flow of life at parties, in church, while working, with friends and lovers, in civil rights demonstrations, in social action. In practically every chapter of the book, there is some music, except in the "Lynne" chapters where Walker seems consciously to replace it with art and poetry. Even the book's structure is naturally based on music. Like a circular rhythmic pattern, short chapters follow long ones, creating syncopated beats. There are starts and stops within every chapter, melodious outpourings, and dissonant sharps. Meridian, as the character who is at the foundation of the book's structure, articulates her most important doubts and revelation in images of music:

> Meridian alone was holding onto something the others had let go. If not completely, then partially—by their words today, their deeds tomorrow. But what none of them seemed to understand was that she felt herself to be, not holding onto something from the past, but *held*— by something in the past: by the memory of old black men in the South, who caught, by surprise in the eye of a camera never shifted their position but looked directly by; by the sight of young girls singing in a country choir, their hair shining with brushings and grease, their voices the voices of angels. When she was transformed in church, it was always by the purity of the singers' souls, which she could actually *hear* the purity that lifted their songs like a flight of doves above her music-drunken head. If they committed murder—and to her even revolutionary murder was murder—*what would the music be like*? She had once jokingly asked Anne-Marion to imagine the Mafia as a singing group.[34]

The emphasis on music in the novel is of course partially based on its central position in black culture. But Walker does not merely rest on this often stated truism, for she shows us that the reason why music is so central to the culture is because it is the deepest connective between the creative force in human beings and nature itself. Through the makings of music, nature is renewed despite man's attacks on it, just as the ripped out tongue of the slave Louvenia becomes the seeds for Sojourner, the Music Tree, the most beautiful magnolia tree in the land.

Meridian's quest reaches its peak when she understands that "it is the song of the people, transformed by the experience of each generation that holds them together, and if any part of it is lost the people suffer and are without soul." It is significant that this realization of Meridian's takes place within the context of social change, as the people come together to honor and remember one of their sons who had struggled for their collective freedom.

> There was a reason for the ceremony she had witnessed in the church. And, as she pursued this reason in her thoughts, it came to her. The people in this church were saying to the red-eyed man that his son had not died for nothing, and that if his son should come again they would protect his life with their own. "Look," they were saying, "we are slow to awaken to the notion that we are only as other women and men, and even slow to move in anger, but we are gathering ourselves to fight for and protect what your son fought for on behalf of us. If you will let us weave your story and your son's life and death into what we already know—into the songs, the sermons, the "brother and sister"—we will soon be so angry we cannot help but move. Understand this, they were saying, "the church (and Meridian knew they did not mean simply "church" as in Baptist, Methodist or what not, but rather communal spirit, togetherness, righteous convergence), "the music, the form of worship that has always sustained us, the kind of ritual you share with us, there are the ways to transformation that we know. We want to take this with us as far as we can."[35]

In this small country church, Meridian sees the totality of experiences that the Civil Rights Movement had been for black folk. As they have always done, the folk have incorporated into their ritual the history of the movement, outward signs that indicate the depth of their experience, the measure of their transformation. So the words of the old songs have changed: the minister speaks in a voice like Martin Luther King about the politics of the nation rather than the omnipotence of God; the traditional painting of Jesus is replaced by a painting of an angered black man called B. B. with sword. The music, the music rises, incorporating all, articulating that which cannot be articulated, manifesting the continuing constancy of the entire tradition.

It is through the black ritual of constancy and change that Meridian comes to know that "she would kill, before she allowed anyone to murder the man's son again," for she realizes that in this hallowed setting, the contemplation of murder would receive the incredible spiritual work necessary to transform it into righteousness. Her realization not only frees her, it gives her health. Her body and spirit are fused in this moment of vision, a moment in which she is no longer apart, no longer alone, but part of a whole that fuses the personal, the political, the spiritual. Such a vision, rooted in ritual, is given only to those who would pass through the terror of conflict to see that the life of all is their life and that their life is the life of all.

The section called "Camara" answers the question Meridian had asked in the first chapter, "The Last Return": "If they committed murder—and to her even revolutionary murder was murder—what would the music be like?" In the ritual, the forces of conservatism and revolution and constancy and change join hands, as the essence of the heritage of black people, the music that articulates their history, is affected by secular and spiritual changes in the present.

Just as the image of music connects the motifs of wholeness that Walker uses throughout the novel, so the concept of guilt encompasses the motifs of fragmentation. Because as Black Elk put it, "the sacred tree is dead," because the mind and the body, the land and its people, are separated from each other; natural basic human relationships are poisoned by the thorns of guilt. Throughout the novel, the relationship between mother and child, man and woman, are distorted by the inability of society to see all life as sacred.

The wondrous fragility of life is compressed into the faces of the many black children, who like mist appear and reappear through the book. Their melodic faces connect the bits and pieces of the South's complexity. What all of these children have in common is the precariousness of their existence. They may be aborted before they even have a chance to live; they may be given away; they may be assaulted or killed. Like The Wild Child, they may be motherless children, or like the child-mother in "Ending," they may be children who kill their own children. Alongside their tentative child bodies stand the seemingly substantial figures of black mothers buttressed by the monumental myth of black motherhood, a myth that is based on the true stories of sacrifice black mothers had had to commit for their children. Walker chronicled the history of the mothers, and their history in turn organizes her analysis of the southern milieu. The history, then, of black Southerners is an essential piece of fabric in this quilt but not as dates of battles or even the accomplishment of singular important black figures but as the natural process of generation and regeneration inherent in all forms of life.

Ironically, however, Walker suggested that the fruits of this struggle may not only be strength or even extraordinary accomplishment but guilt; that we cannot reap the benefits of strength unless we acknowledge the limitations of guilt. Throughout the book we are reminded that the sense of shame develops in the living, not necessarily because they have done something wrong, but also because they know, feel, that others have given up their lives for them. As a hated people living in a land opposed to their regeneration, blacks by their very existence elicited monumental suffering and sacrifices from each other. At the peak of this sacrificial hierarchy stands the relationship between the parent and child, the paradox of life-giving guilt. In giving life to children who were both unwanted and unappreciated by society, Walker's mothers also had to give up much of their own lives to sustain their children's. The children know they survive only because their parents committed acts of extraordinary suffering. In the novel, the relationship among Meridian, her mother, and her maternal ancestors is the major, although not the only, extension through which the motif of guilt is explored:

> Meridian found, when she was not preoccupied with the Movement that her thoughts turned with regularity and necessity to her mother, on whose account she endured wave after wave of an almost primeval guilt. She imagined her mother in church, in which she had invested all that was still energetic in her life, praying for her daughter's soul, and yet, having no concern, no understanding of her daughter's *life* whatsoever; but Meridian did not condemn her for this. Away from her mother, Meridian thought of her as Black Motherhood personified, and of that great institution she was in terrible awe, comprehending as she did the horror, the narrowing of perspective, for mother and for child, it had invariably meant.[36]

Meridian feels that her mother is truly great because she "had persisted in bringing them all (the children, the husband, the family, the race) to a point beyond where she, in her mother's place, her grandmother's place, her great-grandmother's place, would have stopped." Along with life, then, the children receive from their ancestors a heritage of sacrifice and suffering, a heritage that they feel they cannot always maintain.

Since life demands such extraordinary sacrifices, sex, which is its cause, is rife with danger, particularly for the women. Throughout the novel, the role that sex plays in the development of girl-children into women and boy-children into men is at best static, at worst tragic. The body as sensual is almost always problematic. Often too late the girls realize that it is through the fecundity of their bodies their lives can be limited or even ruined. The only worth they find in themselves much of their early life is to make their bodies appealing to men, only to find that the fruits of that appeal come to them before they have even realized who they are:

> For all their bodies assertion, the girls moved protected in a dream. A dream that had little to do with the real boys galloping past them. For they did not perceive them clearly but as they might become in a different world from the one they lived in.[37]

Like the seventeen-year-old Meridian, many girls are dropouts from high school, divorced wives, and young mothers; like her husband, Eddie, many of the men are destined always to be boys, "fetching and carrying, courteously awaiting orders from someone above." Or if they resist, as many would in the civil rights demonstrations, they might be pummeled, kicked, or even killed in their attempt to hold onto their spirit. Given the precariousness of life, the body, as the means through which one's life may be ruined or taken away, is almost always "malingering," its usefulness maintained only through the strict tenets of the Baptist Church, lest everything be lost.

Just as the body can become the tomb of the mind, the mind's anguish can diminish the body, for these two entities are not separate but one. Violence to one is violence to the other. Mental states, particularly the flaccid bubble of guilt, induce dreams and hallucinations, visions that in turn affect the body. The guilt that Meridian feels in not living up to her mother's expectations about motherhood is expressed first in her recurring dream of death and then in her neglect of her own body, later in her "blue spells," in her temporary loss of sight, and finally in her occasional bouts with paralysis. Her body state reveals her spirit, just as the act of nonviolent resistance expresses the spiritual position of the demonstrators.

The thorns of guilt are woven not only into the fabric of Meridian's life but into the heritage of black people as well. That heritage contains within it the quality of powerlessness as well as strength. Thus many would erase aspects of their history from their memory even before they would understand them. In the novel, Walker uses the story of the tree Sojourner to amplify this point. Legend has it that this tree was planted on the ripped-out tongue of the slave storyteller Louvenia:

> Louvenia's tongue was clipped out at the root. Choking on blood, she saw her tongue grounded under the heel of Master Saxon. Mutely, she pleaded for it, because she knew the curse of her native land. Without one's tongue in one's mouth or in a special spot of one's own choosing, the singer in one's soul was lost forever, to grunt and snort through eternity like a pig.
>
> Louvenia's was kicked toward her in a hail of sand. It was like a thick pink rose petal, bloody at the root. In her own cabin she smoked it until it was as soft and pliable as leather. On a certain day, when the sun turned briefly black, she buried it under a scrawny magnolia tree on the Saxon plantation.
>
> Even before her death, forty years later the tree had outgrown all the others around it. Other slaves believed it possessed magic. They claimed the tree could talk, make music, was sacred to birds and possessed the power to obscure vision. Once in its branches, a hiding slave could not be seen.[38]

Louvenia's tragedy is transformed, through the process of Nature, into beauty, for although the Sojourner stands as a reminder of brutal slavery, it stands nevertheless resplendent in its flowering. That the tree is the only thing Meridian's fellow students would destroy in their first social protest at Saxon College illustrates how little they understand and accept their heritage, one of suffering as well as resistance. Although cut to the ground, years later the tree would begin to grow, its tiny sprouts a message of hope.

Like the mystery of the Sojourner, the Civil Rights Movement would transform the agony of black existence into a measure of its persistence. By using the technique of nonviolent resistance, the movement changed the quality of powerlessness into a powerful weapon of protest without doing violence to the spirit. In "volunteering to suffer," the participants of this social revolution confronted the totality of black people's heritage—the strength, the wisdom, and the shame. By insisting that all creation is inhabited by the spirit, the movement harkened back not to a Western Christian tradition, which its enemies also embraced, but to a deeper source, the African concept of animism.

The pervasive feelings of guilt as well as its cause, the philosophical perception of the universe as fragmented, are countered by the attempts of the person Meridian and by a social force, the Civil Rights Movement, to seek wholeness. Meridian is able to pursue her quest, is able to understand the necessity for it because she has been intensely affected by the Movement, and paradoxically, that thrust for social change existed precisely because persons like Meridian, who made it up, came from a tradition that saw creation as one, as inhabited with spirit. The truth that Meridian learns through her quest, the message that she passes unto Truman, at the end of the novel, fuses the motifs of guilt and animism:

> there is water in the world for us
> brought by our friends
> through the rock of mother and god
> vanishes into sand
> and we, cast out alone
> to heal
> and re-create
> ourselves
>
> i want to put an end to guilt
> i want to put an end to shame
> whatever you have done my sister
> (my brother)
> know i wish to forgive you
> love you

it is not the crystal stone
of our innocence
that circles us
not the tooth of our purity
that bites bloody our hearts.[39]

Just as the movement of the plot is a symbol of revolution and the motifs of the novel reiterate the concepts of wholeness and fragmentation, so the characters add another dimension to the novel. The relationship between Meridian Hill, a black woman, Truman Held, a black man, and Lynne Rabinowitz, a white woman, set as it is within the context of a social revolution, is an exploration of the ways in which sexism and racism have affected the people of America. In addition, Walker's analysis of their personal lives indicates why the black woman, the black man, and the white woman were major actors in the Civil Rights Movement.

The units of this novel are in themselves a graph of their relationship. The novel is divided into three parts in which a mind-voice directs the flow of thought and action: "Meridian," which flows through the past and present consciousness of Meridian; "Truman Held," which is dominated by the mind-voice of his wife, Lynne, as well as by his own; and "Ending" in which the voices of Truman and Meridian play with and against one another.

Lest we see these characters primarily as types, however, Walker emphasizes their individuality by introducing other characters who are similar to Meridian, Truman, and Lynne, yet who react differently to similar situations. The most important of these is Anne-Marion, for she persists throughout the novel. Like Meridian she is black and intelligent and is involved in the Civil Rights Movement. She and Meridian are best friends in college and share many political activities. But although Meridian is always groping for meaning, even to the point of illness, Anne-Marion is confident, practical, unquestioning. Meridian is compelled to seek the answer to the dilemma of human beings' injustice to each other, but Anne-Marion is content with being the victor rather than the victim. Throughout the novel, her voice and Meridian's will counterpoint each other. Similarly, other black men like Tommy Odds, and white women like Margaret, will help define Truman and Lynne's particular personalities as well as extend the meaning of their struggle. The novel's characters, major and minor, intersect with each other and are a part of but yet distinct from each other. In unison they all illuminate Meridian's search for wholeness, for their particular actions are alternatives to her distinctly difficult quest. Eventually all of their paths lead back to her, as well as to the ideas that penetrate her existence, the questions that lie unanswered at the core of the movement for human justice.

Why does Walker choose Meridian, a lower-middle-class, southern black woman who could have escaped from her modest condition to be the character compelled to pursue this difficult although illuminating quest? The novel supplies us with the author's reasons, for they are as significant as Meridian's quest.

Meridian's own traditions allow her to be that pilgrim. As a black woman, her antecedents, by their very existence, were deviants of the society—female in that they had breasts, vaginas, and wombs but nonwomen according to the mores of American society, which defined women as nonworkers, asexual, and fair. From Meridian's own personal ancestors, her great-grandmother who had literally starved herself to death to sustain her children, to her racial ancestors, women like Harriet Tubman and Sojourner Truth, Meridian's legacy from the past embodies the idea of personal suffering for a greater good. Within that tradition ". . . black women were always imitating Harriet Tubman escaping to become something unheard of. . . . Outrageous, if even in a more conventional way black women struck out for the unknown." Often that striking out took the form of steadfast devotion to a goal for which one suffered in the ascent to the top, like Langston Hughes's "Mother" whose life "wasn't no crystal staircase," but one of arduous climbing and climbing for the welfare of her children.

Yet black women had not only struck out for the unknown in the territory of suffering for they, as deviants, also sought bodily pleasure, that particular form of ecstasy denied to women in American culture. Clearly, Feather Mae, Meridian's outrageous great-grandmother, had also struck out for the unknown—the pleasure, the ecstasy of the body, she experienced in Indian religion. In either version of the quest, the note is one of unconventionality. Deviants at birth, black women could more easily assume the efficacy of the unknown, test forbidden waters, than other American women who were believed to be normal.

That, however, is not the whole story, for the deviant in any society pays a price, the price of uncertainty, the denial of their experience as valid. So even as black women struck out for the unknown or suffered for a goal, they did so often because they had no choice. Their "extreme purity of life was compelled by necessity" so when they could choose, they naturally chose the norm, sometimes with a vengeance that underscored their long years of suffering. Buttressed by the knowledge that the abysm of hardship was one-half step behind them, many of them galloped to security, girded their loins, starched their homes, and swallowed wholesale the feminine mythology from which they had been excluded. Often they found, like Meridian's mother, that they had exchanged sheer hardship for sheer frustration. Before they *knew* their lives were not their own; later they believed if they improved themselves they would have life, only to find that they were no longer trapped by being outside the norm but by being inside it. Applauded as strong, assailed by the weight of frustration, these women felt themselves caught between the heroism of their past and the mundane boredom of their existence. In both cases, either without or within the norm, the common denominator in their lives was their role as mother. Whether they were slave-women for whom "freedom meant that they could keep their own children," or women like Mrs. Hill who could declare, "I have six children, though I never wanted to have any and I have raised everyone myself," the ones for whom these women sacrificed their lives were their children.

Through Meridian's experiences, Walker examines one of the society's major contradictions about black women. The primary role to which they have been assigned and for which they are perpetually praised is also, para-doxically, the means by which they are cut off from life. Since, in principle, society places motherhood on a pedestal, while, in reality, it rejects indi-vidual mothers as human beings with needs and desires, mothers must both love their role as they are penalized for it. True for all mothers, this double-edged dilemma is heightened for black women because society does not value their children. As they are praised for being mothers, they are also damned as baby machines who spew out their products indiscriminately upon the society.

It is no wonder that Meridian, a sensitive girl-child who understands she had shattered her mother's emerging self, would break the pattern by giving her own child away not only because she wants to go to college (and of course mothers are not permitted there), but also because she knows she will do to her own son as her mother had done to her—poison his growth with thorns of guilt. "When she gave him away, she did so with a light heart. She did not look back, believing that she had saved a small person's life." But in keeping with the long tradition that preceded her, Meridian cannot forget her child as Gwendolyn Brooks' "mother" cannot forget her abor-tions. Meridian's quest is certainly intensified by the search for her child in the faces of all the young children she encounters in the book. Her guilt about her inability to live up to the standard of motherhood that had gone before her shatters her health and propels her on the search for salvation.

Her college years are filled with abortive attempts to give some part of herself as a mother. The first is her encounter with The Wild Child, "a young girl who had managed to live without parents, relatives or friends for all of her thirteen years." Meridian's reaction to this child when she first sees her is the beginning of a pattern in her life:

> The day Meridian saw The Wild Child she withdrew to her room in the honors house for a long time. When the other students looked into her room they were surprised to see her lying like a corpse on the floor beside her bed, eyes closed and hands limp at her sides. While lying there she did not respond to anything; not the call to lunch, not the phone, nothing.[40]

Meridian captures The Wild Child and tries to civilize her only to have her killed by a speeder as she tries to escape. Despite her first failure, Meridian is compelled to try again. Her abortive attempt at motherhood is repeated in her encounter with Anne, the young girl she had called to join her in a Civil Rights demonstration but whose screams Meridian believes she heard in one of the cells after they were arrested. The climax of her abortive mother syndrome is the abortion she must have after Truman Held sleeps with her once and leaves her for Lynne. Ironically, Truman leaves Meridian because he finds out that she had been married, had had a child, and had given it away. "Yet had she approached him on the street dragging her child with her by the hand he would never have glanced at her." But Meridian does not know this. Believing that she cannot sustain motherhood beyond conception and giving birth, she gives it up. She has her tubes tied, an act that intensifies rather than eradicates her guilt.

Meridian is caught between her own tradition, her own personal desire to become a mother, and the fact that motherhood seems to cut her off from the possibilities of life and love. Paradoxically, it is this contradiction that precipitates her quest. In her pilgrimage toward wholeness, she becomes a mother not in the biological sense but in her insistence on nurturing life rather than destroying it. Her philosophical stance is symbolized in the novel by the actions of nonviolent resistance that she commits for the sake of the children in "Ending." By enlarging the concept of motherhood, she is able to absolve her guilt about her inability to live up to the society's standards. She passes on this struggle, the struggle to defend life to Truman, so he, too, may understand that all life is sacred.

Through Meridian's conflicts with society's concept of motherhood, Walker also explores the effects that this view has on the relationship between black men and women. At the core of society's criticism—that all black women are good for is having babies—festers the slightly hidden accusation that they are driven by sexual impulses they cannot control. The criticism of their continuous fecundity is in reality a judgment upon their promiscuity. Yet being a sexual partner to a man, preferably one man, is all society expects of them. No serious attention is given to the development of their minds or imagination, since all girls, particularly black girls, will grow up to be mothers. This line of reasoning is held tautly in place even as society presents sex as sordid.

Due to the ambivalence surrounding sex and its result, motherhood, Meridian's community never instructs her about it. On the one hand, she is told to "keep your panties up and your dress down," and on the other hand, her entire worth as she grows older resides in her ability to get a boyfriend and keep him. Her first sexual experiences, then, take place within the realm of secrecy and sordidness. As a result, Meridian realizes that what was expected of her in sex was not love or mutual affection but "giving in." But "as much as she wanted to—her body, that is—never had any intention of *giving in*. She was suspicious of pleasure. She might approach it, might gaze on it with longing but retreat was inevitable." Since sexual pleasure becomes associated in her mind with giving in rather than sharing, she cannot experience it, for the urge to self-protection is even more instinctive than body pleasure. Yet Meridian knows that her worth is determined by her position as "so-and-so's girlfriend," so she indulges in it.

Sex, as the act of "giving in" for the woman and conquering for the man, characterizes Meridian's relationship with men in this novel. Her deepest involvement with a man, her friendship with Truman Held, develops from a sexual game-play into a truly intense and complex sharing, but only after sex and the possibility of children have been eliminated from it. The nature of their friendship is anticipated by the mystical experience Meridian shares with her father in the Sacred Serpent burial grounds, a sharing that gives them a tangible connection to the past as well as the sensation of body ecstasy.

Meridian's spiritual communion with her father is exceptional, however, for she soon discovers that the men she meets believe it their duty or right to conquer her body. Whether they are the hot-blooded lovers of her teen-age years, or professionals like the doctor who punctuates her abortion with the exclamation, "I could tie your tubes if you'll let me in on some of all this extracurricular activity," their stance is always the same. Nor does their age or intellectual development make any difference in their approach to her. Mr. Raymonds, the old university professor for whom Meridian works during her college years, spends much of his time chasing her around his desk in spite of the fact that he is "very emotional about protecting the virtue of black women from white men."

This old-fashioned "race man" is a foil for Truman Held, an activist and artist in the Civil Rights Movement. As a black man who is consciously struggling for social change, we would think that he should not need, like Eddie, to conquer women. Meridian first meets him when she goes to volunteer for the movement and their relationship initially forms in the crucible of the struggle for social justice:

> Within minutes they had been beaten inside, where the sheriff and his deputies waited to finish them. And she realized why Truman was limping. When the sheriff grabbed her by the hair and someone else began punching her and kicking her in the back, she did not even scream, except very intensely in her own mind, and the scream was Truman's name. And what she meant by it was not even that she was in love with him: What she meant by it was that they were at a time and a place in History that forced the trivial to fall away—and they were absolutely together.[41]

Truman seems to Meridian "unlike any other black man she had known. He was a man who fought against obstacles, a man who could become anything, a man whose words were unintelligible without considerable thought." This was in contrast to her husband, Eddie, who "she thought would always be a boy," and "who was not interested in education but in finishing school." Here certainly is a man, we would think, who has the sensitivity, the desire, to know Meridian, a man who would appreciate her spirit, as well as her body. But although Truman may struggle with Meridian for social change, he is primarily interested in sleeping with her.

It is especially significant that during her pilgrimage, Meridian does not relate to Truman or any other man in a sexual way. Left unresolved in the novel is the way in which men and women may be able creatively to relate to each other if they are sexually involved. Rather Walker provides us with some reasons why such a union is difficult to achieve, for her analysis of Truman's character is set within the context of his understanding of his own heritage as filtered through his relationship with women.

Truman's view of the opposite sex, which is prevalent, reveals the fragmentation that society fosters between men and women. On the one hand, Truman is conditioned to pursue women, but on the other hand, he reveres virginity. Because he is an intellectual as well as a man, he expects his mate to be worldly as well as virginal—that is, to be a woman who is well-to-do enough to know the world without having to endure its hard knocks. The veneer of the world must be there without its messy experiences. Thus he can tell Meridian that the reason why he is interested in the white exchange students is "because they read the New York Times." His wife must be knowledgeable although not sullied; she can be romantically idealistic because she has not had to deal with reality; thus she will admire him as a hero.

Such requirements cannot be met by most southern black women, who, like Meridian, grew up in the confines of a small community in which the women were governed only by the laws of survival and the necessities of motherhood. Because these black women had to be heroic for generations, they would be more informed by reality and less likely to be carried away by waves of adoration. Certainly not as mobile as black men, their provincial background, as well as their contact with sex (reality for a woman), would make them unsuitable for men like Truman who, day-by-day, expected more from life.

The fluid contradiction that Truman and many other black intellectuals like him faced was that the people they sought to save were too narrow, too ordinary, too provincial, for them to live with. As black, he is also seen by American society as a deviant, for in contrast to the prevailing definition that a man is worldly, powerful, and clever, the black man is seen in terms of his penis and his propensity to violence. Truman, however, is a thinker, an activist, an artist, who not only rejects society's definition of him but the lot in life it assigns him. One way in which he can transform the world's definition of him is by being as unlike Afro-American men as he can be, while being the epitome of the group—hence his continuous mouthing of the French language, his playing on the thrill that his blackness, his difference, evokes in liberal whites. It is as if Truman falls in love with his deviancy in society because it makes him exceptional when that uniqueness can be cast in a positive or at least a glamourous glow rather than in the stark light of racism. He does not want to be white, nor does he want to be like ordinary black men. Hence he rejects aspects of black culture like religion (which he calls fanatical) and black women because he wants, as any man would, "a woman perfect in the eyes of the world," a woman who would be the measure of his own worth. He wants to be seen as an exception, as heroic, as the conquering prince, as a man.

Although Truman shares political struggle with Meridian, as black men always have with black women, he wants a woman who knows less than he about reality, a woman who can see him as a prince.

> At times she [Meridian] thought of herself as an adventurer. It thrilled her to think she belonged to the people who produced Harriet Tubman, the only American woman who'd led troops in battle.
> But Truman, alas, did not want a general beside him. He did not want a woman, who tried, however encumbered by guilts, and fears and remorse, to claim her own life. She knew Truman would have liked her better as she had been as Eddie's wife for all that he admired the flash of her face across a picket line—an attractive woman, but asleep.[42]

He leaves her for Lynne who has had the time to read everything, the leisure to be idealistic, and the training to adore him, for Lynne sees her role not as claiming her own life but his life as her own.

Paradoxically, Truman and Meridian both see themselves as exceptional, Meridian because she does not measure up to the standards of her tradition and Truman because he cannot accept much of his tradition. Until their discomfort with themselves is eased, they cannot love each other. Appropriately in the novel, it is left to Lynne in her irrepressible way to describe their emotional condition without really understanding it:

> What's between you is everything that could have happened and didn't because you were both scared to death of each other, you knew. Not your *average* black man and woman, of course who accept each other as natural, but people like you and Truman who have to keep analyzing each other's problems.[43]

Truman Held's section in the novel is primarily concerned with his un-raveling of the effects of sexism and racism upon him. Because he does marry Lynne, he grows increasingly aware of his own discomfort with him-self, for he is forced to do so by the many challenges America presents to any "deviant" couple. But before he can look at himself, the South rivets his attention on Lynne as white and as woman. The chapter "Of Bitches and Wives" is one of the most lucid although complex analyses in the litera-ture of interracial love and marriage. Although Truman is uncomfortable in his relationship with Lynne, he has no context in which to put it until Tommy Odds, one of his friends, loses his arm in a demonstration. Tommy Odds's loss gives him vision: "All white people are motherfuckers." The leap that Truman could now make is that Lynne is unworthy, is guilty, because she is white. But Walker does not let her character off so easily, for Truman knows that to be guilty of a color would necessarily end in racism, which is precisely what he is against. So he moves to the next logical step: "Was Lynne guilty because she was a white woman? Because she was a route to Death? Because she had power over them?" But this Truman feels would be to deny Lynne her humanity and to see her as "some kind of large mys-terious doll." Yet his friends, even the movement, begin to now exclude her from their trust, precisely for this reason.

As he muses, Truman comes closer and closer to the thorn that is really troubling him. It is not whether Lynne is guilty but whether *he* is guilty—of loving a white bitch. Yet would his rejection of Lynne on these grounds mean that he loved black people? His circlings around this question cover much ground:

> He had read in a magazine just the day before that Lamumba Katurim had gotten rid of his. She was his wife, true but apparently she was even in that disguise perceived as evil, a cast off. And people admired Lamumba for his perception. It proved his love of his own people they said. But he was not sure. Perhaps it proved only that Lamumba was fickle. That he married his wife in the first place for shallow reasons. Perhaps he was considering marrying a black woman (as the article said he was) for reasons just as shallow. For how could he state so assuredly that he would marry a black woman next when he did not appear to have any specific black woman in mind?
>
> If his own sister told him of her upcoming marriage to Lamumba he would have to know some answers before the nuptial celebration. Like, how many times would Lamumba require her to appear on tele-vision with him, or how many times would he parade her before his friends as proof of his blackness.[44]

Certainly the reasons must go deeper than that. In attempting to assuage the terrible feeling of rising guilt within him, Truman asks the pivotal question: Is it possible to love the wrong person? When is loving anyone an error?

Tommy Odds's accusations make Truman twist and turn because he knows that his feeling for Lynne had been undergoing subtle changes for some time. Why were they? Was it because of the pressure he was receiving from his friends in the Movement about his loving a white woman? Was it his own guilt that perhaps he did not truly love his own people? Walker amplified his initial analysis in "Of Bitches and Wives," when years later Truman thinks about the differences between Lynne and Meridian:

> Truman had felt hemmed in and pressed down by Lynne's intelligence. Her inability to curb herself, her imagination, her wishes and dreams. It came to her, this lack of restraint, which he so admired at first and had been so refreshed by, because she had never been refused the exercise of it. She assumed that nothing she could discover was capable of destroying her.[45]

So Truman's feeling for Lynne changes for precisely the same reasons it had begun: his desire to have a wife who is both worldly and idealistic, a wife whose intense idealism is based on freedom and security. Truman rejects the part of his heritage that had developed because it was not cradled in freedom and cuts himself off from the strength and control that accompanies such restrictions. In desiring a woman "who is perfection in the eyes of the world," he overlooks the galling fact that *his* world is not perfect in the eyes of the world. From what books was Lynne to learn the specific tradition of strength and poise, that precarious balancing that he identifies with Meridian. Meridian, as she always does in the novel, brings this point home when he tells her years later he loves her:

> "For Lynne's sake alone I couldn't do it," she had said languidly, rocking slowly in her yellow chair. . . .
> "How can you take her side?"
> "Her side? I'm sure she's already taken it. I'm trying to make the acquaintance of my side in all this. What side is mine? . . ."
> "Loving you is different—"
> "Because I'm black?"
> "You make me feel healthy, purposeful—"
> "Because I'm black?"
> "Because you're *you*, damn it! The woman I should have married and didn't!"
> "Should have loved and didn't," she murmured. And Truman sank back staring, as if at a lifeboat receding in the distance.[46]

Truman is unable to love Meridian because she embodies the many aspects of his tradition: the suffering, the lack of freedom, the impotency, the promiscuity, the provinciality, the restrictions. To survive, she, as many others, has to struggle to create beauty out of those limits, a beauty that cannot simply be given but must be earned.

In his attempt to understand this quality, Truman feels compelled to pursue Meridian on her "looney" sojourn through the South. As his teacher in "Ending," she asks him the questions about mother and child, woman and man, the principle of struggle, and the limits of pragmatism that he must confront to be whole. Although she can guide him to the source of his strength and his pain, as a black man he must unravel his own knots. He must pursue his own quest:

> "I meant it when I said it sets you free. You are free to be whichever way you like, to be with whoever, or whatever color or sex you like—and what you risk in being truly yourself, the way you want to be, is not the loss of me."[47]

The other major character that is affected by Meridian's quest is Lynne. At first the relationship among the three characters seems to follow the traditional pattern of a romantic love triangle. But this novel's trio of lovers is not usual, for the emphasis in their relationship is on their respective discovery of self rather than one person's possession of another. Each one of them is illuminated by the others and helps to bring the others closer to self-knowledge. That is why the relationship between Truman and Lynne is presented from Lynne's perspective as well as Truman's and why Lynne reflects on her life with Truman in the presence of Meridian. Each of them has been changed by the other.

Because the subject of a white woman married to a black man is so ridden with stereotypical responses in both the black and white world, Walker's presentation of the character Lynne is done gradually and from varying points of view. We first see her through the eyes of Meridian as she tells Truman about her initial reaction to this northern white woman. Appropriately, the setting is the context of social change. While out together on a register-to-vote drive, the two women encountered Mrs. Mabel Turner, "who is like everybody's grandmother." After feeding the civil rights workers, the old woman informs them, "I don't believe in voting," and insists that "the good lord he takes care of most of my problems." Although Meridian realizes that "Mrs. Turner was well beyond the boundaries of politics," Lynne wants to argue "and alienates Mrs. Turner forevermore." By having Truman, as well as Meridian and Lynne, react to Mrs. Turner's attitude, Walker outlines the relationship that will form among these three characters. Meridian respects the tradition Mrs. Turner represents, but Truman rejects it as backward, and Lynne counters it with pragmatic logic. Although Meridian can tolerate what she perceives as Lynne's ignorance, she cannot abide Truman's disrespect. Truman, on the other hand, is drawn to Lynne's audacious behavior although he has not yet met her. In a sense the northern white woman's response embodies his rebellion against the provincial sounds of Mrs. Turner and her like.

Meridian sees Lynne initially as a white woman, not as a particular person. As a black woman growing up in the South, she has received from her community specific information about the nature of white women:

> But what had her mother said about white women? She could actually remember very little, but her impression had been that they were frivolous, helpless creatures, lazy and without ingenuity. Occasionally, one would rise to the level of bitchery, and this one would be carefully set aside when the "collective Others were discussed. Her grandmother—an erect former maid who was now a midwife—held strong opinions, which she expressed in this way: 1. She had never known a white woman she liked after the age of twelve. 2. White women were useless except as baby machines which would continue to produce little white people who would grow up to oppress her. 3. Without servants all of them would live in pigsties.
>
> Who would dream, in her hometown, of kissing a white girl? Who would want to? What were they good for? What did they do? They only seemed to hang about laughing, after school, until they were sixteen or seventeen they got married. Their pictures appeared in the society column, you saw them pregnant a couple of times, then you were no longer able to recognize them as girls you once "Knew." They sank into a permanent oblivion. One never heard of them *doing* anything that was interesting.[48]

Unlike black women who did "outrageous things," white women, in general, did nothing but produce babies. Ironically, the black female community appropriates to white women the stereotype that had been imposed on them—that all they were good for was having babies—although they took great care to erase from their judgment of white women any trace of sexuality: "White women were like clear dead water." In effect, Meridian's mother and grandmother accept the picture of white women that white society had projected, only they see the emptiness of this image rather than its attractiveness. White women *are* "helpless frivolous creatures," just as they had been billed, Meridian's community seems to say, and who wants to be like that? That is why Meridian is so "bewildered," "embarrassed," when Truman starts dating Lynne. It is incomprehensible to her that a man like Truman would prefer a white woman, a "helpless frivolous creature," to a "woman who claims her own life." When Meridian is trying to figure out Truman's behavior, we have yet to meet Lynne. Nor do we or Meridian know that Truman has rejected Meridian because she is a mother.

When we encounter Lynne again, we see her through the eyes of Truman, first as a white woman who romanticizes black people in the chapter "Truman and Lynne: Time in the South" and then as his white wife for whom his feelings are undergoing subtle changes in the chapter "Of Bitches and Wives." Lynne as a character is beginning to take on flesh; still, she has yet to speak for herself. She does not emerge in the book as her own character, until Meridian strips bare the reasons why Truman is attracted to Lynne, not until Truman tries to come back to Meridian, not until Meridian finally and uncategorically rejects Truman as a lover. Only then does Lynne appear not as a generalization in Meridian's mind or as an extension of Truman but as herself. When she does emerge, she is trying to define herself in relation to Truman and to Meridian, that is, she is trying to define herself as a white woman living in a black world. In keeping with Walker's pattern of interrelated illumination, Lynne muses about her life with Truman in Meridian's house.

Lynne first presents herself as an embittered woman who has been ruined by her husband—for the same reason that he initially desired her, because she is white. By now she has given up her own middle-class Jewish world for her husband and has lost him as well as their child. But Truman is not her only target. She assaults Meridian also, for she believes Truman now pursues her rival because she is black, an attribute that Lynne cannot ever acquire. What is closer to the truth is that Lynne believes she is unworthy because she is white. Thus she respects Meridian because she has what Lynne wants more than anything: blackness and the strength and grace she attributes to that state of grace:

> Even when Truman was leaving her she had been conscious of her size, her body, from years of knowing how he compared it to the bodies of black women, "Black women let themselves go," he said, even as he painted them as magnificent giants, breeding forth the warriors of the new universe. "They are so *fat*, " he would say, even as he sculptured a "Big Bessie Smith" in so soft marble, caressing her monstrous and lovely flanks with an admiring hand.
>
> Her figure then, supple from dancing, was like a straw in the wind, he said, her long hair, a song of lightness—untangled, glistening and free. And yet in the end he had stopped saying those things, at least out loud. It was as if the voluptuous black bodies with breast like melons and hair like a crown of thorns, reached out—creatures of his own creation—and silenced his tongue. They began to claim him. When she walked into a room where he painted a black woman and her

heaving, pulsating, fecund body, he turned his work from her, or covered it up, or ordered her out of the room.

She had loved the figures at first—especially the paintings of women
in the South—the sculptures, enduring and triumphant in spite of everything. But when Truman changed, she had, too. Until she did not want
to look at the women, although many of them she knew, and loved.
And by then she was willing to let him go. Almost. So worthless did
the painted and sculptured women make her feel, so sure was she that
Truman, having fought through his art to the reality of his own mother,
aunts, sisters, lovers, to their beauty, their greatness, would naturally
seek them again in the flesh.[49]

Lynne does not want to be a white woman, a member of that delicate
group for whose benefit the most violent acts of racism are performed. It is
supposedly to protect her virtue that white men systematically deny black
men their freedom, for the white woman in southern mythology is the white
man's most valuable possession. Because of this deeply entrenched societal
value, Lynne cannot merely be a person; she is a white woman not only in
the minds of white Southerners, but necessarily in the mind of the black
community and increasingly in her own mind. She cannot escape her caste,
for too much blood has been spilled over it. She leaves her young innocent
room in her mother's house to confront reality through her involvement
with Truman and the Civil Rights Movement. The reality she discovers,
begins to experience, is racism, not only as it affects black people but also
as it affects her. She is as much defined by the philosophy of racism as they
are. In her desire to be worthy, to be on the side of righteousness, she allies
herself with black people, sees them as the ultimate perfection. But she cannot erase her own history or the history of America by merely making a
personal choice. In fact, by making that choice, she becomes the white
woman who has stepped outside the confines of decency. By marrying a
black man and living in Mississippi, Lynne gives up the protection of the
white man and therefore becomes in the eyes of the world a slut. As a woman,
her righteousness lies not in her intellectual or her political activity but in
her sexual choices.

When she allows Tommy Odds to rape her, because she feels the guilt of
being a white woman, Lynne strips herself of any romantic illusions she
might have had about her connection with black men. In forgiving him the
rape, she responds to his manhood by taking away *its* essence—the responsibility he has for his own actions. Instead, she validates society's beliefs
that her only worth lies in her pussy. She reduces him and herself to a one-
dimensional stereotype, as much as the southern racists who shot off his
arm. Appropriately, Odds reacts to her forgiveness with rage, as if he had

attempted to rape her to verify what he already knew, but wanted to disprove:

> "Black men get preferential treatment, man, to make up for all we been denied. She ain't been fucking you, she's been atoning for her sins."
>
> "That's not true," said Truman, sounding weak, even to himself.
>
> "She felt sorry for me because I'm black, man," said Tommy Odds and for the first time there was dejection in his voice. "The one thing that gives me some consolation in this stupid world, and she thinks she has to make up for it out of the bountifulness of her pussy." His voice hardened. "I should have killed her."[50]

Truman responds to Tommy Odds's assessment of Lynne's love for him by leaving her to herself, to become what she really is. Exposed both physically and psychologically, Lynne loses the sense of her own worth and gives herself up to the image the South has constructed for her. She sees her relationship to black men and women only in terms of sexuality—her only source of power. She sleeps with black men, tantalizes black women with her power to waylay their men—only to discover that she is not seen as a powerful person but as an object of pity or hate. Ironically, she steps down from her shaky pedestal only to put black men on it, although she knows through her own personal experiences that a pedestal does not lift; rather it dehumanizes. Finally, the only viable connection she has to the community she reveres is her and Truman's child.

Lynne's experience of the effects that the long tradition of American racism has on her illustrates how deep the connection is between racism and sexism. She cannot be what she wants to be because she is perceived by society as a White Woman, a person whose value lies in the preciousness of her pussy. One of the most consistent ways in which black people are made to understand that they are not valued in this country is the vehemence with which this precious object is denied them, whether or not they desire it. Like Marilene O'Shay in the first chapter of this novel, Lynne as a white woman who betrays her own "divinity" must be reduced to the opposite. As a white woman who does not guard her precious possession from all unworthy intruders, who, in fact, gives it away as if it has no value, she becomes a slut, a female devil, in the eyes of the South.

It is thematically as well as structurally significant that the only time Truman, Lynne, and Meridian come together is in their groping attempts to mourn the death of their child. Camara joins the long line of children in this book whose existence is snuffed out by society's violence. Together these three persons whose lives had so passionately affected each other unite to ask forgiveness of each other. Meridian is finally able to feel again for

Truman: "with a love totally free of possessiveness or contempt, a love that is forgiveness." She and Lynne become sisters, not over their wrangling about Truman but in their desire for the freedom of, in their love for, the land and the people, of the South.

> There was a scene on the television of a long, shady river bank and people—mothers and fathers, children, grandparents—almost elegantly fishing, and then the face, close up of a beautiful young black man with eyes as deceptively bright as dying stars. Now that he had just won the vote, he was saying, where was he to get the money to pay for his food? Looks like this whole Movement for the vote and to get into motels was just to teach them that everything in this country from the vote to motels, has to be changed. In fact, he said, looks like what he needed was a gun.
>
> To them both this was obvious. That the country was owned by the rich and that the rich must be relieved of this ownership before "Freedom" meant anything was something so basic to their understanding of America they felt naive even discussing it. Still, the face got to them. It was the kind of face they had seen only in the South. A face in which the fever of suffering had left an immense warmth, and the heat of pain had lighted a candle behind the eyes. It sought to understand, to encompass everything, and the struggle to live honorably and understand everything at the same time, to allow for every inconsistency in nature, every weird possibility and personality had given it a weary serenity that was so entrenched and stable it could be mistaken for stupidity. It made them want to love. It made them want to weep. It made them want to cry out to the young man to run away, or at least warn him about how deeply he would be hurt. It made them homesick.[51]

It is only after this coming together through the land that Walker has Lynne reflect on her own tradition, her own Jewishness. Ironically, the land she loves has taught her that she, too, is part of a tradition that it will not accept. The South would not tolerate blacks, Indians, or Jews, seeing their difference as deviancy, a threat to the established order. Lynne's experience in the South, her relationship with Truman and Meridian, with black men and women within the context of the Civil Rights Movement, has helped her to discover an aspect of her own heritage that her blood relatives erroneously turn away from—the quality of struggle rather than accommodation. In discovering her own history and reinterpreting her life in the face of her own family, her own sex, as well as her minglings with the black South, Lynne begins to understand her own humanity:

"Black folks aren't so special," she said. "I hate to admit it. But they're not."

"Maybe," said Meridian, as if she had been wide awake all along, "the time for being special has passed." . . . "Good God, this is depressing," said Lynne. "It's even more depressing than knowing I want Truman back." "That is depressing," said Meridian. "Oh, I know he's not much," she said. "But he saved me from a fate worse than death. Because of him, I can never be as dumb as my mother was. Even if I practiced not knowing what the world was like, even if I lived in Scarsdale or some other weird place, and never had to eat welfare food in my life. I'd still *know*. By nature I'm not cut out to be a member of the oppressors. I don't like them; they make me feel guilty all the time. They're ugly and don't know poor people laugh at them and are just waiting to drag them out." "No, Truman isn't much, but he is *instructional*," said Lynne. "Besides," she continued, "nobody's perfect." "Except white women," said Meridian, and winked. "Yes," said Lynne, "but their time will come."[52]

These are the last words Lynne speaks in the novel. Her words reiterate the concept that white women too must accept a struggle that will rid them of their pedestal, their "perfection," and allow them to be human without risk or rebuke, without the scent of blood rising from mutilated bodies and souls at their feet. To give up the aura of perfection, the cloak of perfection, may seem a loss until one glimpses the wonder of one's own humanity. Until the assertion of that humanity is seen as a most precious gift, a most valuable responsibility, either perfection at the price of human blood or wantonness at the price of guilt will keep the pedestal and the foundation upon which it rests intact.

Lynne's discovery of the preciousness of her own humanity has come as much through her engagement in social struggle as through psychological searching. In bringing together individuals like Meridian, Lynne, and Truman, the Civil Rights Movement is the impetus for personal change and therefore deep and lasting social change. Whatever Lynne might become beyond the space of this novel, she cannot be, as she was before she went to Georgia or Mississippi, ignorant of the restrictions that this society's attitude toward black people and women have placed on her life. She knows, too, that she is a victim as well as a part of the wheels of oppression. What she will do to extricate herself from these restrictions is yet unknown. But she knows that no matter what her relationships are, she is not black. She knows that she is no missionary, no appreciator of the art in the lives of the oppressed. She cannot give what she does not have.

Nor can Meridian or Truman. The major characters in this novel all discover that they cannot give what they do not have. That in order to transform their society, they must understand their own heritage and transform themselves. And that, paradoxically, it is in the process of attempting social change that they discover their own personal and cultural paths. This discovery is itself the core of the novel, the essence of its focal idea.

The major elements of *Meridian*, the circular plot movement, the use of motifs that delineate the spirit within all living things, the focus on the black woman in her struggle for social and personal transformation, and the relationship between its major characters and the Civil Rights Movement reiterate the novel's theme that the personal and societal quests for health and freedom are interrelated; that it is a continuing process rather than an adventure that ends in a neat resolution.

Thus the book ends with Truman replacing Meridian as that part of the pattern who must understand and try to change the entire pattern so he might be whole. Although Meridian has restored herself to health for the moment, Walker's ending suggests that even *her* dearly won salvation is not sure unless we others sort out the tangled roots of our past and pursue our own health. In other words, until the pattern of this society is transformed, no part of it is free, though the whole society will not change unless each of us pursue our own wholeness. By making the end of the novel the beginning of another such quest, Walker invites us to use the novel as a contemplative and analytical tool in our own individual search. For the questions that she gives flesh to in this novel, questions that are rooted in this country's past, persist in the present.

PART III

The Third Life of Grange Copeland and Meridian: Patterns for Change

> To acknowledge our ancestors means
> we are aware that we did not make ourselves, that the line stretches
> all the way back, perhaps to God:
> or to Gods. We remember them
> because it is an easy thing to forget: that we are not the first
> to suffer, rebel, fight, love and die: The grace with which we
> embrace life, in spite of the pain, the sorrows, is always a measure
> of what has gone before.[53]

Alice Walker is a poet, short-story writer, and essayist, as well as a novelist. Because her works in these different genre complement each other and contain many of the same thematic and structural elements, they can be discussed as a whole. Her book of poetry, *Revolutionary Petunias*, for example, can be read as a companion piece to *Meridian*. Nevertheless, I think that her first two novels, *The Third Life of Grange Copeland* and *Meridian* are peculiarly characterized in thematic and structural terms by their emphasis on the possibilities of change.

In both novels, the focal ideas are similar, although from the first to the second, there is a progression in theme and structure. Grange Copeland is a man who experiences three lives, one in which he hates himself, one in which he hates his oppressor, and the final one in which he is able to love his granddaughter and, therefore, himself. The pattern of Grange's life is a series of psychological stages brought on by the oppression that is inflicted upon him and his family. Although much of the Copeland history is painful and horrible, the novel itself is optimistic, for in spite of all this, Grange is able to change. By taking responsibility for his own life, he is able to love himself and pass on the possibility of "surviving whole" to his granddaughter.

Similarly, *Meridian* is about personal change. Its major characters—Meridian, Truman, and Lynne—all attain some measure of self-discovery. Meridian, as the character in the novel who is compelled to pursue wholeness, transforms herself even as she affects the other major characters. She also passes on the possibility of "surviving whole" to Truman. But although *The Third Life of Grange Copeland* remains primarily within the context of the Copeland family, *Meridian* encompasses the history of oppression of black people in America, as well as the possibility of change on a societal level. The analysis of societal forces and their philosophical underpinnings that are implicit in the first novel are explicitly explored in the second. Thus Meridian, the character, is a synthesis of the many aspects of black southern heritage. The change that she undergoes is not only personal. It is set within the tradition of resistance (in this particular instance, the Civil Rights Movement) that is as much a part of that heritage as is oppression. Like many of her ancestors, Meridian takes responsibility for the injustices in her society. Because of this emphasis, *Meridian* is a novel about the relationship between personal change and movements for social change.

Both Walker novels also focus on the major characters' perception of their past as crucial to their personal transformation in the present and the possibility of change in the future. In *The Third Life of Grange Copeland*, Walker accomplishes this by having her major character live through three generations. By reflecting on his past, he is able to understand the nature of his own existence in relation to the world in which he lives. In sorting out the repetition of tragedy in his family as it extends through a period of sixty years, Grange is able to effect his own personal change, which in turn may change the future of his descendants. In *Meridian*, the concept of the present as "a measure of what has gone before" is not limited to one family. It is extended to the history of black women in the South as reflected through Meridian Hill's maternal ancestors. In concentrating on the "mothers" of the people, their suffering, wisdom, and triumphs, Walker illuminates the heritage of the folk. The character Meridian embraces that past so she might attain grace in the present and help to effect change in the future. In both novels, Walker's use of time as circular and progressive is central to her major character's capacity for change.

Walker's use of the past is also reflected in her characterizations of black women. The significant development of this theme from her first novel to her second is especially dramatic. In both novels, the way in which the women are treated and the way in which they define themselves are related to the possibility of change. Grange and Brownfield participate in their own degeneration through their assault on their wives. Because Margaret, Mem, and Josie accept society's definition of woman as a passive wife, or a manipulative whore, they are unable to call on the wisdom and strength that is a part of their ancestral tradition. As a result, their family is in continual danger of being destroyed. Only when Grange is able to define his own manhood for himself rather than in societal terms is the process of degeneration halted and regeneration a possibility. None of the adult women, however, is able to withstand the assaults that are inflicted upon them. Only Ruth may be able to "survive whole," primarily because of Grange's personal change. But she, too, must, in the final analysis, define herself for herself.

That is what the character Meridian does do in Walker's second novel. Like Margaret and Mem, Meridian at first accepts society's definition of a woman. But her understanding of the past, her involvement in the Civil Rights Movement, and her willingness to use her traditions helps her redefine herself in her own terms as a woman and as a mother. In her first novel Walker emphasized the oppression that has destroyed many black women; in her second novel, she shows the relationship between that oppression and the creative sparks that have enabled black women to define themselves.

Paradoxically, although both novels show how the past is related to the possibility of change, they also focus on how the past is an obstacle to change. In *The Third Life of Grange Copeland*, Brownfield is incapable of growth because he cannot reach beyond the pain of his past. He destroys much of his family and himself because he comes to believe in his oppressor and in the inevitability of his oppression. Interestingly, Mem falls somewhere between Brownfield's inability to change and his father's realization of his right to grow, for she is destroyed by her husband, precisely because she has gotten a glimpse of her own possibilities. Similarly, although many of the characters in *Meridian* are affected by the Civil Rights Movement, society remains recalcitrant because its past is so rooted in violence.

In both novels, then, Walker emphasizes the element of struggle, which she sees as a prerequisite to real and lasting change. The persons who do achieve wholeness are beacons of this possibility within human beings. Both Grange and Meridian commit acts that they perceive as destructive. It is in their struggle to transcend their own violations against life that they come to the vision they achieve. In *Meridian*, the emphasis is not only on the ordeal that the individual person must endure, but on how that struggle is intimately connected to the collective struggle that society must bear.

Although there is a progression in theme from *The Third Life of Grange Copeland* to *Meridian*, these two novels reveal Walker's insistence on penetrating the essence of her characters rather than creating types who stand for a political or philosophical idea. Although *Meridian* concentrates on the conflict between two philosophical views of the world, Walker embodies this conflict in the actions of her characters rather than in extraneous asides. Above all, Walker is, in both novels, a storyteller. The telling of the story is as important as what she tells; the structuring of her tales are themselves possible patterns for change.

In *The Third Life of Grange Copeland*, Walker lays out, arranges and examines bits and pieces of waste in the lives of the Copelands so we might see the overall design. Then she remakes these very same pieces into a different pattern, one of rebirth. Her use of thrifty units, much like the compression of poetry, enables her economically to develop her overall design so the major elements could be clearly seen and intensely felt. By using these same elements to create a new pattern, she suggests that the pain in life must be understood and used, if the new pattern is to endure.

In *Meridian*, the quilt that Walker creates is more intricate, for she uses the elements of pain and strength of an entire tradition as the bases for her design. Nevertheless, she again uses economical units and the repetition of motifs in creating her pattern. But because she is demonstrating the relationship between personal and societal change, between the past and the present of the South, and between the conflicting philosophies of animism and fragmentation, her major structural elements are strongly outlined. In charting a pattern for change she creates a design of circles that are continually intersecting with each other but that also move forward and upward toward the highest spiritual point. Ascension is impossible, she suggests, without the struggle to go backward in order to come forward. Nor is spiritual growth possible unless all life is seen as interdependent, as a circle of wholeness.

In creating this design, Walker also indicates that focus is as important as movement. Meridian, a sensitive black woman, is the median point of the circular patterns in the novel, for she has experienced sexism and racism, major obstacles to societal wholeness. For this author, the black woman, as a result of her history and her experience, must be in struggle against these two distortions of life. Until she is free, her people cannot be free, and until her people are free, she cannot be free. Walker stresses the interrelatedness of these two obstacles to wholeness, for the struggle against them is not merely a question of replacing whoever is in power; rather it is a struggle to release the spirit that inhabits all life. Walker's quilts reiterate the basic concept that "the greatest value a person can attain is full humanity which is a state of oneness with all things,"[54] and that until this is possible for all living beings, those of us who seek wholeness must be willing to struggle toward that end.

7

_____ Pass It On _____

It's always seemed to me black people's grace has been
what they do with language.
                                        —*Toni Morrison*[1]

Whatever their differences, and there are many, the novels of Paule Marshall, Toni Morrison, and Alice Walker tell the stories of their mothers—
perhaps not specifically *their* mothers but certainly the women who came
before them. Their novels are the literary counterparts of their communities'
oral traditions, which in the Americas have become more and more the
domain of women. The history of these communities, seldom related in text-
books, are incorporated into tales that emphasize the marvelous, sometimes
the outrageous, as a means of teaching a lesson. In concert with their African
ancestors, these storytellers, both oral and literary, transform gossip, happenings, into composites of factual events, images, fantasies, and fables.

Not that any of these novelists are merely reporting stories; they are obviously creating fiction. Rather they tell their mothers' stories through their
crafted articulation of the particular imaginative style their respective communities use to manifest their experience. Nor are these stories and fables
merely glorifications of the community. They are critical not only of an individual but of the entire social fabric. Yet the style, the merging of images
and events, constitutes a particular value system.

I am not equating the communities these authors present with the Black
Community. That term is often used to express the unity that black people
have as a culture. Implicit in that term is the definition of black culture in
contrast to other cultures. What is emphasized then is the distinction between
it and other group expressions. Black culture, as a concept, was not easily
accepted by the majority American culture. By the late 1960s, however,

the cumulative effect of works such as *Invisible Man* along with a resurgence of black nationalism made it possible no longer to have to prove its existence. In defining their culture, however, black artists have had to make it into an abstraction and thus have felt compelled to deemphasize variations that existed among black communities. Noting too many variations would make it difficult to assert the existence of the general configuration. The result has been a rather homogenized picture of black culture.

Marshall, Morrison, and Walker, however, do not begin with this abstraction. The communities these authors present are more particular. The world of their first novels is the network of persons through which their major characters receive their sustenance and their belief systems, and these communities vary according to their age, location, size, and past. The particular community in each work has its own unique style, legends, and rituals, although it also contains basic elements that it shares with other black communities. Instead of defining itself in contrast to white culture, it emphasizes its own past, its own forms. White culture, of course, has an impact on these communities, for it inflicts psychic terror upon them. But the definition of the community does not come solely from its confrontation with white culture. Whites are usually presented as emblems rather than fully developed characters, for they are important to the community as role figures rather than individuals. The result of this approach is that we arrive at an understanding of the larger configuration, black culture, by focusing on the particular, and, at the same time, we do not lose the richness that variations have to offer.

The style of each of these three writers reflects certain qualities of the community in their novels as well as their own personal vision. The allegorical approach is especially strong in the novels of Toni Morrison, where nature and human beings converse and where the images of the stories dance to create their own structure, their own parables. Especially in her novels, the process of naming, of capturing the spirit through the word, is paramount. Although the novels of Marshall are more psychological than imagistic, she, too, investigates the folk history of her characters as they grope toward self-understanding. Again, communal action, in this case rituals of the West Indian community, are her guides. Walker's theme is the pursuit of personal and societal wholeness, as she analyzes a major dilemma of black Southerners, the relationship between one's responsibility for one's life and the restrictions of sexism and racism. By revealing the fantasies, myths, and dreams of her characters, she attempts to penetrate what she calls "the historical subconscious" of their communities.

These three novelists' immersion into the nature of their communities' styles and their communities' way of grasping meaning as the dramatized word, action, or thought helps to explain why their first novels are so insular. At first, one could say that *Browngirl, Brownstones, The Bluest Eye,* and

the *Third Life of Grange Copeland* are novels about the trials and tribula-
tions some black girls encounter on the road to adulthood. They are certainly
that. But they are also the stories of their communities, as they recreate
themselves. In attempting self-definition, Selina, Pecola, and Ruth must
necessarily ask their respective communities what is expected of them. The
response reveals much about each community's sense of womanhood and
adulthood, as well as about the natural process of growth.

It is significant that few prominent black male novelists have concentrated
on this particular phase of their characters' lives. James Baldwin did it in
Go Tell It on the Mountain. But in many classic novels written by black
males the protagonists quickly move from the insularity of their natal communities into confrontations with the outer world. It is through this confrontation, buttressed by their often imperfect understanding of their own
communities, that they seek their identity. These male protagonists discover
their identity as racial beings, that is, that they are black rather than white,
and their experience as members of a particular community, or of a particular family, is not as critical. Of course, men, even boy-men, are considerably
more mobile than girl-women. But it is not only the degree of mobility that
is different; it is also the greater emphasis the female authors place on their
characters' communities as the primary source of their definition. Even when
they present women like Sula or men like Grange, who leave their communities, these characters ultimately return.

This insularity, particularly in Marshall, Morrison, and Walker's first novels, affects the structure of their works. Critics have noted that the ending
of many classic black novels, such as *Invisible Man* and *Native Son*, differ
from the usual picaresque novel in that the hero finds no satisfactory resolution. As one of my colleagues has so adroitly pointed out, how could it be
otherwise, since the fate of the protagonist is so linked to the destiny of his
people, a destiny that has yet to reach its point of resolution.[2] Having stepped
beyond their communities in an attempt to exert some control over their
lives, the male protagonists find themselves in a hole. These classic novels,
then, move outward and then downward as the hero gradually acknowledges
his predicament. But in the first novels of Marshall, Morrison, and Walker,
the structure tends to be circular in movement. Their characters' stories are
inevitably tied to the life of their communities. Their protagonists, like Zora
Neale Hurston's Janie, give the meaning of their stories back to the community. Selina gives her mother and the Barbadian community its due,
Grange Copeland gives Ruth the sum of his people's wisdom so she might
continue on, and Claudia tells us that the cause of Pecola's tragedy is the
land of her town.

I do not want to overstate this point, for clearly the distinction between
male and female writers can be a factious one. Writers are free to imagine
anything, as Toni Morrison so beautifully illustrated in her *Song of Solomon.*

Nonetheless, these women writers' first novels seem to emphasize the major character's psychic connection to her natal community, as well as their desire to articulate their mother's stories as a metaphor for human existence. Their emphasis on their own communities, then, while seeming to be narrow, is more complex, perhaps even broader than many works in which the white world is prominent.[3]

Not surprisingly, these three first novels are about continuity, at first as reflected through the girl-woman's perception of her parents and then in the discovery of her sexuality. Such an exploration inevitably revises the images of black women and men that have been prevalent in the literature. These girl-women view the man primarily as father, rather than worker or conqueror of the outside world, and their view of woman is charged by the realization that they, too, will be called upon to be women and probably mothers. Central to all of these books is the point of view of a child: Selina, Claudia, Pecola, Brownfield, Ruth. That Claudia, although not Pecola, continues, that Selina develops into an independent person, that we are cautious although hopeful that Ruth will be able to transcend her family's bloody history, illustrates the many variations on this theme. Yet all three works do not restrict the process of their stories to a child's understanding, for as point of view characters, the children's perspectives are filtered through the omniscient view of the adult writer.

The child feels the mother, the father, and tries to understand them so she can become herself. That is at the core of each book's yearnings. To develop further, these children must penetrate the stereotypes that their parents appear to be. All of these writers present black women and men characters that at first appear to be the worn-out images of old, a testament to the effect that persistent images have on reality. Then each novelist proceeds to crack the stereotypes, revealing the complexity of the human beings beneath. Again, there are variations on this process. Marshall is intensely concerned with the image of the dominant, bitter black mother, at least as she appears to the young girl, and graphically charts Selina's gradual understanding of her mother. Although Selina begins to understand how her mother's and father's own sensibilities have been restricted by society, Marshall does not allow her to ignore her parents' unique personalities as they respond to the world. Morrison's treatment of her women characters is more expansive, less particular than Marshall's, for there are many women figures in *The Bluest Eye*. They vary in the degree to which their sensibilities have been damaged by their internalizations of stereotypes. Morrison shows us the relationship between the degree of their wasted lives and the tragedies of their children. Pauline Breedlove's accommodations to her condition produce decay rather than continuity, but Mrs. McTeer is somehow able to sustain her children, Claudia and Frieda. Pauline comes closer than Marshall's Silla to becoming the image of the mammy of antiquity, for she prefers little white girl-dolls to her own black children. Yet in acknowledging Pauline Breedlove's existence, Morrison beautifully dramatizes the relationship between this black woman's repressed creativity and her mutilated children.

Walker's mothers are more deranged, more pathetically abused, than Marshall's or Morrison's. Silla, after all, has a consuming ambition to own a brownstone, and that ambition at the very least charges her life with fire and energy. Pecola's mother has her employer's house as a canvas where she can arrange and rearrange beautiful things. But both Margaret and Mem are isolated, cut off from any energizing force, although Mem at first plants flowers and for a time manages to acquire a presentable house. Walker's mothers are victims, the strong black woman image shattered. Yet they do live on in Ruth who at least is an offering of hope.

In each novel loose woman images inject a particular view of sensuality into the girl-woman's world. In *Browngirl, Brownstones*, Suggie is Selina's instructor on the virtues of pleasure, a sphere of reality that the young girl's mother has had to reject in her relentless pursuit of material stability. This loose Barbadian woman is good-natured and generous, and she represents that aspect of Barbadian culture that the newly arrived immigrants believe they cannot afford. To the young Selina, Suggie is Deighton's counterpart, for both lend magic to everything they touch. But neither Suggie nor Deighton, in spite of their rebellion against their community, survive in this hard-knocks world. They therefore are not viable models for the strong-willed Selina.

In contrast to Suggie, the whores in *The Bluest Eye* are not at all good-hearted. They are tough women who realize that the world around them is both crazy and false. Pecola wonders if they are real, and perhaps they are the only real people in this world of schizoid values. They are her only grownup friends, for they accept her as she is. But since they themselves are unacceptable, she can hardly be expected to find her ideal woman image reflected in them.

Fat Josie is the thorn in the side of the Copeland women, for she helps to destroy their relationship to their husbands. Kindhearted although tough, she falls prey to the whore's image without being able to live up to it, for she wants more than anything to be loved.

None of these characters, however, not even the voracious Josie, duplicates the loose, black woman images in the novels of the past. Certainly Morrison's whores are clearly whores, but they are completely aware that supposedly decent women are whores, too. Suggie is not so much obsessed by sex, as she is in living as much as she can in the few hours that she is not a drudge. Fat Josie is so much in search of her father's love that she becomes stupid in her sexiness.

The male images in these novels are also revisions. Considering the myth that there are only mothers and children in black families, it is interesting that all three novelists choose to include two parents in their troubled families. Marshall seems consciously to present the "primitive," sensual stereotype of the black man in her characterization of Deighton. But of course we soon discover his complexity and that his fun-loving guise is only that. He both fears and desires the values he says he rejects. His complete turnabout from sensualist to ascetic is an incisive stroke on Marshall's part, revealing the frustration of his need to create his own world.

Morrison's Cholly Breedlove is also presented initially as a "primitive," only a more sordid type than Deighton. He is almost godlike in his narcissism, for he has no sense of either family or community. Freed as he is from any human context that will allow him a structure for his imagination, he inverts his godlike narcissism into a demonic mask. His rape of Pecola is certainly marked by this inversion. Yet the rape is the only thing he has to give her, according to the stereotypes that have been inflicted on him. Finally, it is the only love his daughter is to know.

Brownfield and the first Grange Copeland are also variations on this theme. Unable to exert any power over their lives, they turn in on themselves and on their wives and children. Grange, however, who leaves his manic life, learns something (even if it is based on hatred) about the nature of responsibility. Confronted with his granddaughter's innocence, he is able to regenerate himself, to live another life, this time as himself. He is the only male in these first novels who manages to transcend the restrictions of his environment and the invidiousness of stereotypes. In this he is guided by a child.

In conjunction with the images of women and men in these novels, much attention is given to why the relationships between the mother and the father are so violent. Black men and women do inflict physical and psychological harm on each other. Of course, this is also true of other groups, but the stigma of violence attached to the black man-woman relationship has been so devastating that few authors before Richard Wright dared to approach it. Wright and Ann Petry both presented violence between black men and women (Bigger kills Bessie in *Native Son*; Lutie kills Boots when he attempts to rape her in *The Street*). But they did not penetrate the nature of that violence besides indicating that it is a result of the pent-up anger black people feel toward the white world. Since their sexual counterparts are the only ones they can get close enough to, men and women release their anger on each other.

Marshall, Morrison, and Walker go further than that. All three of course present the rage, the frustration, and the resulting violence. But they take great care to point out that one of the most insidious effects of racism is that it is so pervasive, it becomes elusive. Few of the major characters understand that their personal lives are indeed affected by this problem. So these characters are not prepared to meet the onslaught, to understand what effects it is having on them, and therefore to change their mode of behavior.

Silla is angry because she expected more from her husband, more from this new country to which she had come. She wants to be taken care of with grace and dignity. But she knows Deighton's insatiable need to express himself, his belief that a man must do big things, and that making a little money at a time, saving, working under the heel of a white man, is no big thing to him. She falls in love with his magic, yet is unable to understand until it is too late that Deighton cannot be himself and a successful black man, too.

Pauline is also totally unprepared for the privations that would greet her when she moves from the richer cultural scene of the South to the more fragmented North. Gradually she internalizes the very stereotypes that threaten to dehumanize her. She believes that she is ugly and unworthy since ugly, unworthy things happen to her. Further, like Silla she expects her husband to support her both emotionally and financially when he can hardly do either for himself.

Margaret and Mem are also women who are trapped by the stereotype inflicted on blacks and on women. They believe that if they are faithful, good wives who take care of their husband's physical needs, they will be cherished. They relate initially to their husbands as if they are seen as men in society, as if they have access to power. Misguided, they, too, are unprepared for the avalanche of misery that falls upon them.

Implicit in all of these women's lives is the authors' criticism that their communities have not absorbed the reality that awaits the black woman; that the community has itself internalized the image of the lovely, faithful, beloved wife who stays at home, rears neat, well-behaved children, and presents her husband with luscious meals and clean-smelling sheets. That particular stereotype is inflicted as well on white women, who in many cases have achieved it with a vengeance. But given the conditions under which many black communities struggle, this image is a corrupted fantasy, seldom attainable, if it is desirable at all. Nonetheless, the community reinforces this stereotype as an ideal, having suffered so much from being seen as different, and therefore of lower quality, that the community seeks normality, a discernable and appreciated order.

It is fascinating that this ideal is most strongly held by the characters in *The Bluest Eye*. Neither southern nor northern, neither rural nor urban, they have scarcely had enough time to figure out what their new life-style is. In a vacuum with few functional traditions, they are more intolerant of any deviations from the norm. That is perhaps why the Western concepts of beauty and romantic love, particularly since they are usually coupled with rewards of love and security, are so overwhelmingly important in their lives.

All of the major women characters in these first novels, to some extent, however, share this confusion, until gradually they begin to become the stereotypes they had hoped to avoid. Silla becomes a bitter, domineering woman, her ideal woman image drowned in the ocean; Pauline Breedlove becomes a mammy to some white girl-doll and treats her home like a dungheap; and Mem must threaten her husband with castration to survive. Their communities, meanwhile, seem to offer no solution except to say, what can you expect from such ugliness.

There is some relief for the girl-children in these novels, some in viable ways, some not. Although Selina's community is restrictive, it does allow her protection and love, until she is able to stand by herself, for its rituals ignite her imagination and give her a strong core. Ruth, too, learns through her grandfather's tales something about the culture of her people, the nature of racism, and the possibility of change. By the end of these novels, these girl-women are well on their way to self-discovery. Only Pecola completely accepts the lie of her society, for she is neither cherished nor protected and therefore does not survive long enough to discover the lie. Her relief is her desire for and receipt of blue eyes, the final judgment on her community's distortions of reality. In addition, Morrison suggests that all communities need such failures as scapegoats for their own weaknesses.

The stories of these girl-children illustrate how far away we are from the novels of Frances Harper, Jessie Fauset, Nella Larsen, and even Ann Petry. Marshall, Morrison, and Walker are not interested in creating counterimages to the stereotypes imposed on black women. Nor are they concerned only with protesting to whites the conditions of blacks. Their language, their characters, their analyses, seem to be directed at their own communities or more precisely at that part of themselves that is their community. In this respect their novels are more strongly connected to Zora Neale Hurston's novels and to Jean Toomer's *Cane* than they are to other writers of the past. These contemporary novels are evidence that black women are plumbing their own imaginations, creating their own sentences, structuring the content of their own experiences, to instruct their own communities. They are fulfilling the promise of creativity that Toomer predicted for black women. Yet because they do delve into themselves, they also express perennial questions that are uniquely human, for they do not question or need to prove their characters' humanity.

Their second novels are further testament to the strengths of their first. They go on to present the black woman as rebellious rather than misguided. All three major characters—Merle, Sula, and Meridian—are women who have for a time left the confines of their communities and returned to them. Each is deepened although wounded in a particular way. Defiled by her British sojourn, Merle has lost her child and her husband. Sula has learned that men may be your lovers but not your friends, that all of the other communities she has been to are similar to the Bottom in that her imagination, as a woman, is restricted and mistrusted. Meridian has given her child away to escape her mother's fate only to find that she feels she has betrayed her maternal ancestors. Each has paid a price for her acquisition of knowledge and each seeks wholeness. Not surprisingly, much of their conflict with themselves or with the world has to do with the concept of motherhood and how that defines them as women.

Why do these women return to the communities they left? Partially they return because they have nowhere else to go and partially because they love their homes. But it is an agonized love they feel, for their communities are too restricted in their commitment to mere survival. Sula is the most rebellious of the three, and she returns to the Bottom to see Nel, the only friend she ever had. But she challenges her community's definition of a woman, and since that definition is intrinsic to their philosophy of life, they turn her into a witch. Her insistence on living for herself is unimaginable to a community that stresses continuity and survival rather than creativity and experiment. Morrison's novels criticize the conservatism of her characters' communities, which use the strong, deep tradition they possess to restrict rather than to free individuals. Yet she insists on the importance of the community without which the creative imagination cannot survive, for it has no framework in which to structure its tremendous energy.

Meridian is similar to Sula in that she, too, refuses to be a mother. But her choice is more complicated than Sula's, for her rejection of motherhood is based on her strong belief in the tradition of motherhood that her maternal ancestors held to and her inability to live up to their standards. Meridian's past points up why some, like Sula, might reject motherhood without shame, for it seems to cut them off from the possibilities of life. Yet there is a great difference between Sula's and Meridian's perspectives. Not only is Meridian too much involved with her community's history to dismiss it; her self-awareness also takes place with the context of the struggle for social change. Although Sula's choice is primarily a personal one based on her own experiences, Meridian's acts of rebellion, her continued nonviolent resistance, is based on personal and political awareness.

All of these "second" novels, *Sula* and *Meridian* and *The Chosen Place, The Timeless People*, show the relationship between the personal and the social spheres of life, a relationship that many women writers are prone to express. I hesitate to give simple reasons for this tendency. Perhaps it is because women have been, until recently, so bound to their own communities that they somehow understand that unless there is personal change, political or social change is apparent rather than real. Perhaps it is because they have usually been left out of the race for power and therefore are not as fooled by it. Or perhaps because their roles have been so rigidly defined by their respective communities and for so long that they understand that political changes may seem to happen, but unless they are really internalized, they are quickly diverted. Or perhaps they realize, as Gwendolyn Brooks's poetry so wondrously expresses, that both good and evil are ordinary phenomena based on the deeply etched images that a particular person responds to.

In any case, Sula, in her intensity, challenges her community not because she calls herself a feminist. Her act of rebellion is based on her own personal experiences. But in opposing it, she makes a statement about the restrictive structures that she believes it imposes on her. In challenging its definition of woman, she challenges the whole social structure.

Perhaps Sula's act occurs within a vacuum because she and her cousins, for there must be others like her, are ahead of their time, or maybe because her community itself seems to exist in itself so completely that she has no other rebels with whom to identify. Meridian, however, is opened up, renewed by the Movement of the sixties. Essentially her story is the effect of the Movement on her personal life and her personal life on it. Because the Movement reaches out beyond the southern black community for some of its energy, Meridian's personal and political values are challenged by other value systems. Without the political movements that occurred during her young adulthood, Meridian's life would have been quite different.

Although Marshall's character Merle in *The Chosen Place, The Timeless People* is extremely self-directed, her characterization heightens an aspect of both Sula and Meridian's journey into the outside world. Merle is a crossroads character between the natives of Bournehills and the visitors from the outside. Because she knows both cultures, she understands the strengths and limitations of the two. But because she has become a part of both cultures, she is split. She resembles the past images of black women in literature in that she finds herself caught between two worlds. Yet that position gives her insight and becomes a metaphor for the black person who has been educated in the West but has also been a part of the tradition of her people. Rather than resembling the images of old, she is closer to the black men Wright describes in his essay, "The Miracle of Nationalism on the African Gold Coast," who are no longer tribal but neither are they Western. "They share a third but not quite clearly defined point of view."[4] Although Merle returns to her community, it is a world that for centuries has been invaded by the outside world. So the characters she encounters come from all over the West. Her story then is scarcely insular in scope. As a crossroads character, she understands how political-philosophical systems based on imperialism and racism have raped her community, and yet she admires the degree to which Bournehills has retained its identity. The making of history as a unity of the personal and political is central to Marshall's *Chosen Place*, for only when the people believe they can take personal responsibility for the course of history can they change it. Although Merle sees the relationship between the personal and the political, she herself cannot give her people her knowledge until she, too, is whole. In her case, that means she must find her lost child; she must regain her hold on continuity in her own personal life.

Clearly each of these novelists extends her world further in her second novel, and each weaves stories that heighten the dangers as well as the benefits of venturing out. The benefits may be broadening in scope, but the dangers for these women are primarily sexual. Merle loses her husband and child because he has been told by her English benefactress that they had a sexual relationship. Sula has learned that sex is the only experience in her life where she can feel herself as powerful and that men whether they are in the Bottom or in New York do not see women as their equals. Meridian finds out that whether her lover is her provincial teenage husband, Eddie, or the intellectual Truman, neither is much interested in her personal growth.

Although the results are quite different, all of these novelists stress their major character's exploration of their sexuality as one of their most important means to self-discovery. Sula wants sex to be a mutual sharing between man and woman, but she discovers that men do not seek that sharing. Rather than give herself up to their power, their pleasure, she seeks her own. But her experience of power in the sexual act also expresses her utter aloneness. Meridian, on the other hand, is never able to experience pleasure in sex, for she feels that men want women to give in, to lose their essence rather than find themselves. For Merle, sex is healing and her sexual relationship with Saul, a white man, is her attempt to heal the wounds of mistrust that she had suffered as a result of her sexual encounter with her English benefactress.

In each of these novels, there are interracial sexual minglings. In *Sula*, such touching is only hinted at, for the community insists that Sula, the witch, sleeps with white men. That is enough of a charge to relegate her to the company of devils. In *Chosen Place* and in *Meridian*, the relationship between a black woman and a white man and a white woman and a black man is carefully outlined. In both cases, with Merle and Saul and Truman and Lynne, the relationship results in heightened self-awareness. Especially in *Meridian*, it is the fulcrum through which the values of the movement are put to a test. Walker asks whether Truman and Lynne's relationship is a result of their distorted perceptions of each other that have been fostered by a world where black and white are kept apart, whether such a relationship is possible at all. Her insistence on looking at this relationship as a result of personal value systems of her characters as they are affected by sociopolitical structures is another variation on the theme of the personal-social vortex. Can such a relationship, she asks, given the context of this society, develop in a natural way?

As a result of their developing knowledge of the world and themselves, each major character exhibits a certain "looniness." Merle becomes catatonic from time to time; Sula is as "quirky" as Nature, and Meridian has

recurrent bouts of paralysis. Their bodies manifest their grieving spirits. In
Sula and *Meridian* the community characterizes their "looniness" as other-
worldly. Sula is seen as a witch by her community, a drastic revision in the
image of the conjure woman. Morrison suggests that such images are created
by a particular community as a dumping ground for their fears and as a
means of keeping the community together. When the deviant is a woman,
the community is threatened particularly since its continuity is at stake. In
contrast, Meridian is seen as a saint, a bit crazy but close to God. She becomes one of those figures who carries the weight of the community's sorrows and sins. Merle, on the other hand, is loved by her community; they
absorb her "craziness" and call it by its right name. They see it as a grieving,
because she stands for their land, which has been defiled. Merle and Meridian differ from Sula in that somehow they manage to regenerate themselves through their communities even as they rebel against them; yet the
witch Sula refuses to live for any other and cannot be absorbed into the
community. Cut off from her source, she dies. But so does the community,
for it has need of creative spirits like hers to stay alive.

Because their communities' view of women is related intrinsically to their
view of Nature, and the course of human history, the structures of these
novels are based on the interaction between the novelists and the communities' definition of Nature and Time. In Morrison's works, Nature is mean
but precious, magical but indifferent, very much like Sula. In the *Chosen
Place*, the land has been defiled by the outside world as Merle has been;
yet both retain their integrity because they refuse to accept life unless it
is really life. In *Meridian*, Nature reacts to the unnatural philosophies of
sexism and racism by grieving. Yet it, like the character Meridian is regenerative, but only as a result of struggle.

Time in its timelessness is also intrinsic to the structure of these novels.
The communities of these three women do not see Time as chronology.
They name it "significant process." Because of their definition of time, their
proper naming of it, these communities understand its importance. This
definition is particularly strong in *Chosen Place* as the rhythms of nature
remain constant. But it is also crucial to the structure of *Sula*, for Nature's
actions unite with the actions of human beings to produce significance, and
events are presented not as chronology but as moments of impact. In *Meridian*, Walker's presentation of time as circular and progressive structures
her theme that social change can last only if it is connected to the songs,
the communal creations of the people, and the link between them and Nature.

Although Nature is central to these communities' philosophy of life, Marshall, Morrison, and Walker suggest that the folk often misrepresent it, for
they are too static in their understanding of it; often they view Nature as a
rationalization for inaction, as a dam against necessary change. Sula's community, for example, believes that Nature is good and evil, and that the way

to deal with evil is to outlast it. That traditional value, effective when there is no other possibility but perserverance, is no longer viable in a world where they can make their own history. The same observation can be made about Bournehills, which in its timelessness ignores the possibilities of timeliness. Meridian's community has been so caught up with the difficulty of survival that it feels caught between Nature and the process of human history.

These works assert that although Nature is a constant and the past is a part of the present, there are also variations within the constant, possibilities of choice within the present. Motherhood has always been used as a metaphor for Nature's process in the human realm and as such women have been called upon to reiterate the relationship between Nature and human beings. It is not surprising then that these authors approach this subject with extreme care. Toni Morrison's *Sula* suggests that Nature is life; that it is, finally, beyond the crazy inversions to which human society is prone; and that since it is forever constant, it cannot be outlasted. Rather it is the human mind with its facility for imagination and experiment that must continually renew the community's understanding of life. The novel then insists that creativity might be not only physical but spiritual as well. Sula, the character, proclaims that her mind is her own, a statement central to this book's content. But her complete inordinate obsession with her mind is the result of an idle imagination. Like Pauline Breedlove in *The Bluest Eye*, she becomes dangerous because she has no form within which to structure her spiritual creativity. Her natural gifts are not even acknowledged, for no one has thought to look for them. Since she is a woman, she has her womb; what more does she need to be creative? Sula then is seen by her community as a *quirk* of nature because she does not fit into the folk's definition of a woman.

Merle, on the other hand, judges herself. She feels she has not lived up to her community's definition of woman because she has slept with another woman for material gain. Her judgment on herself is reinforced by her husband's shame. He leaves her and takes their child with him. But she learns from her equally defiled land, Bournehills, that her value is based on her own assessment of the past, on her ability to create her own history, on her refusal to be a victim of the past.

In *Meridian* as in *Chosen Place*, Nature does reflect the human condition. The land grieves as humankind refuses to acknowledge its wisdom and continues to corrupt the natural order by holding onto the unnatural philosophy of racism. Within this context, motherhood is demanded of women, although not respected. It cuts them off rather than opens them up to the possibilities of life. The word *mother* is enlarged in *Meridian* for it comes to mean not only those that give physical birth but those who are willing to struggle to make life possible and to preserve its fullness against unnatural restriction.

In all three novels, the concept of woman each community believes in is based on their concept of Nature as the creative force. But they see Nature, and therefore women, primarily as physically creative. They do not extend their concept of creativity in woman or Nature to the spiritual realm and therefore do not grasp the meaning of Nature itself. All three books then challenge the definition of female creativity as solely residing in the womb and graphically chart the effects of this pervasive definition on the spiritual growth of these communities. These works attempt to redefine the words *mother, Nature, woman,* and *creativity.* They suggest that if women cannot fulfill their nature, the creative spirit within them, they become dangerous like Sula, or catatonic with rage like Merle, or paralyzed by guilt like Meridian. Their respective communities suffer, then, for they stunt the natural growth of their members.

The images of black women in the literature articulate this loss. The racism that black people have had to suffer is almost always presented in peculiarly sexist terms. That is, the wholeness of a person is basically threatened by an assault on the definition of herself or himself, as female or male. The literature suggests that this holds true not only for black women but for black men as well.

The pattern that emerges from *Iola LeRoy* to the present is amazingly revealing. First, black women writers try to prove that the black woman is a woman, their definition of course derived from the prevailing definition of the white woman. But the contradictions between the images and reality lead to an even greater psychic gap, for black women cannot possibly attain the uniquely Western values that this definition projected and survive. Finally, black contemporary women writers are challenging the very definition of woman and are beginning to project their own definitions of themselves as a means of transforming the content of their own communities' views on the nature of woman and therefore on the nature of life. They are doing it in a most profound way for they are using language, the correct naming of things as a means of renewing the traditions of their communities while sustaining them. They express the value of the word as the repository for the wisdom of their communities and therefore deepen the content of human experiences. As creative writers, then, they exemplify the redefinitions they present. Perhaps because of their works, the word *writer* will not have to be qualified by the word *woman.*

Notes

CHAPTER I

1. James Weldon Johnson, *The Black Mammy*, in *St. Peter Relates an Incident* (New York: Viking Press, 1917).

2. Frances Harper's *Iola LeRoy, Shadows Uplifted*, 3rd ed. (Boston: James H. Earle, 1895), is usually listed in surveys of Afro-American literature, such as Brown, Davis, and Lee, eds., *Negro Caravan* (New York: Dryden, 1941) and Roger Whitlow's *Black American Literature: A Critical History* (Totowa, N.J.: Littlefield Adams,1974), as the first novel published by an Afro-American woman. There is some question, however, whether a novel by Amelia Johnson, *In God's Way* (Rochester, N.Y.: American Baptist Publishing), was not published before 1892. I recently saw a copy of this novel at an exhibit of rare black books done by Daphne Muse at Mills College. The publication date was 1891. This novel is not listed in most bibliographies. It, like *Iola LeRoy*, is about an octoroon.

3. William Still, Introduction to Harper, *Iola LeRoy*.

4. Frances Harper, "Black Women in the Reconstruction South," reprinted in *Black Women in White America: A Documentary History*, ed. Gerda Lerner (New York: Vintage, 1973), p. 247.

5. Ibid., pp. 249-50.

6. Winthrop D. Jordan, *White Over Black: American Attitudes Toward the Negro, 1550-1812* (New York: Penguin Books, 1969), p. 101.

7. Ibid., p. 143.

8. Milton Cantor, "The Image of the Negro in Colonial Literature," in *Images of the Negro in American Literature*, ed. Seymour Gross and John E. Hardy (Chicago: University of Chicago Press, 1966), p. 29.

9. Jordan, *White Over Black*, p. 79.

10. Ibid., p. 31.

11. Cantor, "The Image of the Negro in Colonial Literature," pp. 29-53.

12. Jordan, *White Over Black*, p. 32.

13. Ibid., p. 31.

14. George Stocking, *Race, Culture and Evolution: Essays in the History of Anthropology* (New York: The Free Press, 1968), pp. 37-38.

15. Jordan, *White Over Black*, pp. 429-81.

16. Ibid., p. 142.

17. Ibid., p. 148.

18. Ibid., p. 149.

19. Herbert G. Gutman, *The Black Family in Slavery and Freedom, 1750-1925* (New York: Pantheon Books, 1976), p. 75. Although historians make a great distinction between breeding in the Caribbean and the practices of United States slaveholders who encouraged promiscuity among slaves, there are a few points worth considering: (1) that the distinction they make between the Caribbean and the United States is somewhat muted by the continuous contact between the slaves and planters of these two areas. The United States was as much a part of the New World as the Caribbean; (2) that slave narratives include many references to slaves who said they were forced to mate with a particular slave; (3) that there are many advertisements for breeder slaves, written by men as famous as Benjamin Franklin. Although forced mating may not have been widespread in the United States, there seems to be some indication that breeding was not "rare." But I defer to the historians. See Lerner, *Black Women in White America*, pp. 47-48. See Norman R. Yetman, *Life Under the "Peculiar Institution": Selections from the Slave Narrative Collection* (New York: Holt, Rinehart and Winston, 1970). See Eugene D. Genovese, *Roll, Jordan, Roll: The World the Slaves Made* (New York: Pantheon Books, 1974), p. 464.

20. Jordan, *White Over Black*, p. 160.

21. Ibid., p. 77.

22. Ibid.

23. Anne Firor Scott, *The Southern Lady: From Pedestal to Politics, 1830-1930* (Chicago: University of Chicago Press, 1970), p. 4.

24. Ibid., pp. 23-44. Also, Julia Cherry Spruill, *Women's Life and Work in the Southern Colonies* (Chapel Hill: University of North Carolina Press, 1938).

25. George Frederickson, *The Black Image in the White Mind: The Debate on Afro-American Character, 1817-1914* (New York: Harper and Row, 1971), pp. 43-70.

26. Ibid., pp. 76-78.

27. Severn Duvall, " 'Uncle Tom's Cabin': The Sinister Side of the Patriarchy," in *Images of the Negro in American Literature*, ed. Gross and Hardy, p. 166.

28. Frederickson, *The Black Image in the White Mind*, pp. 66-69.

29. Stocking, *Race, Culture and Evolution*, pp. 49-50.

30. Lerner, *Black Women in White America*, p. 5.

31. Duvall, " 'Uncle Tom's Cabin': The Sinister Side of the Patriarchy," pp. 165-67.

32. Three notations must accompany this statement. First, I am using the concept of African philosophy in much the same way that writers use, with ease, the concept of a European world view. There are obviously differences between the many peoples of Africa as there are between the many peoples of Europe. Scholars such as John Mbiti, *African Religions and Philosophy* (New York: Double-

day Anchor, 1970), and Janheinz Jahn, *Muntu* (New York: Grove, 1961), have envisioned African peoples as sharing some basic philosophical concepts that are distinct, either in content or style, from European and Asian peoples. Second, I am referring, in this specific instance, to the concept of mother as pivotal to the African world view. See Denise Paulme, ed., *Women of Tropical Africa* (Berkeley: University of California, 1971), and the first chapter, "Mother and Child," of Wilfred Cartey, *Whispers from a Continent* (New York: Vintage, 1969), an in-depth study of this theme in contemporary African literature. Third, I am obviously in agreement with the concept of African survivalism in the United States, as well as the New World. See Herkovits, *The Myth of the Negro Past* (New York: Harper, 1941); John Blassingame, *The Slave Community: Plantation Life in the Ante Bellum South* (New York: Oxford University Press, 1972), pp. 18-40; Lorenzo Turner's "African Survivals in the New World with Special Emphasis on the Arts," in *Africa Seen by American Negroes*, ed. John Davis (Paris: Presence Africaine, 1958); Lawrence Levine's *Black Culture and Black Consciousness: Afro-American Folk Thought from Slavery to Freedom* (New York: Oxford University Press, 1977); as well as Genovese's *Roll, Jordan, Roll*, particularly the section on folk religion.

33. Genovese, *Roll, Jordan, Roll*, p. 496.

34. Sterling Brown, *The Negro in American Fiction* (1937; reprint, New York: Atheneum, 1969), p. 21.

35. Ibid., pp. 1-189.

36. Ibid., pp. 23-24.

37. Scott, *The Southern Lady*, pp. 46-54. See also Genovese, *Roll, Jordan. Roll*, pp. 353-61.

38. Genovese, *Roll, Jordan, Roll*, p. 353.

39. Scott, *The Southern Lady*, p. 37.

40. Jordan, *White Over Black*, p. 151.

41. Blassingame, *The Slave Community*, pp. 82-84.

42. Jordan, *White Over Black*, p. 150.

43. Scott, *The Southern Lady*, p. 52.

44. Jordan, *White Over Black*, p. 475.

45. William Wells Brown, *Clotel* (Miami: Mnemosyne Publishing, 1969). Reprint of *Clotel, or the Colored Heroine: A Tale of the Southern States* (Boston: Lee and Shepard 1867), p. 5. The first version of this book was published as *Clotel; or the President's Daughter* (London: Patridge and Dakey, 1853). Other versions are *Miralda, or the Beautiful Quadroon* (New York: *The Weekly Anglo-African Magazine* 1860); *Clotelle: A Tale of the Southern States* (Boston: James Redpath, 1864).

46. Lerner, *Black Women in White America*, pp. 45-53. See also Genovese, *Roll, Jordan, Roll*, p. 419.

47. Again, the comments I made in footnote 32, in relation to African philosophy and African survivalism in the United States, apply here. On the question of sex, see Genovese, *Roll, Jordan, Roll*, pp. 234, 246-47, 259; Mbiti, *African Religions and Philosophy*, pp. 160-64, 191-94, William Lew Hansberry, "Indigenous African Religions," *Africa Seen by American Negroes*, esp. pp. 90-93.

48. Brown, *The Negro in American Fiction*, p. 8.

49. Eric Patridge, *Origins: A Short Etymological Dictionary of Modern English* (New York: Macmillan Co., 1958), p. 420.

50. Frederickson, *The Black Image in the White Mind*, p. 75.

51. Jordan, *White Over Black*, pp. 20-24, 180-82, 191-93.

52. Levine, *Black Culture and Black Consciousness*, p. 74.

53. Blassingame, *The Slave Community*, p. 48.

54. Levine, *Black Culture and Black Consciousness*, p. 75.

55. Ibid., pp. 59-60.

56. Scott, *The Southern Lady*, pp. 7-14.

57. Mbiti, *African Religions and Philosophy*, p. 88.

58. Scott, *The Southern Lady*, p. 21.

59. Benjamin Quarles, *Black Abolitionists* (New York: Oxford University Press, 1969), pp. 43-46, 177-80.

60. James Baldwin, "Everybody's Protest Novel," in *Notes of a Native Son*, by James Baldwin (New York: Bantam Books, 1955), pp. 9-17.

61. Severn Duvall, " 'Uncle Tom's Cabin': The Sinister Side of the Patriarchy," p. 164.

62. Ibid., pp. 174-75.

63. Ibid., p. 176.

64. Ibid., p. 178.

65. Frederickson, *The Black Image in the White Mind*, pp. 114-15.

66. Ibid., pp. 108-9.

67. Ibid., p. 115.

68. Brown, *The Negro in American Fiction*, p. 45.

69. Brown, *Clotel*, p. 70.

70. Ibid., p. 5.

71. Quarles, *Black Abolitionists*, pp. 62-63.

72. Ibid., pp. 218-22. Quarles noted that some abolitionist blacks, primarily those in the African Civilization Society, supported colonization.

73. Frederickson, *The Black Image in the White Mind*, p. 5.

74. Quarles, *Black Abolitionists*, pp. 90-115.

75. W. E. B. Du Bois, *Black Reconstruction in America, 1860-1880* (1935; reprint, New York: Meridian Books, 1962), p. 128.

76. Frederickson, *The Black Image in the White Mind*, pp. 184-85.

77. John Hope Franklin, *From Slavery to Freedom* (1947; reprint, New York: Vintage, 1969), pp. 297-343.

78. Frederickson, *The Black Image in the White Mind*, pp. 187-99.

79. Ibid., pp. 228-55.

80. Ibid., pp. 259-61.

81. Lerner, *Black Women in White America*, pp. 193-215.

82. Ibid., p. 194.

83. Frederickson, *The Black Image in the White Mind*, p. 211.

84. Harper, *Iola LeRoy*, p. 281.

85. Ibid., p. 38.

86. Lerner, *Black Women in White America*, pp. 172-93.

87. Harper, *Iola LeRoy*, p. 64.

88. Ibid., p. 243.

89. Ibid.

90. Ibid., p. 254.

91. Ibid., p. 279.

92. Lerner, *Black Women in White America*, pp. 7-72. See also Yetman, *Life Under the "Peculiar Institution."*

93. Ibid., pp. 7-72.

94. Howard Odum and Guy Johnson, *Negro Workaday Songs* (Chapel Hill: University of North Carolina Press, 1926), p. 145.

95. Ibid., pp. 142-43.

96. Ibid., pp. 153-54.

97. Ibid., p. 146.

98. Robert M. Farnsworth, Introduction to *The Marrow of Tradition*, by Charles Chestnut (Ann Arbor, Mich.: Ann Arbor Paperbacks, 1969).

CHAPTER II

1. Claude McKay, *Selected Poems of Claude McKay* (Harcourt, Brace and World, 1953), p. 61. Critics such as Sterling Brown chose 1917, the publication date of this poem, to designate the beginning of the Harlem Renaissance.

2. Floretti Henri, *Black Migration: Movement North, 1900-1920* (New York: Doubleday Anchor, 1975). Henri's book gives a detailed account of the causes and results of the black migration.

3. Ibid., p. 231.

4. Ibid., p. 51.

5. Alain Locke, "The New Negro," in *The New Negro*, ed. Alain Locke (1925; reprint, New York: Atheneum, 1969), pp. 6-7.

6. Nathan Huggins, *Harlem Renaissance* (New York: Oxford University Press, 1971), pp. 22-31.

7. George Kent, "Patterns of the Harlem Renaissance," in *The Harlem Renaissance Remembered*, ed. Arna Bontemps (New York: Dodd, Mead and Co., 1972), p. 27.

8. Langston Hughes, "The Negro Artist and the Racial Mountain," *The Nation* 122 (June 1926): 692-94.

9. Locke, "The New Negro," pp. 11-12.

10. Huggins, *Harlem Renaissance*, p. 52.

11. George Frederickson, *The Black Image in the White Mind: The Debate on Afro-American Character, 1817-1914* (New York: Harper and Row, 1971), p. 327.

12. Kent, "Patterns of the Harlem Renaissance," p. 33.

13. James Weldon Johnson, *The Book of American Negro Poetry* (New York: Harcourt, Brace and World, 1922), p. 9.

14. Frederickson, *The Black Image in the White Mind*, p. 327.

15. McKay, *Selected Poems*, p. 60.

16. Langston Hughes, *The Big Sea* (New York: Hill and Wang, 1963), p. 218.

17. Jessie Fauset, "The Gift of Laughter," in *The New Negro*, ed. Locke, p. 162.

18. Ibid., p. 166.

19. Zona Gale, Introduction to *The Chinaberry Tree*, by Jessie Fauset (New York: Frederick A. Stokes Co., 1931), p. viii.

20. Sterling Brown, *The Negro in American Fiction* (1937; reprint, New York: Atheneum, 1969), p. 142.

21. Jessie Redmon Fauset, Foreword to *The Chinaberry Tree*, by Jessie Redmon Fauset (New York: Frederick A. Stokes Co., 1931), p. ix.

22. Ibid., p. x.

23. Arthur Davis, *From the Dark Tower* (Washington, D.C.: Howard University Press, 1974), pp. 90-91.

24. Hiroko Sato, "Under the Harlem Shadow: A Study of Jessie Fauset and Nella Larsen," *The Harlem Renaissance Remembered*, ed. Arna Bontemps (New York: Dodd, Mead and Co., 1972), p. 67.

25. Marion L. Starkey, "Jessie Fauset," *The Southern Workman* 61, no. 5 (May 1932): 219.

26. Fauset, *The Chinaberry Tree*, p. 2.

27. Brown, *The Negro in American Fiction*, pp. 144-45.

28. Fauset, *The Chinaberry Tree*, pp. 340-41, final lines of the novel.

29. Ibid., p. 278.

30. Sato, "Under the Harlem Shadow," pp. 67-68.

31. Adelaide Cromwell Hill, Introduction to *Quicksand*, by Nella Larsen (New York: Knopf, 1929; reprint, New York: Collier Books, 1971), pp. 11-17.

32. Ibid., p. 16.

33. Larsen, *Quicksand*, p. 24.

34. Ibid., pp. 28-29.

35. Ibid., pp. 42-43.

36. Ibid., p. 52.

37. Ibid., p. 82.

38. Ibid., p. 93.

39. Ibid., p. 150.

40. Ibid., p. 158.

41. Ibid., p. 222, final lines of the novel.

42. Ibid., p. 206.

43. Arna Bontemps, Introduction to *Cane*, by Jean Toomer (New York: Harper and Row, 1969), pp. vii-xvi.

44. See Darwin Turner's Introduction to *Cane*, by Jean Toomer (New York: Liveright, 1975), pp. ix-xxv. See Larry Thompson, "Jean Toomer: A Modern Man," in *The Harlem Renaissance Remembered*, ed. Bontemps, pp. 52-55.

45. Huggins, *Harlem Renaissance*, p. 179.

46. Jean Toomer, "Avey," in *Cane*, by Jean Toomer (New York: Boni and Liveright, 1923; reprint, New York: Harper and Row, 1969), pp. 86-87.

47. Toomer, "Carma," in *Cane*, 1969, pp. 17-18.

48. Robert Hemenway, *Zora Neale Hurston: A Literary Biography* (Champaign: University of Illinois Press, 1977).

49. Robert Hemenway, "Zora Neale Hurston and the Eatonville Anthropology," in *The Harlem Renaissance Remembered*, ed. Bontemps, pp. 194-95.

50. George Stocking, *Race, Culture and Evolution: Essays in the History of Anthropology* (New York: The Free Press, 1968), pp. 232-33.

51. Hemenway, *Zora Neale Hurston*, p. 88.

52. Zora Neale Hurston, *Their Eyes Were Watching God* (New York: J. B. Lippincott, 1937; reprint, New York: Fawcett Publications, 1965), p. 16.

53. Ibid., pp. 40-41.

54. Ibid., p. 62.

55. Ibid., p. 159, final lines of the novel.

56. Ibid., p. 11.

57. Quoted in Hemenway, "Zora Neale Hurston and the Eatonville Anthropology," p. 201.

58. Hemenway, *Zora Neale Hurston*, pp. 320-21.

59. Ibid., p. 322.

60. Alice Walker, Foreword to *Zora Neale Hurston*, by Hemenway.

61. Hemenway, *Zora Neale Hurston*, p. 348.

CHAPTER III

1. Richard Wright, *Native Son* (1941; reprint, New York: Harper and Row, 1966), p. 170.

2. Robert Hemenway, *Zora Neale Hurston: A Literary Biography* (Champaign: University of Illinois Press, 1977), p. 241.

3. Ibid.

4. George Frederickson, *The White Image in the Black Mind: The Debate on Afro-American Character, 1817-1914* (New York: Harper and Row, 1971), p. 329.

5. Richard Wright, "A Blueprint for Negro Writing," *New Challenge* 11 (1937): 53-65.

6. Ibid.

7. Arthur Davis, *From the Dark Tower* (Washington, D.C.: Howard University Press, 1974), pp. 193-94.

8. Ann Petry, *The Street* (Boston: Houghton Mifflin, 1946; reprint, New York: Pyramid Books, 1961), p. 7.

9. Ibid., p. 42.

10. Ibid., p. 32.

11. Ibid., p. 266.

12. Ibid., p. 269.

13. Gwendolyn Brooks, "Maud Martha," in *The World of Gwendolyn Brooks* (New York: Harper and Row, 1971), pp. 127-28.

14. Ibid., pp. 178-79.

15. Ibid., pp. 226-27.

16. Margaret Walker, *How I Wrote Jubilee* (Chicago: Third World Press, 1972), p. 16.

BOOK II

1. Margaret Walker, *How I Wrote Jubilee* (Chicago: Third World Press, 1972), p. 24.

2. Robert Staples, *The Black Woman in America: Sex, Marriage and the Family* (Chicago: Nelson Hall Publishers, 1973), p. 27.

3. See Andrew Billingsley, *Black Families in White America* (New York: Prentice, 1968); Angela Davis, "Reflections on the Black Woman's Role in the Community of Slaves," *The Black Scholar* 3, no. 4 (December 1971); Joyce Ladner, *Tomorrow's Tomorrow: The Black Woman* (New York: Doubleday, 1971); Inez Reid, *Together Black Woman* (New York: Emerson Hall, 1972).

CHAPTER IV

1. Paule Marshall, *Browngirl, Brownstones* (New York: Avon Books, 1959), p. 69.

2. Ibid., p. 7.

3. Ibid., pp. 11-12.

4. Ibid., p. 18.

5. Ibid., p. 19.

6. Ibid., p. 22.

7. Ibid., p. 28.

8. Ibid., p. 37.

9. Ibid., p. 60.

10. Ibid., p. 85.

11. Ibid., p. 86.

12. Ibid., p. 89.

13. Ibid., pp. 70-71.

14. Ibid., p. 71.

15. Ibid., p. 96.

16. Ibid., p. 97.

17. Ibid., pp. 113-14.

18. Ibid., pp. 121-22.

19. Ibid., p. 126.

20. Ibid., p. 141.

21. Ibid., p. 146.

22. Ibid., p. 152.

23. Ibid., p. 154.

24. Ibid., p. 156.

25. Ibid., p. 163.

26. Ibid., p. 165.

27. Ibid., p. 217.

28. Ibid., p. 219.

29. Ibid., p. 252.

30. Paule Marshall, *The Chosen Place, The Timeless People* (New York: Harcourt, Brace and World, 1969), epithet.

31. Ibid., pp. 4-5.
32. Ibid., p. 5.
33. Ibid., p. 17.
34. Ibid., p. 19.
35. Ibid., p. 21.
36. Ibid., p. 17.
37. Ibid., p. 103.
38. Ibid., pp. 162-63.
39. Ibid., pp. 209-10.
40. Ibid., p. 225.
41. Ibid., pp. 142-43.
42. Ibid., p. 242.
43. Ibid., p. 185.
44. Ibid., p. 275.
45. Ibid., p. 276.
46. Ibid., pp. 239-40.
47. Ibid., p. 309.
48. Ibid., pp. 96-97.
49. Ibid., p. 146.
50. Ibid., pp. 295-97.
51. Ibid., p. 237.
52. Ibid., p. 459.
53. Ibid., p. 454.
54. Ibid., p. 164.
55. Ibid., p. 315.
56. Ibid., p. 337.
57. Ibid., p. 402.
58. Ibid., p. 407.

CHAPTER V

1. Toni Morrison, *The Bluest Eye* (New York: Holt, Rinehart and Winston, 1970), p. 40.
2. Ibid., p. 30.
3. Ibid.
4. Ibid., p. 146.
5. Ibid., p. 78.
6. Ibid., p. 92.
7. Ibid., p. 97.
8. Ibid., pp. 109-10.
9. Ibid., p. 133.
10. Ibid., p. 134.
11. Ibid., p. 68.
12. Ibid., p. 16.
13. Ibid., p. 125.

14. Toni Morrison, *Sula* (New York: Knopf, 1974), pp. 52-53.
15. Ibid., pp. 89-90.
16. Ibid., p. 29.
17. Ibid., p. 68.
18. Ibid., pp. 71-72.
19. Ibid., p. 52.
20. Ibid., p. 66.
21. Ibid., p. 82.
22. Ibid., pp. 92-94.
23. Ibid., pp. 118-19.
24. Ibid., p. 121.
25. Ibid., p. 117.
26. Ibid., p. 94.
27. Ibid., p. 110.
28. Ibid., pp. 121-22.
29. Ibid., p. 134.
30. Ibid., p. 142.
31. Ibid., p. 143.
32. Ibid., p. 146.
33. Ibid., p. 160.

CHAPTER VI

1. Alice Walker, "In Our Mothers' Gardens," *Ms.* 2, no. 11 (May 1974): 65.
2. Ibid., p. 70.
3. Alice Walker, *The Third Life of Grange Copeland* (New York: Harcourt Brace Jovanovich, 1970), p. 207.
4. Ibid., pp. 11-13.
5. Ibid., pp. 53-54.
6. Ibid., p. 55.
7. Ibid., p. 82.
8. Ibid., p. 83.
9. Ibid.
10. Ibid.
11. Ibid., p. 84.
12. Ibid., p. 86.
13. Ibid., p. 91.
14. Ibid., p. 92.
15. Ibid., p. 107.
16. Ibid., p. 162.
17. Ibid., p. 40.
18. Ibid., p. 21.
19. Ibid., pp. 224-25.
20. Ibid., pp. 17-18.
21. Ibid., p. 111.
22. Ibid., pp. 133-34.

23. Ibid., pp. 138-39.

24. Ibid., p. 196.

25. Ibid., p. 166.

26. Ibid., p. 209.

27. Ibid., p. 214.

28. Alice Walker, *Meridian* (New York: Harcourt, Brace Jovanovich, 1976), pp. 13-14.

29. Ibid., p. 19.

30. Ibid., pp. 54-55.

31. John O'Brien, ed. *Interviews with Black Writers* (New York: Liveright, 1973), p. 193.

32. Black Elk, *Black Elk Speaks; Being the Life Story of a Holy Man of the Oalala Sioux*, as told through John G. Neihardt [Flaming Rainbow] (Lincoln: University of Nebraska Press, 1961).

33. O'Brien, *Interviews with Black Writers*, p. 204.

34. Walker, *Meridian*, pp. 14-15.

35. Ibid., p. 204.

36. Ibid., pp. 92-93.

37. Ibid., p. 70.

38. Ibid., pp. 33-34.

39. Ibid., p. 219.

40. Ibid., p. 24.

41. Ibid., p. 80.

42. Ibid., pp. 106-7.

43. Ibid., p. 145.

44. Ibid., pp. 133-34.

45. Ibid., p. 138.

46. Ibid., pp. 137-38.

47. Ibid., p. 223.

48. Ibid., pp. 104-5.

49. Ibid., pp. 170-71.

50. Ibid., pp. 165-66.

51. Ibid., pp. 176-77.

52. Ibid., p. 185.

53. Alice Walker, "Fundamental Difference," in *Revolutionary Petunias*, by Alice Walker (New York: Harcourt Brace Jovanovich, 1973), p. 1.

54. O'Brien, *Interviews with Black Writers*, p. 205.

CHAPTER VII

1. Mel Watkins, "Talk with Toni Morrison," *The New York Times Book Review*, September 11, 1977, p. 48.

2. Professor Erskine Peters, Afro-American Studies, University of California, Berkeley, presented this point in a lecture on "The Critical Interpretation

of Black Literature: Reasons for Caution in Approaching Aesthetic and Historical Informants," 1976.

3. Perhaps few books written by black male authors on this question of the
relationship of the young black boy's identity to his natal community have been
published, since many critics believe this theme is parochial and narrow. Mel
Watkins in the *New York Times* interview with Toni Morrison, cited in footnote 1, calls the theme of her first two novels "a narrower theme" than the scope
of her book *Song of Solomon* (New York: Knopf, 1977). Morrison's *Song of
Solomon* does not include whites but it does present men in a more prominent
way and emphasizes an external journey (adventure) as well as the more internalized style of her first two novels.

4. Richard Wright, *White Man Listen* (New York: Doubleday, 1964), p. 115.

Bibliography

Baldwin, James. *Notes of a Native Son.* New York: Bantam Books, 1955.

Blassingame, John. *The Slave Community: Plantation Life in the Ante Bellum South.* New York: Oxford University Press, 1972.

Bontemps, Arna, ed. *The Harlem Renaissance Remembered.* New York: Dodd, Mead and Co., 1972.

Brooks, Gwendolyn. *Report from Part I.* Detroit: Broadside Press, 1972.

————. *The World of Gwendolyn Brooks.* New York: Harper and Row, 1976.

Brown, Sterling. *The Negro in American Fiction.* 1937. Reprint, New York: Atheneum, 1969.

Brown, William Wells. *Clotel.* Miami: Mnemosyne Publishing, 1969. Reprint of *Clotel, or the Colored Heroine: A Tale of the Southern States,* Boston: Lee and Shepard 1867. The first version of this book was published as *Clotel; or the President's Daughter.* London: Patridge and Dakey, 1853.

Butterfield, Stephen. *Black Autobiography of America.* Amherst: University of Massachusetts Press, 1974.

Cade, Toni. *The Black Woman.* New York: New American Library, 1970.

Cartey, Wilfred. *Whispers From a Continent.* New York: Vintage, 1969.

Chesnutt, Charles. *The Conjure Woman and Other Stories.* Boston: Houghton Mifflin, 1899.

————. *The Wife of His Youth and Other Stories of the Color Line.* 1899.

————. *House Behind the Cedars.* Boston: Houghton Mifflin, 1900.

————. *The Marrow of Tradition.* Boston: Houghton Mifflin, 1901.

————. *The Colonel's Dream.* New York: Doubleday, 1905.

Davis, Angela, "Reflections on the Black Woman's Role in the Community of Slaves." *The Black Scholar* 3, no. 4 (December 1971).

Davis, Arthur. *From the Dark Tower.* Washington, D.C.: Howard University Press, 1974.

Davis, John, ed. *Africa Seen by American Negroes.* Paris: Présence Africaine, 1958.

Du Bois, W. E. B. *Black Reconstruction in America, 1860-1880.* 1935. Reprint, New York: Meridian Books, 1962.

Fauset, Jessie Redmon. *There Is Confusion.* New York: Boni and Liveright, 1924.

————. *Plum Bun.* New York: Frederick A. Stokes Co., 1929.

————. *The Chinaberry Tree.* New York: Frederick A. Stokes Co., 1931.

————. *Comedy, American Style.* New York: Frederick A. Stokes Co., 1933.

Franklin, John Hope. *From Slavery to Freedom.* 1947. Reprint, New York: Vintage, 1969.

Frederickson, George. *The Black Image in the White Mind: The Debate on Afro-American Character, 1817-1914.* New York: Harper and Row, 1971.

Genovese, Eugene. *Roll, Jordan, Roll: The World the Slaves Made.* New York: Pantheon Books, 1974.

Gross, Seymour and John Hardy, eds. *Images of the Negro in American Literature.* Chicago: University of Chicago Press, 1966.

Gutman, Herbert G. *The Black Family in Slavery and Freedom, 1750-1925.* New York: Pantheon Books, 1976.

Harper, Frances. *Iola LeRoy, Shadows Uplifted.* 3rd ed. Boston: James H. Earle, 1895.

Hemenway, Robert. *Zora Neale Hurston: A Literary Biography.* Champaign, University of Illinois Press, 1978.

Henri, Floretti. *Black Migration: Movement North, 1900-1920.* New York: Anchor Press/Doubleday, 1975.

Huggins, Nathan. *Harlem Renaissance.* New York: Oxford University Press, 1971.

Hughes, Langston. "The Negro Artist and the Racial Mountain." *The Nation* 112 (June 26, 1926).

Hurston, Zora Neale. *Jonah's Gourd Vine.* New York: J. B. Lippincott, 1934.

————. *Mules and Men.* New York: J. B. Lippincott, 1935.

————. *Their Eyes Were Watching God.* New York: J. B. Lippincott, 1937. Reprint, New York: Fawcett Publications, 1965.

————. *Tell My Horse.* New York: J. B. Lippincott, 1938.

————. *Moses, Man of the Mountain.* New York: J. B. Lippincott, 1942.

————. *Dust Tracks on a Road.* 1942. Reprint, New York: J. B. Lippincott, 1971.

————. *Seraph on the Suwannee.* New York: Scribner, 1948.

Johnson, James Weldon. *St. Peter Relates an Incident.* New York: Viking Press, 1917.

————. *The Book of American Negro Poetry.* New York: Harcourt, Brace and World, 1922.

Jordan, June. "On Richard Wright and Zora Neale Hurston: Notes Toward a Balancing of Love and Hatred." *Black World* 23, no. 10 (August 1974).

Jordan, Winthrop D. *White Over Black: American Attitudes Toward the Negro, 1550-1812.* New York: Penguin Books, 1969.

Ladner, Joyce. *Tomorrow's Tomorrow: The Black Woman.* New York: Doubleday, 1971.

Larsen, Nella. *Passing*. New York: Knopf, 1929. Reprint, New York: Collier Books, 1971.

———. *Quicksand*. New York: Knopf, 1928. Reprint, New York: Collier Books, 1971.

Lerner, Gerda, ed. *Black Women in White America: A Documentary History*. New York: Vintage, 1973.

Levine, Lawrence. *Black Culture and Black Consciousness: Afro-American Folk Thought from Slavery to Freedom*. New York: Oxford University Press, 1977.

Locke, Alain, ed. *The New Negro*. 1925. Reprint, New York: Atheneum, 1969.

Marshall, Paule. *Browngirl, Brownstones*. New York: Avon Books, 1959.

———. *Soul Clap Hands and Sing*. New York: Atheneum, 1961.

———. *The Chosen Place, The Timeless People*. New York: Harcourt, Brace and World, 1969.

Mbiti, John. *African Religions and Philosophy*. New York: Doubleday Anchor, 1970.

McKay, Claude. *Selected Poems of Claude McKay*. New York: Harcourt, Brace and World, 1953.

Morrison, Toni. *The Bluest Eye*. New York: Holt, Rinehart and Winston, 1970.

———. *Sula*. New York: Knopf, 1974.

———. *Song of Solomon*. New York: Knopf, 1977.

O'Brien, John, ed. *Interviews with Black Writers*. New York: Liveright, 1973.

Odum, Howard and Guy Johnson. *Negro Workaday Songs*. Chapel Hill: University of North Carolina Press, 1926.

Paulme, Denise, ed. *Women of Tropical Africa*. Berkeley: University of California Press, 1971.

Petry, Ann. *The Street*. Boston: Houghton Mifflin, 1946.

———. *Country Place*. Boston: Houghton Mifflin, 1947.

———. *The Narrows*. Boston: Houghton Mifflin, 1953.

———. *Harriet Tubman: Conductor on the Underground Railroad*. New York: Crowell, 1955.

———. *Tituba of Salem Village*. New York: Crowell, 1964.

———. *Miss Muriel and Other Stories*. Boston: Houghton Mifflin, 1971.

Quarles, Benjamin. *Black Abolitionists*. New York: Oxford University Press, 1969.

Rushing, Andrea. "Images of Black Women in Afro-American Poetry." *Black World* 24, no. 11 (September 1975).

Russell, Charles. "Poetry, History and Humanism: An Interview with Margaret Walker." *Black World* 25, no. 2 (December 1975).

Scott, Anne Firor. *The Southern Lady: From Pedestal to Politics, 1830-1930*. Chicago: University of Chicago Press, 1970.

Southerland, Ellease. "The Novelist-Anthropologist: Life and Works: Zora Neale Hurston." *Black World* 25, no. 2 (December 1975).

Spruill, Julia Cherry. *Women's Life and Work in the Southern Colonies*. Chapel Hill: University of North Carolina Press, 1938.

Staples, Robert. *The Black Woman in America: Sex, Marriage and the Family*. Chicago: Nelson-Hall Publishers, 1973.

Stark, Catherine J. *Black Portraiture in American Fiction*. New York: Basic Books, 1971.

Stepto, Robert B. "Intimate Things in Place, A Conversation with Toni Morrison." *Massachusetts Review*, September 1977.

Stocking, George. *Race, Culture and Evolution: Essays in the History of Anthropology*. New York: The Free Press, 1968.

Walker, Alice. *Once*. New York: Harcourt Brace Jovanovich, 1968.

———. *The Third Life of Grange Copeland*. New York: Harcourt Brace Jovanovich, 1970.

———. *In Love and Trouble: Stories for Black Women*. New York: Harcourt Brace Jovanovich, 1973.

———. *Revolutionary Petunias*. New York: Harcourt Brace Jovanovich, 1973.

———. "In Our Mothers' Gardens." *Ms*. 2, no. 11 (May 1974).

———. "In Search of Zora Neale Hurston." *Ms*. 3, no. 9 (March 1975).

———. *Meridian*. New York: Harcourt Brace Jovanovich, 1976.

———. "Lulls—A Native Daughter Returns to the Black South." *Ms*. 5, no. 7 (January 1977).

———. *Good Night, Willie Lee, I'll See You in the Morning*. New York: Dial Press, 1979.

———. ed. *I Love Myself When I Am Laughing, a Zora Neale Hurston Reader*. Westbury, New York: The Feminist Press, 1979.

Walker, Margaret. *For My People*. New Haven, Conn.: Yale University Press, 1942.

———. *Jubilee*. Boston: Houghton Mifflin, 1966.

———. *Prophets for a New Day*. Detroit: Broadside Press, 1970.

———. *How I Wrote Jubilee*. Chicago: Third World Press, 1972.

———. *A Poetic Equation*. Washington, D.C.: Howard University Press, 1974.

Washington, Mary Helen. "Black Women Image Makers." *Black World* 23, no. 10 (August 1974).

Watkins, Mel. "Talk with Toni Morrison." *The New York Times Book Review*, September 11, 1977.

Wright, Richard. "A Blueprint for Negro Writing." *New Challenge* 2 (1937).

Index

269

blacks; as reference to subtitle of *Clotel, The President's Daughter,* 26
Johnson, Amelia, black woman novelist of late 19th century, 253n2
Johnson, James Weldon, black writer and philosopher of early 20th century, 37, 39
Jubilee, (Walker, Margaret): as folk novel, 71-72; as historical novel, 71-72; in comparison to novels of Harper, Fauset, Larsen and Hurston, 72; revision of black woman images, 72. *See also* Walker, Margaret

Kennedy, J.P., antebellum southern novelist, 11
Lady, image of: in abolitionist literature, 22, 23, 26-30; in antebellum southern literature, 8-11, 12, 13-15, 16, 17-18; in *The Bluest Eye,* 150-51, 177; in *The Chosen Place, The Timeless People,* 110-11, 121-27; in *Meridian,* 207, 219-220, 223, 228, 231; in novels of Fauset, 43-47, 72; in novels of Larsen, 43-47, 72; in novels of Marshall, Morrison and Walker, 245; in *Their Eyes Were Watching God,* 58-59; in *The Third Life of Grange Copeland,* 188, 194
Larsen, Nella, 1920s black woman novelist. 47-53: biographical notes, 47-48, 61; discussed in "In Search of Our Mother's Gardens," 181; *Quicksand,* author of, 48-53. *See also Quicksand*
LaVeau, Marie, as conjure woman, 97; as powerful black woman, 33
Locke, Alain, Harlem Renaissance writer and philosopher: *The New Negro,* author of, 37-38; *Their Eyes Were Watching God,* review of, 62
Loose black woman image in: abolitionist literature, 23, 26-27, 29; antebellum literature, 6, 12-15; *The Bluest Eye,* 144; *Browngirl, Brownstones,* 85; *The Chosen Place, The Timeless People,* 109; *Jubilee,* 72; *Meridian,* 223; novels of Fauset, 40; novels of Nella Larsen, 40, 50, 52, 53; novels of Marshall, Morrison and Walker, 243; *The Street,* 65, 66; *Sula,* 159-160, 166, 170, 176; *The Third Life of Grange Copeland,* 194-196. *See also* Sexuality

Mammy, image of: in abolitionist literature, 21, 24, 29; in antebellum literature, 7-12; in *The Bluest Eye,* 144, 146; in *Jubilee,* 72; in novels of Marhall, Morrison and Walker, 242, 246; in oral tradition, 30; in *The Street,* 65; in *Sula,* 158. *See also* Motherhood
Manhood, definition of: in *The Bluest Eye,* 147-48; *Browngirl, Brownstones,* 82, 86, 87, 89-91, 96-97, 101-03; 244; *The Chosen*

Place, The Timeless People, 116, 119, 120; in *Meridian,* 223-24; in novels of Marshall, Morrison and Walker, 243-44; in *The Street,* 66; in *Sula,* 170-71; in *Third Life of Grange Copeland,* 185-188, 191-93, 197-99, 202. *See also* Black male images; Fatherhood
Marshall, Paule, Contemporary black woman novelist, 80-137, 239-253. *See also: Browngirl, Brownstones; The Chosen Place, The Timeless People*
Matriarch, image of: 78, 84-85. *See also* Mammy, image of
Maud Martha (Brooks, Gwendolyn), 68-71: community in, use of, 68; motherhood, theme of, 70; ordinary woman, theme of, 70
Meridian, discussion of, 204-234
—Characters: black girl as focal character, 206, 210, 215-16, 220; black men, 218, 222-27; black woman as focal character, 205-206, 218, 219-222, 223, 236, 237-38; children, 205-05, 214-15, 220-21, 231, 246-252; major characters, relationship between, 218, 220, 222-233; white women, 218, 227-233, 249
—Plot, movement in relation to theme, 206-11
—Structure, 206, 237: characters, in relation to, 206, 218; concept of guilt, in relation to, 214-218, 248; motifs, in relation to, 209-18; music image, in relation to, 212-14; nature, use of, 211, 216-17, 250-251; ritual, use of, 212-14; time, use of, 207-11, 250
—Themes: animism, 211-12, 237-38; black woman's search for elf, 206, 209-11, 213-14, 218-23, 233-34, 236, 237-38; body and mind, relationship of, 212, 215-16, 250; creativity of black women, 206, 234, 238, 251; fatherhood, 222; guilt, 214-18; manhood, definition of, 223-24; motherhood, 206, 214-15, 219-21, 251; past and present, relationship of, 204 5, 207, 209, 235-37, 250; quest for wholenes ӽ 205, 213-14, 217, 234-37, 247, 251; sexism and racism, relationship be,ween, 207, 215-16, 218-33, 236, 237-38, 251; social and personal change, relationshp be,ween, 205, 209-10, 213-14, 217, 234, 235 38, 247; violence and change, relationship between, 205, 217, 232-33, 234, 236, 237; womanhood, definition of, 206, 219-31
Miscegenation, 6-7, 15-16, 26, 55. *See also* Interracial sexual relationships
Morrison, Toni, contemporary black woman novelist: 137-180, 239-253. *See also The*

About the author

BARBARA CHRISTIAN is associate professor of Afro-American studies at the University of California, Berkeley. Her articles have appeared in such journals as *Women's Studies, Black World*, and the *Journal of Ethnic Studies.*

Recent Titles in
Contributions in Afro-American and African Studies
Series Adviser: Hollis R. Lynch